MORE
OFF-BROADWAY
PLAYS

ALSO BY PHILIP FREUND

NOVELS

The Volcano God
The Zoltans, *a Trilogy*
The Dark Shore
The Evening Heron
Dreams of Youth
Easter Island
Searching

SHORT STORIES

The Devious Ways
The Beholder
The Snow
Three Exotic Tales
A Man of Taste
The Young Greek and the Creole
The Spymaster
The Young Artists

FANTASY

The Merry Communist

PLAYS

Prince Hamlet
Three Off-Broadway Plays
Three Poetic Plays
Mario's Well
Black Velvet
Simon Simon

CRITICISM

Myths of Creation
The Art of Reading the Novel
Preface to
Joseph Conrad's *Lord Jim*
Preface to Otto Rank's
*The Myth of the Birth of the Hero
and other Essays*
Preface to Kimi Gengo's
*To One who Mourns at
the Death of the Emperor*

PHILIP FREUND

MORE
OFF-BROADWAY
PLAYS

W. H. ALLEN
LONDON
1974

Library of Congress Cataloging in Publication Data

Freund, Philip, 1909-
    More off-Broadway plays.

    CONTENTS: Charles IV.--Edge of the jungle.--Miss
Lucy in town.
    I. Title.
PS3511.R66M6   812'.5'2   74-10774

ISBN 0 491 01762 6

Printed and bound in Great Britain by
T. & A. Constable Ltd., Edinburgh

CONTENTS

CHARLES IV

PREFATORY NOTE

Those who read chronicle plays (and my story of Charles pretends to be nothing more than a chronicle in the old-fashioned tradition of Shakespeare's Richards and Henries) are apt to ask themselves how closely the dramatic account adheres to historic fact. The answer here is that Charles and all the circumstances and persons that surrounded him in Spain are depicted with almost complete fidelity to truth. Little of the interpretation, even, is my own: the record is so definite. The visitor to the Hispanic Museum in New York City may hold in his hands an ancient copy of Charles's translation of Aristotle, and his appended commentary. He may pore over the poems of Ausias March (quite unintelligible, in their fifteenth-century Catalan dialect). He may read careful accounts of Carbonero's picture of the prince. Not much was left for my invention: only those minor people, once living—and not minor to themselves—who are now reduced to mere names on a hurried page of historical text. Such simplification of fact as may exist in the play is mostly that accomplished by the passing of five hundred years. I must admit, however, that my French King is a more fanciful creation.

Charles was the artist in a political world: not the important artist, but the minor one. He was, though less definitely, the liberal. He was also the fated leader in a time of transition, a time whose rapid changes would make short shrift of him. I have seen this, through analogy, and in the medium of allegory, as topical material: his inner conflict is the same as that known to a goodly number of modern men, however much or little circumstances may have altered. But even the circumstances themselves have not altered so much, if one examines them closely, choosing new names for old ones.

The prince has my apology for this attempt to read a little modern meaning in his life. But then, Charles himself tried to bring Aristotle up to date. I think, therefore, he was not entirely an enemy to presumption.   P. F.

CHARLES IV

A Play in Two Acts

THE PERSONS OF THE PLAY

John, *King of Navarre, and afterward of Aragon*

Joanna Henriquez, *his second wife, Queen of Navarre, and daughter of the Admiral of Castile*

Blanche, *divorced wife of the Prince of Asturias, later Henry IV of Castile*

Charles, *Prince of Viana, sometimes called Charles IV of Navarre*

Eleanor, *Countess de Foix*

    } *children of John by his first wife*

Gaston, *Count de Foix, husband of Eleanor*

Don Pedro de Navarra, *Marshal of Navarre, head of the Agramont faction*

Mossen Pierres de Peralta, *cousin of the Marshal*

Don Juan de Beaumont, *Constable and Grand Prior of Navarre*

Dona Brianda de Vaca

Ausias March, *a Valencian poet*

Moreno Carbonero, *a court painter*

Charles VII, *King of France*

The French Ambassador to Castile

Louis XI, *King of France, son of Charles VII*

Nicolau Vinot, *a Catalan*

Fray Juan Christoval de Guelvès, *a Dominican*

Other members of the Catalan deputation

A company of French musicians

SYNOPSIS OF SCENES

ACT ONE: *Scene One:* France, 1453
Scene Two: Aragon, 1453
Scene Three: France, 1458
Scene Four: Sicily, 1459
Scene Five: Barcelona, January 1460

ACT TWO: *Scene One:* Barcelona, June 1460
Scene Two: France, June 1461
Scene Three: Morella, June 1461
Scene Four: Barcelona, September 1461
Scene Five: France, 1467

ACT ONE

SCENE ONE: CHARLES VII, *the ironical King of France, is dressed in green velvet. Seated, he extends his hand to his kneeling ambassador.*

THE KING: Welcome to France.

AMBASSADOR (*rising*): I thank Your Majesty and pray my services have been of value.

THE KING: You're my ambassador to Castile? What's the news from there?

AMBASSADOR: The war continues.

THE KING: What war's that? Do the Spanish never cease fighting? They're cruel, barbarous.

AMBASSADOR: No crueler, no more barbarous than most. These emotions are in every man. He'd discover them, if he also had courage.

THE KING: I don't pretend to understand Spanish politics. Dynasty against dynasty. Province against province. This has always gone on.

AMBASSADOR: Spain's a most unhappy country.

THE KING: I insist, the Spanish are cruel and barbarous. They delight in killing one another.

AMBASSADOR: Does Your Majesty think they also delight in being killed?

THE KING: We must make some effort to understand, I suppose.

AMBASSADOR: Your Majesty's renowned for his understanding.

THE KING: I hope your diplomacy's better in Castile. Tell me the story in simple words.

AMBASSADOR: It'll be harder to grasp in simple words. That'd be a plain recital of names and dates. Too bare. It'd be better if I gave you the characters and destinies of those involved. That method's longer but more vivid. The details aren't important. You can afford to forget most of them at once.

THE KING: Then why bother me with them? I'm your audience, my

[7]

dear Ambassador. Spare me. I don't like to think any more than I need to.

AMBASSADOR: In any explanation, I think, the *feel* is more important than the facts. But you must accumulate the facts, most of them, to get that.

THE KING: Facts. Petty details. Let me send a man to Spain, immediately he becomes engrossed in Spanish history. You're like all my other ambassadors. They bore me.

AMBASSADOR: Sire, the history of Spain may be the history of France.

THE KING: I've a few minutes to spare you. But only a few minutes. Tell me the whole story quickly. From the beginning. In simple words.

AMBASSADOR: Spain's divided into many countries.

THE KING: Are you going to explain the political situations in all of them!

AMBASSADOR: No, Sire. Only of Castile, Navarre, Aragon, and Catalonia. And, of course, Naples and Sicily.

THE KING: In simple words? And in a few minutes?

AMBASSADOR: Yes, Sire, if you insist.

THE KING: Well, hurry.

AMBASSADOR: In all these countries, as you know, there're inner dissensions. In Castile, civil war. In Navarre, a quarrel over the accession. In Aragon, war against Castile. And in Castile, war against Aragon. Meanwhile, the people of Barcelona are a rebellious and independent lot who trouble their absent King. And in the south, we've Moorish Grenada.

THE KING: These're the facts? You were right. Forget these facts. Tell me about men. I can remember them better.

AMBASSADOR: One man. John, King of Navarre, who's very unpopular with his people.

THE KING: That's a little too simple.

AMBASSADOR: I beg Your Majesty to have patience.

THE KING: An unpopular king? I've heard of others.

AMBASSADOR: He's unpopular for good reasons. He is ambitious, arrogant, quarrelsome. Though a man of ability.

THE KING: If he has ability, he'd most certainly be unpopular.

AMBASSADOR: He's also an interloper. And an alien in Navarre.

THE KING: Ambitious, arrogant, quarrelsome, an interloper, and an alien?

AMBASSADOR: All these, Your Majesty. But, I repeat, a man of ability.

THE KING: I'd like to know him. Men of ability are rare. I could use him.

AMBASSADOR: Now, Sire, look on this map. You'll see that Navarre's the smallest and least important of all these countries. But, because of the character of John, it holds promise of a great enterprise. For John's the younger brother of Alfonso, King of Aragon, which borders on Navarre. And Alfonso, as you know, has spread his dominion over Catalonia, Naples and Sicily.

THE KING: Alfonso's in Naples.

AMBASSADOR: Yes, Your Majesty. And John's in Spain. At the moment, Alfonso's queen is his vice-roy in Catalonia. And John is his vice-roy in Aragon. And while John's in Aragon, his own son Charles is vice-roy in Navarre.

THE KING: How much of this shall I remember? I hate looking at maps. They seduce kings. It's so easy to make patterns with them.

AMBASSADOR: Only this, something which isn't on the map at all. John has three children. Charles, his vice-roy in Navarre. Blanche, named for her mother. And Eleanor.

THE KING: John's children. Charles, Blanche, and Eleanor.

AMBASSADOR: Yes, Your Majesty.

THE KING: Charles, Blanche, and Eleanor.

AMBASSADOR: You are thorough, Sire.

THE KING: Charles, Blanche, and Eleanor. I repeat everything three times, so I shall not forget.

AMBASSADOR: Blanche is married to the royal house of Castile. To Henry, the son of the king.

THE KING: Must I remember that?

AMBASSADOR: I shall soon remind you of it. Now, Your Majesty, look again on this map. If Alfonso were to die before John, then John would inherit Naples, Sicily, Catalonia, and Aragon. And could unite them to Navarre. Besides, John has personal claims in Castile. You grasp, then, what ideas work in the mind of this man.

THE KING: John of Navarre?

AMBASSADOR: But meanwhile, he is almost no one. Alfonso lives. Catalonia's hard to govern. And John's not even the legitimate King of Navarre. Besides, he wars on Castile and loses.

THE KING: Wars on Castile?

AMBASSADOR: Over personal claims. Even though his daughter Blanche is married to the royal house of Castile. So that the father-in-law wars on his own son-in-law.

THE KING: That's not unusual.

AMBASSADOR: John carries on his war from Aragon, because the people of Navarre do not want him at home. His son Charles governs for him there. And the people of Navarre want Charles as their king, to preserve the independence of their royal line.

THE KING: The son instead of the father?

AMBASSADOR: You forget, Sire, John became King of Navarre only by marriage.

THE KING: I did not forget. You didn't tell me.

AMBASSADOR: The marriage contract provided that John was to step aside in favor of his son when his wife died. She died nine years ago, but John still refuses to give up the throne. Though he stays away from Navarre, letting Charles rule in his place.

THE KING: The son is satisfied with this?

AMBASSADOR: The people, no. The son, yes. He obeys the dying request of his mother to do nothing. Charles waits.

THE KING: Out of respect to his dead mother?

AMBASSADOR: And to his father. And also to his own temperament.

THE KING: He waits? How long?

AMBASSADOR: Nine years.

THE KING: Would that I had such a son.

AMBASSADOR: But not all goes well between father and son. Between John and his children.

THE KING: That's easier to believe.

AMBASSADOR: For one thing, both Charles and Blanche are angry about the war John is waging on Blanche's husband.

THE KING: Henry of Castile?

AMBASSADOR: Yes, Sire. And that's not all. For, since this war started, John has married again. This further enrages his children.

THE KING: A resourceful man. But it's never hard to enrage one's children.

AMBASSADOR: Look again at the map. I've told you there's dissension in Castile itself. Between the king and a party headed by the admiral.

THE KING: The Admiral of Castile?

AMBASSADOR: John's second marriage is one of policy, as well as natural attraction. His new wife's Joanna Henriquez, the daughter of the Admiral of Castile. Thus, by this alliance, the King of Castile's enemies at home and abroad are brought under one banner.

THE KING: In simple words, John, the father-in-law, who's warring on his son-in-law, Henry, now joins forces with his own father-in-law, the Admiral of Castile?

AMBASSADOR: Your Majesty puts it well. But you see how complicated these simple words can be.

THE KING (rises): These Spanish astound me. Was there ever such a people?

AMBASSADOR: Joanna, the new queen, is a woman of unusual qualities. She helps John, even to commanding his armies. She's borne him a son, Prince Ferdinand. Naturally, John's children by his first wife dislike this and suspect her.

THE KING: Children are selfish. What don't they resent? They even resent other children.

AMBASSADOR: They do.

THE KING: John's children suspect their stepmother? Of infidelity?

AMBASSADOR: No, Your Majesty. Her virtue's unquestioned. It's her ambitions that're wondered at.

THE KING: What are her ambitions?

AMBASSADOR: I don't know enough about women to answer that with assurance.

THE KING: At a court where the queen moves men, a knowledge of women is important.

AMBASSADOR: The queen's in Aragon. I'm Ambassador to Castile. At my court there's the Princess Blanche, the unhappy daughter of John. Her position, as you can understand, isn't an easy one. Thus far Navarre, under the governorship of Prince Charles, has remained neutral. But now John has declared war for Navarre, too, and Blanche's husband, Prince Henry, goes to march against her brother.

THE KING: Then it's father-in-law with son-in-law . . .

AMBASSADOR: The Admiral of Castile and the King of Navarre . . .

THE KING: Against the son-in-law of the son-in-law . . .

AMBASSADOR: Henry of Castile . . .

THE KING: And brother-in-law against brother-in-law . . .

AMBASSADOR: Henry, the Prince of Castile, against Charles, the Prince of Navarre.

THE KING: Thank you for making everything so clear to me.

AMBASSADOR: But there's something else, Your Majesty. In Navarre, there're two factions, as in Castile. Those in Navarre are called the Agramonts and the Beaumontais. The Agramonts serve the king. And the Beaumonts serve the prince.

THE KING: The king being absent in Aragon. And the prince being at home.

AMBASSADOR: Your Majesty grasps it quickly. There's also the second daughter of the king by his first wife.

THE KING: My dear Ambassador, you shall tell me of her on some other occasion. The next time there's a war in Spain.

AMBASSADOR: It's really all one war, that'll never end until Spain is united.

THE KING: Or until someone's able to remember all the elementary facts. Bring me that map.

AMBASSADOR (*carries it to him*): Sire.

THE KING (*tears the map in small pieces*): Spain! Now let us go hunting. I repeat, I hate maps. They're too seductive. And I hate facts. There're too many of them.

AMBASSADOR: I think you may safely forget most of them, Your Majesty. But, in a way, they're interesting. To help get the *feel* of things.

THE KING: Kings. Queens. Dynasties. Factions.

AMBASSADOR: And perhaps economics. Of such things are the histories of kingdoms compounded. Yes. But let's forget for the moment that we're living only a few miles from Spain. Let's imagine we're living at a great distance, or at some time far removed, four or five hundred years in the future. In that way we'd gain the proper objectivity.

THE KING: The proper subjectivity.

AMBASSADOR: Well, then?

THE KING: The question we'd ask, if any, is what does all this mean to us? (*He scatters the last pieces of the map.*)

SCENE TWO: The MARSHAL OF NAVARRE, *arriving at the royal court in Aragon, received there by his cousin,* MOSSEN PIERRES DE PERALTA.

DE PERALTA (*observing the dust beaten from the Marshal's cloak*): You've brought your share of Navarre with you.

DON PEDRO: And something more. (*With a final brush.*) All of Navarre! (*He cleanses his ear with a soldierly finger.*)

DE PERALTA: Welcome to Aragon! What's your news, Cousin?

DON PEDRO: Charles refuses to fight against Castile.

DE PERALTA: Does he!

DON PEDRO: Beaumont joins Charles in this. Best of all, they've already made a separate peace with Castile.

DE PERALTA: This's wonderful! The king'll be furious.

DON PEDRO: We must hope so.

DE PERALTA: Oh yes, he will be!

DON PEDRO: I thought Beaumont would be more clever. But he has more heart than brain. Why'd Charles choose him as his Constable?

DE PERALTA: Yours is the best way to lay plans. Base them on the characters of men!

DON PEDRO: It's strange I know so much about character, when I've so little myself.

DE PERALTA: You've pride of family. We're Agramonts.

DON PEDRO: Is that it?

DE PERALTA: We've fared badly at the hands of the Beaumontais. You're Marshal of Navarre, but ought to be the Constable.

DON PEDRO: So, to revenge ourselves, we'll let Navarre and Aragon perish, set father against son?

DE PERALTA: A royal house is better divided; for when kings grow too strong, nobles are set down. The Beaumontais bow to the prince too quickly. That's our true quarrel.

DON PEDRO: Anyhow, we quarrel. That's enough. After awhile, the quarrel itself suffices. We no longer need reasons for it.

DE PERALTA: I have already sent word to the queen of your arrival.

DON PEDRO: Shall I see her first?

DE PERALTA: You'll speak well, as always, and we'll profit.

DON PEDRO: The act speaks for us. But Charles fears the Castilians in Navarre more than his father in Aragon.

DE PERALTA: You foresaw that.

DON PEDRO: I considered it this way. Beaumont . . . courage but little more. Charles . . . brains, but that's all. With them, one isn't added to one to get two. One's subtracted from one, leaving nothing. Now, if the Castilians are troubled no further with Navarre, they'll be free to turn on Aragon in full force. They'll defeat the king again, as at Olomedo. He can thank his son Charles for that. And he can thank Beamont, his son's Constable.

DE PERALTA: Yes, John wished Navarre attacked as a diversion from Aragon.

DON PEDRO: Good strategy. But the prince has a most unstrategic stomach for the smell of battle. He's fond of sweeter music. Like Saul, he sits all day listening to the French singers at his court.

DE PERALTA: How was the peace reached?

DON PEDRO: Charles remained in Olite, sent word to his dear brother-in-law he felt only love for him, as Henry of Castile is his own sister's husband—

DE PERALTA (*who has other knowledge*): Did he say that!

DON PEDRO: Considerably more. He even deplores his father's conduct, since coming to Aragon as his uncle Alfonso's governor.

DE PERALTA: Unless I'm much mistaken, his father's conduct from now on will be even more deplorable.

DON PEDRO: You're not mistaken. The king'll not enjoy hearing the full terms of the prince's statement.

DE PERALTA: Enjoy? You don't know what's happened in Aragon in your absence. His Majesty is already in enormous bad humour. He has a new and deeper grievance against Castile.

DON PEDRO: What's this?

DE PERALTA: You've clearer wits than mine, Cousin Pedro. How does this fit together? Henry, whom Charles calls his "dearly

[14]

beloved brother-in-law", has divorced Charles's sister and sent her home.

DON PEDRO (*astonished*): Divorced her? On what pretext?

DE PERALTA: Witchcraft. Henry, with whom Charles has just made peace behind the king's back, and against the king's orders. . . . Is this good fortune or bad for us?

DON PEDRO (*his mind seizing upon the most amazing part of this information*): Witchcraft?

DE PERALTA: He calls it that. In thirteen years she's given him no child.

DON PEDRO: Knowing Prince Henry, I can think of better reasons.

DE PERALTA: Yes, look upon Blanche, you can find them. But the pope was told she worked a spell that left the prince quite unable to enter her.

DON PEDRO: It'd be easier for a camel to go through the eye of a needle, than for Henry of Castile to enter any woman. He started too early.

DE PERALTA: The pope granted the divorce. Henry's seeking a new marriage alliance with Portugal. And Blanche's here, raising her lamentations against her father. She's with him now. A bottomless well of tears. Her father cannot draw up buckets enough to empty her.

DON PEDRO: I can remember Princess Blanche as a pale, thin girl, so shy she dared to peek only from behind her mother's skirts. The king'll not accept this insult!

DE PERALTA: The queen won't let him? She has little love for her stepdaughter, and Blanche none for her. But the more she can incense the king against the Castilian court, the more she assists her father. Joanna is Queen of Navarre, but she's also the daughter of the Admiral of Castile, and never forgets it.

DON PEDRO: She is Blanche's advocate?

DE PERALTA: Because she's her father's advocate.

DON PEDRO: John might wish such loyalty in his own children.

DE PERALTA: I do admire him. He's tireless, never wearied by misfortune or truly routed by defeat. He studies all new events to learn how he can use them to advantage.

DON PEDRO: He's our man. The realist. Our easy-going prince has charm of manner, seduces your sympathy when you're with him. But dreamers are riderless horses. (*pauses*) I wish it were otherwise.

DE PERALTA: We must emulate the king.

DON PEDRO: In a world of realists, only the weakling dreams.

DE PERALTA: I meant, what advantage, if any, lies in this turn?

DON PEDRO (*slowly*): The danger now is that Charles, when he learns what has happened, may turn on Castile to rehabilitate his sister.

DE PERALTA (*agreeing*): Yes.

DON PEDRO: We must prevent that.

DE PERALTA: How?

DON PEDRO: Through the queen.

DE PERALTA: Be careful how you speak to her. She's neither so guileless as she seems, nor as womanly as she would appear. And she'll not betray herself by a single word.

DON PEDRO: One word would do.

DE PERALTA: You'll not have it from her. But watch her, and you'll understand.

DON PEDRO: How do things continue between them?

DE PERALTA: The king grows blind. Slowly, but each day he sees a little less. The queen has become his eyes. She has also become his ears. Perhaps his mind. They are verily flesh of each other's flesh. It's a miraculous transformation. And none knows which is the sun and which is the moon at this court.

DON PEDRO: Well, we shall observe these heavenly bodies.

DE PERALTA: There never shone a fairer one than our queen anywhere. But don't trust her!

DON PEDRO: I'll not. (*pauses*) I'm very tired. It's a long ride from Navarre to Aragon, and I'm old. I envy the king. He renews himself in the spirit of his young wife.

(*They stand back as* JOANNA HENRIQUEZ *enters. She is now in her middle thirties and a famous beauty.*)

JOANNA: My Lord Marshal. You come from Navarre.

DON PEDRO (*kneels to kiss her hand*): Your Majesty.

JOANNA: Don Pedro, what brings you here when the king's enemies knock at the gates of Estella?

DON PEDRO: The Castilian armies have turned away. They vanished at a wave of your stepson's hand.

JOANNA: I can hardly believe this!

DON PEDRO: The hand held a pen. Your stepson is once more writing poems.

JOANNA: What's your news, Marshal?

DON PEDRO: The best and the worst. And better suited to reach your ears before it reaches the king's. You'll know better how to tell him. Your stepson, as governor of Navarre, has made peace with Castile. A separate treaty, with the aid of the Beaumontais.

JOANNA (*after a moment, softly*): Then Navarre is saved.

DON PEDRO: And Aragon left open to attack. And your father's cause in Castile quite lost for the moment.

JOANNA (*a long pause*): We shall know how to defend Aragon. As for my father, he has held his own against the King of Castile for as long as I can remember. He will keep on. (*another pause*) I was born of that struggle. That war was my childhood game.

DON PEDRO: You learned to play it well.

JOANNA: From birth. It's the royal game. My stepson denies his birthright. Peace at any price is a softer way of life.

DON PEDRO: Way of life? You borrow your stepson's language and translate his action into philosophy. In Navarre, some speak of it as treason. Silent rebellion. At least, cowardice.

JOANNA: To some it might seem so. But then, those who need a philosophy are cowards. My father taught me that.

DON PEDRO: The Admiral of Castile was a good preceptor.

JOANNA: What else do they say in Navarre?

DON PEDRO: That the king will be furious to learn his son has betrayed him.

JOANNA: Who prays for that? The Agramonts? You believe what most pleases you. My stepson's rebellion is deeper. In the game he plays, his mind makes war on his impulses. If he commits treason, that's where it takes place. He makes peace with Castile, but not with himself.

DON PEDRO: He yields to the Beaumontais. And the Beaumontais yield to him. We Agramonts would've followed a different policy. But only the Beaumonts shine at your stepson's court. The Agramonts stand in shadow.

JOANNA: An old grievance.

DON PEDRO: Which I think might be allied to yours.

JOANNA: Have I a grievance?

DON PEDRO: Your Majesty is so subtle that candor's the best diplomacy.

JOANNA: Or flattery?

DON PEDRO: Two causes most dear to Your Majesty suffer by your stepson's act. That of your father. And that of your son, Prince Ferdinand.

JOANNA: My son? An infant. What cause has he?

DON PEDRO: While Charles remains heir to Navarre, and after him Blanche and Eleanor, Prince Ferdinand—descended of the most royal blood of Spain, yours and the king's, Madame—takes his place in the world with not a single province to rule.

JOANNA: Do you, in this way, presume to read my mind?

DON PEDRO: I read a mother's heart.

JOANNA: I'm not a mother but a queen. All my loyalty to my father and son, combined, does not equal the loyalty I bear my husband.

DON PEDRO: Are they not synonymous?

JOANNA: My son's still at the breast.

DON PEDRO: It's then that a mother dreams most.

JOANNA: You mistake my feeling toward my stepson. By marriage, Prince Charles, too, is my son. Should I not hold him in close affection?

DON PEDRO: That'd be unnatural, Madame. Since you're almost of an age.

JOANNA: What is natural to others, is not natural to the blood royal. We are a race apart.

DE PERALTA: In what affection do the king's children hold you?

DON PEDRO: They resented your marriage!

JOANNA: Because of the love they bore their mother. Since my marriage, I've striven to keep the most friendly relations between the king and prince.

DE PERALTA: You came too late. Hasn't the prince always been jealous and forever desirous of his father's throne in Navarre? Doesn't he claim, by his mother's will, sole right to that throne?

JOANNA: Not openly. His mind's treason is not his heart's. He stays his hand.

DON PEDRO: Many others speak openly. They encourage him in his ambition; they misconstrue the king's every deed as tyranny.

JOANNA: For this reason, the king accepted his brother's offer of governorship in Aragon. He has generously left Navarre to the prince's rule.

DON PEDRO: Prince Charles has made a treacherous peace with Castile. Has he not flouted his trust?

JOANNA: The king alone shall judge his son's act. As father. And as king.

DON PEDRO: This maternal affection for your stepson compliments you. But a time has come when espousal of the prince's cause is disloyalty to the king.

JOANNA: I am determined to intervene before that happens.

DON PEDRO: Madame, my family's the strongest in Navarre. You hold its allegiance.

DE PERALTA: We offer that.

JOANNA: Thank you, Lord Marshal. And, de Peralta, thank you. We've long believed we can count on the Agramonts. And the Beaumontais?

DON PEDRO: That's the prince's party.

JOANNA: I hope there is only a king's party. And that all the feudal families of Navarre belong to it.

DON PEDRO: That'll not be attained by hope alone.

(JOHN, KING OF NAVARRE, *enters. He gropes a bit uncertainly. He is not wholly blind, but sees with difficulty. The queen goes to him, takes his hand, leads him.*

The king is bearded, fifty-seven, pale, handsome. The "laconic gravity" of his manner hides his irascible temper and active mind. He is a man of impressive presence, though with the small, white delicate hands of a woman. At times he is capable of an insinuating smile.)

JOHN: Where are you, Joanna? Will no one deliver me from that girl!

JOANNA: Have pity on her!

JOHN: Let her have pity on me. I am besieged by my own daughter in my own palace. Tears! Wailings! Complaints! Lamentations! Bring your army, Joanna, to rescue me. Shall I weep with her? What does she want?

(*He is followed by the* PRINCESS BLANCHE, *his tall, gaunt daughter by his first wife. The princess is twenty-nine.*)

BLANCHE: Am I truly a witch?

JOHN: You are!

BLANCHE: All Europe witnesses my indignity. And you'll do nothing?

JOHN: I'm already at war with your husband! What more can I do?

BLANCHE: Send me to the pope. I'll plead my own case.

JOHN: Where did she learn to speak this rude dialect? She was always the weakest, most timid of my children. What'd they feed you in Castile?

BLANCHE: Bitterness. Thirteen years of insult!

JOHN: Thirteen was always an unlucky number.

BLANCHE: You jest at my sorrow? Are you my father? Have you nothing in your heart but amusement at what's been said of me?

JOHN: Who's here?

JOANNA: Don Mosson. And his cousin, the Marshal of Navarre.

JOHN: Let my daughter be silent.

BLANCHE: Is my shame a secret? Am I not laughed at in all the courts of Spain and Italy? Has not the Marshal of Navarre heard and smiled at my story? Has he not asked what redress my father promises me?

JOHN: Am I a Christian? Or the Moorish King of Granada? Shall I make war on the pope?

BLANCHE: Send me to Rome!

JOHN: She will carry on the war single-handed! Henry returns his wife, but not her dowry. Where've I money for presents to the pope? Ask your brother. He's rich in Navarre, while I'm poor in Aragon. (angrily) With his help, we shall prevail on Castile.

BLANCHE: As a princess in Castile, I was not happy to see my father make war on my husband. What I want is restoration to my place. But not war.

JOHN: I've claims in Castile. And I'll win them.

BLANCHE: Once Henry has married again, nothing can be done.

JOHN: I'll marry you elsewhere.

BLANCHE: I wish no other husband.

JOHN: You miss him. He's not much to miss.

BLANCHE: Let Prince Henry take me back.

JOHN: And then?

BLANCHE: We shall live together, hating each other. That is what I would enjoy.

JOHN: If you talk this way, I can believe you are a virgin.

BLANCHE: For the rest of our lives. He has taught me insult. But if he cannot be free of me, he'll be my prisoner.

JOHN: What did my first wife leave me? A daughter who hates like a man. And a son who loves like a woman.

JOANNA: The Marshal brings news from Navarre.

JOHN: Why's the Marshal here! Are not the Castilians marching against Estella?

DON PEDRO (*kneeling*): Sire, Navarre's at peace.

JOHN: Peace?

DON PEDRO (*rising*): Your son and his Constable have signed a separate treaty with Prince Henry. Castile withdraws from Navarre and turns again toward Aragon.

JOHN: Peace? Signed?

(*They stand silent. The king passes his hand before his face.*)

I can still see my hand. And I know a lie when I hear one! Don Pedro, you've come with some scheme.

DON PEDRO: No scheme, Sire. Is the king so blind he doesn't know the truth in Navarre!

JOHN: Peace? I swore to forget the word. My son would destroy me? What was his price?

DON PEDRO: Only the love he bore his brother-in-law, husband of his sister Blanche.

BLANCHE: He did that for me!

JOHN: Does he place his sister before his father? What agreements have my children against me, that they opposed my marriage, secretly deny my right to the throne, now seek to destroy me?

BLANCHE: Charles doesn't seek that!

JOHN (*to her*): You, too! (*turns on Don Pedro*) Was that all? Beaumont? My son's Constable. What love does he bear for Henry of Castile?

DON PEDRO: That was but a preface. The prince repudiates your war with Castile. He deplores the money and men you have spent for your claims there. He says you act chiefly at the instigation of the queen, who makes use of you to further her father's cause.

JOHN: And you? Why did you not warn me?

DON PEDRO: The prince asks no counsel of the Agramonts. Are we not the king's friends?

JOHN: And how do they receive this in Navarre?

DON PEDRO: Some welcome it.

BLANCHE: They welcome peace. My brother has thought of his people.

JOHN: Are they not my people?

BLANCHE: You know Charles to be gentle, more suited for music than war.

JOHN: Yes, gentle. But how gentle? His music makes a peculiar sound. I detect a discordant note.

BLANCHE: He loves peace.

JOHN: And hates his father. My children all know how to hate me. Castile is not the enemy now. But Navarre. My own kingdom. And my son. (pauses) We shall need a truce with Castile. My son's inaction marches against us. We're forced to it.

BLANCHE: Peace! That is all he ever desired.

JOHN: And during the truce, I'll go to Navarre.

BLANCHE: Do not!

JOHN: Am I so unwelcome? Is my name so hateful there? Our Beaumont shall no longer be Constable. I'll depose him. He'll forfeit his lands.

BLANCHE: You're already the queen's fool. Do not be the fool of the Agramonts.

JOANNA: Don't say that, Blanche!

DON PEDRO: Your son not only betrays you. He betrays his intentions. Does he not live in the style of a king, display a king's prerogatives? Is not his court the most lavish in Spain, while you're forced to beg money from Navarre for your wars? Does he send men to assist you? Does he not expect you to stay away from Navarre, while he conspires with Beaumont?

BLANCHE: Dare you speak thus of your prince, who's the rightful ruler of Navarre! Does my father support this!

JOHN: Whose is the treason? Yours! That you support your brother against me! By what right does he rule, save by my sufferance!

[22]

BLANCHE: Do you say that, Father? Are you not King of Navarre only because Charles permits you to keep the title!

JOHN: By the law of Navarre, as head of a family, the rights of my children are mine.

BLANCHE: That was never my mother's intention, nor the wish of Navarre, nor your first profession.

JOHN (*bitterly*): I've long guessed my children's thoughts.

BLANCHE: Charles has been a good son. He's checked the feeling of his people against you.

JOHN: You've been taught this hostility in Castile? Or have you always nurtured it? (*freeing himself from the queen's warning hand*) My subjects in Navarre say I've been a bad father and a worse king? You agree with them?

BLANCHE: You've allowed my stepmother to employ you as her father's instrument, while she schemes to dispose of us for her own son's sake.

JOANNA: This last, my lord, is your daughter's true complaint! Your children fear me. And the child at my breast.

BLANCHE: Should we not?

JOHN: Charles is the acknowledged heir of my kingdom. But he'll be governor no longer. I'll return to Navarre.

BLANCHE: Were my brother king, had I my rights, I'd go to Rome. There'd be no war with Castile. And there'd be enough money.

JOANNA: This also prompts her.

JOHN (*to Blanche*): I shall send you to your gentle brother. You be the messenger of my coming.

BLANCHE: I should choose to be with him.

DON PEDRO: Are not the Agramonts your most loyal vassals? Haven't we followed you to Aragon and placed our swords at your command? But how does your son treat us? Not only does he favor the Beaumontais but he deprives us of office and despoils us of our fiefs. Does that suggest nothing to Your Majesty?

BLANCHE: This can't be true.

JOHN (*to Don Pedro*): You shall return to Navarre with me. I'll study your complaints. If they're real, they shall be righted.

JOANNA: Do not take harsh action, my lord. Do not be hasty or misread what motives lie in your son's heart. Nor forget the genuine

[23]

love the people of Navarre bear to their prince. You don't wish to offend them.

BLANCHE (*fiercely*): Does the queen speak?

JOANNA: You'll forgive Blanche's impetuous tongue. She's unnerved by her sorrow. She is the more frustrate that we find ourselves helpless to right her wrong. It's a true wrong. Your honor, as well as hers, has been slighted.

BLANCHE: This's the daughter of the Admiral of Castile. She's relentless. Only a continued war will please her.

JOANNA: It's you who are relentless, Blanche. And an even poorer sister to Charles than you're a daughter to the king. Why've you raised the king's anger against him? Your talk's foolish. And when you accuse me, do you not know you cross the king further? Not for my sake, but your father's, shouldn't you spare me?

BLANCHE: My father's sight fails him. Not mine.

JOANNA: When his sight's gone, my eyes shall be his. He shall look at you kindly. (*to John*) You know your son well. He's loved because he's good. He is generous. A scholar more than a statesman. An artist more than a practical ruler. But the King of Navarre too is good. He's even more generous. If Charles has purchased peace for Navarre, it's his father who must pay for it. Let me go to Navarre and tell this to the people, without breaking your pact to leave Charles in authority there. Appoint me governor jointly with Charles, sharing his office and revenues, that I may help guide him, while vigilant to your best interests, and keep friendship between father and son.

BLANCHE: My stepmother's cunning. She knows neither Charles nor Navarre would accept her. Under the pretense of seeking peace and friendship, she provokes civil war.

JOANNA: For thirteen years my stepdaughter was the enemy of the Admiral of Castile. She can think of me in only one way.

DON PEDRO (*to John*): Your Majesty, the queen's proposal is wise. It's admirable.

BLANCHE: I warn you. She's hated more than you! Civil war.

JOANNA: What do you say, my lord?

JOHN: So be it.

SCENE THREE: CHARLES VII *of France receives his ambassador.*

THE KING: Welcome to France.

AMBASSADOR (*rising*): I thank Your Majesty and pray my services have been of value.

THE KING: You're my ambassador to Castile? It's five years since you were here last.

AMBASSADOR: Your Majesty commanded me to learn something of women. That's not done quickly.

THE KING: I could have told it all to you in a sentence.

AMBASSADOR: What would that be, Sire?

THE KING: Some other time. What is the news from Castile?

AMBASSADOR: The war continues.

THE KING: What war's that?

AMBASSADOR: With Navarre and Aragon. But, for the moment, all three countries observe a truce.

THE KING: These Spanish are harsh. A violent, intractable people.

AMBASSADOR: Braver than most, Your Majesty. But they're divided, when they should really be one.

THE KING: That'd make Spain a strong neighbor. It's not good policy for France.

AMBASSADOR: Their division is deep. Once it was father-in-law against son-in-law. But now, for the past five years in Navarre, it has been father against son.

THE KING: What's this?

AMBASSADOR: Civil war. And most bloody.

THE KING: I can't pretend to follow these complicated Spanish quarrels.

AMBASSADOR: The story is this, Your Majesty. The rightful heir to Navarre is Prince Charles. But his father, the younger brother of Alfonso of Aragon, has continued to hold the throne . . .

THE KING (*interrupting*): I recall something of this. You've told it to me before.

AMBASSADOR: I fear to weary you by repetition.

THE KING: History and politics. They're the same thing over and over again. Always repetition.

AMBASSADOR: I speak of John and Charles . . .

THE KING: And that's also an old story. Timeless. David and Absalom. But you ring a few changes.

AMBASSADOR: This change. John sent his second wife to Navarre to keep watch on Charles and share his governorship. The people were hostile to the new queen, and particularly the ruling party, the Beaumontais, were opposed to the Agramonts, the queen's supporters. After bickering, there was civil war.

THE KING: I've a son, too. His name is Louis. He can scarcely wait until I die. But he doesn't take openly to the field against me.

AMBASSADOR: Both the king and his son sought to prevent the war, but their followers got out of hand. You see, the trouble was not really between the king and his son. It was between the Beaumontais and the Agramonts. The Beaumonts represent a part of Navarre that lives in the mountains. The Agramonts, a part that lives on the plains. Between the mountain people and those on the plains there have long been differences. . . .

THE KING: We only think ourselves kings. And deceive ourselves, when we seek to name royal causes for the wars we declare. We don't even make wars. They're made for us.

AMBASSADOR: That was true of Prince Charles. He had no heart for the struggle against his father. He was soon defeated and imprisoned. But the Beaumonts fought on. They besieged the queen, who with a naked sword in her hand withstood her enemies.

THE KING: This's distressing. I do not like to see the authority of kings challenged. And especially by princes. As I said before, I have a son named Louis . . .

AMBASSADOR: His subjects in Navarre forced the king to release the prince. They rallied around Charles again, and the war began once more.

THE KING: No more about it! Civil war in Spain. If a people living four or five hundred years after us heard this story, wouldn't they ask what did all this mean to them? We must do the same.

AMBASSADOR: Your Majesty seeks to be objective.

THE KING: And subjective.

AMBASSADOR: Does Your Majesty wish to be objective and subjective at the same time? I only wish I had a map. You'd find it very interesting.

THE KING: A map of Spain? (*points*) Against the wall.

AMBASSADOR: On my last visit, you destroyed the map.

THE KING: That was five years ago. Time enough since then for a new one to be drawn. But I hate maps. There're too many lines on them.

AMBASSADOR: Some lines on maps are rivers. They can't be changed. But other lines are boundaries. They can always be removed.

THE KING: Lines. Lines.

AMBASSADOR: And there're also lines not shown on maps.

THE KING: What lines are those?

AMBASSADOR: Why, Sire, royal lines. Fathers, sons, and daughters.

THE KING: The succession?

AMBASSADOR: Inheritance, Your Majesty, is the easiest form of conquest. And the least expensive.

THE KING: Speak up!

AMBASSADOR: John of Navarre has three children by his first wife.

THE KING: Charles, Blanche, and Eleanor. It comes to me now. If I repeat anything three times, I don't forget.

AMBASSADOR: Blanche is the divorced wife of Henry of Castile. There's civil war in Navarre, and she has taken sides with her brother. But the younger daughter, Eleanor, has joined her father.

THE KING: Eleanor is a good daughter.

AMBASSADOR: For a price. The king has named Eleanor as his successor.

THE KING: Denouncing Charles and Blanche?

AMBASSADOR: Yes, Your Majesty. And Eleanor's married to Gaston, the Count de Foix, who's your vassal.

THE KING: Why then, if Eleanor succeeds to the throne of Navarre, that country comes under my dominion?

AMBASSADOR: Precisely, Sire.

THE KING: Show me on the map!

AMBASSADOR: Gaston's land lies here. This's Navarre.

THE KING: Give me the map!

AMBASSADOR: At your command, Sire.

THE KING: Spain's many colors.

AMBASSADOR: Too many.

THE KING: And Navarre's this brown patch?

AMBASSADOR: It might better be shown as blood-red.

THE KING: I hate maps. They seduce me. (*He makes as though to destroy the map, but the Ambassador snatches it from him.*)

AMBASSADOR: Not yet, Your Majesty. Not yet. A moment!

THE KING: Do you dare!

AMBASSADOR: We must save it, Your Majesty, until I've finished my exposition. I'd dare anything for that. When I'm done, Sire, I'm sure you will not be offended by my action.

THE KING: Well, give it back to me.

AMBASSADOR (*hands him the map*): At your command.

THE KING: You were showing me Gaston's lands. And Navarre.

AMBASSADOR: Let me show you something else. And continue my account.

THE KING: Well, do it quickly. And in the simplest words. I'd like to go hunting.

AMBASSADOR: Yes, Sire. (*Reaches over the King's shoulder to point.*) Look. Here's Naples. John's brother, Alfonso, was king there. When Prince Charles grew weary of the war, he left his sister behind him as governor of Navarre, and went to Italy, to the Neapolitan court of his uncle.

THE KING: I knew Alfonso.

AMBASSADOR: That magnanimous man welcomed his nephew. They were kindred spirits. Both shared a love of classical learning. Both kept poets and scholars at their court. While he was imprisoned at Monroy, the prince even occupied himself with writing a history of the Kings of Navarre.

THE KING: I wish my son would busy himself with history. But the few words my son can spell aren't to my liking. They're his father's death. And his father's throne.

AMBASSADOR: We see ourselves better when we know history. And one of our deepest delights is to read some likeness to our own story in the story of the past. But let's continue with the history before us. Charles was too gentle to fight. He went to Naples. He asked his uncle's help.

THE KING: You've already told me that.

AMBASSADOR: Alfonso upbraided him for his unfilial acts towards his father.

THE KING: That was proper.

AMBASSADOR: But Alfonso also knew that his brother John was wholly in the wrong. He forced an immediate truce on the warring parties, and threatened John with loss of the governorship of Aragon, if he did not restore the rights of his son and daughter in Navarre.

THE KING: Charles and Blanche? But Eleanor's my vassal.

AMBASSADOR: We're remembering that, Sire.

THE KING: She's married to Gaston de Foix? I know him. He's a noble scoundrel. But it doesn't matter, as long as Gaston's my vassal. For I'm a good king.

AMBASSADOR: Yes, Sire. Gaston's a scoundrel. But if he should become King of Navarre, it'd come under your liberal dominion. And more than Navarre. Open your map, Sire . . . The truth is, Gaston waited to see which way the war was going, before taking sides.

THE KING: He's a true Frenchman.

AMBASSADOR: He did this, although he and Prince Charles, as neighbors, had been lifelong friends. Two young men the same age . . .

THE KING: Friendship is not for princes.

AMBASSADOR: That's how the affair stood two months ago, when as you know, Alfonso suddenly died. Is your map ready? By his will, his brother John inherited all his territories except Naples, which went to a bastard son. John is now King of Aragon, Catalonia, Majorca, Sicily. Prince Charles has not only lost his protector, but is again wholly in the power of his father.

THE KING: And Eleanor might inherit all this? Together with Navarre!

AMBASSADOR: She might. And she might not. There's Prince Charles to be considered.

THE KING: Where is he?

AMBASSADOR: Prince Charles is loved everywhere. Immediately the Neapolitans asked him to be their king.

THE KING: King of Naples?

AMBASSADOR: The prince refused. He has retired to Sicily, where he holds court in a monastery and devotes himself to translating the *Ethics* of Aristotle.

THE KING: *Ethics*? Who is Aristotle?

AMBASSADOR: A Greek philosopher. Long dead.

THE KING: Then we need not concern ourselves about him.

AMBASSADOR: In Sicily, too, Prince Charles is loved. And it's said that the people there plan to offer him their throne. This worries his father. Not only the Sicilians, but the Catalonians declare their affection for him.

THE KING: My affection is suddenly towards his sister Eleanor. I think I shall name her husband Gaston as my ambassador to King John, so that he may be always at his court, and have a hand in whatever may happen.

AMBASSADOR: Sire, you gaze long at the map.

THE KING: I'd thought these Spanish quarrels remote. But now, properly read, they concern us deeply. Remember, my friend, the question we must always ask ourselves is what does all this mean to us?

SCENE FOUR: The Beautiful DONA BRIANDA *works at her tapestry, while* DON MORENO CARBONERO *prepares his canvas, watched by the aged Valencian poet,* AUSIAS MARCH.

MARCH: Why paint the prince in those robes?

CARBONERO: The world, Master March, has an idea how a prince should look.

MARCH: Better portray the royalty of his mind.

CARBONERO: That comes less easily to the brush.

BRIANDA: Don Moreno is right. I love to see the prince in his finest velvets, with a gold chain about his neck.

CARBONERO: You see. There's the prince as even our Brianda beholds him.

MARCH (*softly*): I too see the prince with a gold chain 'round his neck.

BRIANDA: Not "our Brianda". *His* Brianda. My lord's jealous.

CARBONERO (*after he has crossed and kissed her*): He has no reason to be.

MARCH: You wrong a good man. A generous man. One who has done much for you.

[30]

CARBONERO (*returning to his canvas*): Shall Charles be less generous than his mistress?

BRIANDA: If the prince loves me, as he says, why does he not marry me?

MARCH: He's a prince. And that, for him, is something more than a velvet suit and a gold chain.

CARBONERO: It's only the velvet I see. The color. The feel of it. I shall paint the prince for the future. And when men and women look upon him, they shall say, "What a beautiful suit! Look how the artist has caught the texture and folds of the garment. Look at the opulent glint of the gold jewel!" In the world of my senses, my friend, these things are most important.

MARCH: Physical beauty. There'll be many more velvet suits. And many more gold chains. But when again a man of his qualities?

CARBONERO: Of his moral qualities, you shall write poems. But the prince too loves the things I love. (*with a nod to the prince's mistress*) Even Brianda. And that love we'll share on canvas.

MARCH: I think, did you paint him as he is, men would look at him and say, "This was the perfect prince. And the most unfortunate prince. The most loved. And the most sinned against. Charles IV, the uncrowned King of Navarre. Charles, the uncrowned King of Naples. Of Sicily. Of Barcelona. Of Aragon."

CARBONERO: Charles has chosen the wrong enemies.

MARCH: And the wrong friends.

CARBONERO: We're both his friends, Master March. But in different ways. You're the friend of his mind. And I'm the friend of his senses. Yet we both love him for what he is. The philosopher. The artist.

MARCH: I'm thinking of Beaumont, who also loves him. And of his sister Blanche, who comes to him today. They love him for what he's not, and was never intended to be. They love him because they hate others and must balance their emotions. Any man, weighed in the wrong scale, may be found wanting.

CARBONERO: What does the world's opinion count?

MARCH: To him, everything. Princes are born to the world. They're born to adulation and the crowd's applause.

CARBONERO: He has refused the crown of Naples and sought a monastery.

MARCH: And lives in a monastery with a mistress, a court painter, musicians, poets such as myself, secretaries, a treasurer, a major-domo. That's hardly an ascetic life. He doesn't belong here but in Naples.

CARBONERO: He doesn't like the climate there. It's malarial.

BRIANDA: I hear the prince.

(CHARLES *is thirty-nine, and like his father, pale and handsome. His grey eyes and long, straight nose give his expression a natural melancholy. He is elegantly dressed and bears a rolled parchment in his hand.*)

CHARLES (*he crosses to Brianda and kisses her softly on the brow*): Your tapestry advances. (*to Carbonero*) You're an artist, Don Moreno. You shall pass judgment on Brianda's pattern.

CARBONERO: I greatly admire the pattern.

CHARLES (*passing the parchment to March*): I've written a poem, Master. (*He turns to regard Carbonero's canvas.*) You shall paint me as a king today, Don Moreno. My sister comes. And a deputation from Catalonia. Besides, I've news for you. We're leaving Sicily.

BRIANDA: Leaving?

CARBONERO: You're tired of Sicily?

CHARLES: Of the orange trees? The limes? The blue sea? Do you think I've grown weary of conversation with Ausias March, the greatest poet in Spain, or the chatter of Don Moreno, who loves color and paint as a man loves a woman? But my father's anger pursues me. I'm too much loved in Sicily. And so I've received a message from him. We go to Majorca.

MARCH: The king fears the Sicilians might offer you their throne as did the Neapolitans!

CHARLES: The Sicilians might. They remember my mother as the noblest, most gracious of queens. And were the Devil her son, they'd welcome him.

MARCH: If you refused the king's order?

CHARLES: Would you take up arms in my behalf, Don Ausias?

MARCH: I'm an old man. But Beaumont, in Navarre? And the Sicilians?

CHARLES: My father's too powerful. And I'm now too poor. He's the legitimate King of Aragon and Catalonia. My brother-in-law helps him. Beaumont scarcely holds his own in Navarre. I've already provoked five years of hopeless civil war. Shall I provoke more, because the climate of Sicily agrees with me?

MARCH: If only your uncle had lived!

CHARLES: Why then I should not be translating the *Ethics* of Aristotle. I should doubtless have caught malaria in Naples. Or I should be back in Navarre, directing that endless game of intrigue between Constable Beaumont and the Marshal, Don Pedro. Each protesting he loves me, or loves the king, when his amorous emotion, if he has any, is more likely for himself and the interests of his faction. No, we shall go quietly to Majorca. Perhaps you'll come with me? The sea there's almost as blue. There'll be olive trees. The Spanish orange. And Aristotle reads as well in Majorca as in Messina.

MARCH: But here in Sicily you've been granted a financial bounty by the people.

CHARLES: That's true. In Majorca we'll have to consider economics as well as philosophy. And economics is something which has never appealed to me. You've forgotten my poem, Master March? (*to Brianda*) You'll come with me to Majorca, Brianda. And the boy.

BRIANDA: I pray, my lord, you shall never desert our son.

CHARLES: I know what it is to be a son disowned by his father. Your boy's my natural son. He'll not have an unnatural father.

MARCH (*glancing up from the parchment*): You've used the Petrarchan form.

CHARLES: Come, Master! Can't you see I tremble so that Don Moreno can scarcely follow me with his brush?

CARBONERO: My lord, if you could remain more still.

CHARLES: A poet's first sonnet is a novitiate's marriage with Christ. I've taken the veil.

MARCH: It's a good poem.

CHARLES: Which speaks? The critic or courtier?

MARCH: Did you write as the man or the prince?

CHARLES: A good question.

MARCH: The poet's both critic and courtier. He's also man and prince in one. He likewise reigns by divine right. Over the heart. The mind. The passions.

CHARLES: You believe in the divine right of princes?

MARCH: Do you not?

CHARLES: A man's a prince by some divine chance. That the royal seed of his father swells in a royal womb. That he, and he alone, is the consequence. Who can deny a certain divine ordination in that?

MARCH: None.

CHARLES: And yet they speak of the blood royal as though it were something you could recognize in the man. A special quality. A destiny quite apart from circumstance. Do you believe in that, too?

MARCH: I'm a poet, my lord, and I do believe in it.

CHARLES: And you, Don Moreno? You've a painter's eye. You see what other men cannot .

CARBONERO: I admire your lordship's taste in clothes. And your fine taste in jewelery.

CHARLES: That's a truthful answer.

MARCH: No, my prince. It's less than truthful. There are princes among men. There're men endowed with a special quality. It's a quality for which they are loved—it may be by those who scarcely know them. As you were loved in Navarre.

CHARLES: For the piety of my cause.

MARCH: As you were loved in Naples . . .

CHARLES: For the affection in which my uncle held me.

MARCH: As you are loved in Sicily . . .

CHARLES: Because of my mother.

MARCH: Those who are princes among men have a higher intelligence and a special sensitivity. They are born with a "divine" or superior faculty. Men turn to such " princes" for help and leadership.

CHARLES: Do men love me? I've little love for them.

MARCH: You're in a bad mood. You, who love the beauty that man can produce, and the morality of great minds—painting and philosophy—must love what it is in men that makes beauty and morality. Must love men themselves.

CHARLES: Not as subjects. Everywhere I've gone, men have wanted me to be their king.

MARCH: You turn from your destiny.

CHARLES: The mob of Naples! Who would rule them? Did you smell, as I did, the stench of the Neapolitan mob?

MARCH: There're many hungry and naked in Naples. Not only the poets and painters need kings. And the lovers of freedom. The hungry and naked need them.

CHARLES: We feel sorry for the troubles of others, if they're far enough away from us. When they're near us, we dislike them.

MARCH: Near troubles are a danger. What we feel then is fear.

CHARLES: Then to pity asks a courage I lack.

MARCH: You have it. As you have love for men. It is *that* you fear. But you are one of those princes among men who must accept not only your divine privileges but also your divine duties. That is why I have told Don Moreno to paint you not in these costly trappings but in your naked merit.

CHARLES: No, Moreno. Paint me as you see me. And as I see myself. In this velour suit. And a book beside me. We love these things. (*to March*) Spare me your harsh poetry, my friend.

MARCH: If you'll spare me your empty sonnets. And the outward princely spectacle.

CHARLES: It's not necessary for me to be profound, while I know enough Greek to render Aristotle into Spanish.

MARCH: Any monkish clerk can do that. You're a prince. In the past, have princes been known for their knowledge of Greek!

CHARLES: This's a new age. In the past, men of royal birth needed political power, because they did not have the power of knowledge. But we're in the fifteenth century. The century of new light in Europe! When the pagan glories of the ancients are to be married to the new glories of Christianity!

MARCH: Men are neither Christian nor pagan in these times. They're so fashioned of sense and spirit, the one quite cancels out the other, leaving nothing.

CHARLES: Men are learning to love philosophical truth.

MARCH: Abstract truth is a hag. A Niobe with tears from a stone face. A Gorgon with a petrifying gaze.

CHARLES: There's also physical beauty.

MARCH: Physical beauty? That's all deception.

CHARLES: You must forgive my saying it, Master March. But Don Moreno and I are young.

MARCH: It is true. I'm old. I no longer suck at the hasps of beauty.

But you'll learn what I've learned. The greatest poetry, the highest beauty, is right action.

CHARLES: You're a poet with one theme. (*Rises.*) We cannot argue about these things. If I'm anything, I'm beauty's fool. (*to his mistress*) Even your fool, Brianda. Why am I so jealous of you, who am myself so unfaithful? Because yours is a pure, a virginal beauty. And I cannot bear the thought that beauty could deceive me. I must believe the evidence of my eyes and trust the testimony of my senses. These guide my impulses. That's my character. My religion. My philosophy.

MARCH: A love of physical beauty?

CHARLES: What's more divine? More royal? More princely?

BRIANDA: And do you think I deceive you, my lord?

CHARLES: I pray not. (*Resumes his pose.*) (*to Brianda*) Does Don Moreno never cast sheep's eyes at you?

CARBONERO (*working*): He does not, my lord.

CHARLES: Then he's no artist. He does not know a pretty face when he sees one. (*after a moment*) At the same time, Moreno, there is no danger that you will be petrified by that Gorgon truth of Don Ausias' invention. (*to March*) Let's declare a truce, Master March. The Catalans come. It's not hard to guess their mission. My sister is arrived in Sicily and will march against me with an army of tears and memories. Of all enemies, a sister's tears are the most difficult to rout. A woman's tears are the most persuasive poetry.

MARCH: May they convince you!

CHARLES: Is this a truce? (*pauses*) My sister is Niobe. She is the stone body and endless weeping. What does love, turned aside, do to a woman?

MARCH: Shall you, like your sister, miss your destiny?

CHARLES: You speak of destiny as though it were something known, measurable, definite.

MARCH: There's only one destiny for princes.

CHARLES: What's that? (*as March is silent*) You don't answer my question.

MARCH: Those whose destiny it is to serve the common man, must expect the gratitude of common men. The favor of kings is fickle. But the favor of the mob is more fickle. Kings have it in their power to grant rewards. But the mob is poor. It has nothing. It can give no rewards.

CHARLES: You do not tempt me.

MARCH: I'm old. For whom do I write poetry? For the mob? For the common man? For fame? I am not tempted by these. I write for myself. I follow my predestined course, as you must, too.

CHARLES: Why is this predestined?

MARCH: Because you're Charles of Navarre. Because you're not only a prince by natural quality but by circumstance as well. By the divine chance of which you spoke.

CHARLES: Cannot the people be served by those princes among men in whom there is no royal blood? Let the mob produce its own leaders.

MARCH: In future centuries, perhaps. But not in ours. With us, because the people are still not ready, the leader must come dressed in all the royal and symbolic trappings with which Don Moreno has adorned you. He has betrayed, by his words, the common mind.

(*Softly a bell chimes.*)

CHARLES: What time?

BRIANDA: An hour before noon.

CHARLES: Then Blanche comes. (*rises*) Leave me, please. Let me look on the image Don Moreno has painted. The world's image.

(*They retire to left. He continues staring at the canvas in silence, until the door opens at right and* BLANCHE *enters. He looks up and addresses her.*)

There is another image, Blanche, that I read in your eyes.

(*He crosses to her and bends to kiss her hand.*)

Welcome, Blanche.

BLANCHE: For how long? They tell me you leave.

CHARLES: For Majorca. Yes.

BLANCHE: Are you not loved in Sicily?

CHARLES: Too much loved. (*pauses*) What's the news in Navarre? How does Beaumont?

BLANCHE: He keeps the truce, for he dare not do otherwise.

CHARLES: And the king?

BLANCHE: In Aragon.

CHARLES: And the queen?

BLANCHE: With him. Our sister Eleanor holds forth in Navarre. She has been named governor there.

CHARLES: So it has been sister against sister! Are we of this family human? There're weird fish that swallow their young. And great plants, with a royal smell, that entice men and capture them whole in their imprisoning leaves, where they're held to rot and decay. We of Navarre are equally strange and offensive.

BLANCHE: There's a royal smell in Navarre. And a woman who entices and captures men.

CHARLES: You believe this of our stepmother?

BLANCHE: You're another caught by that soft voice and smiling face.

CHARLES: She has beauty. But, I believe, means us no harm. Our father had no need to borrow her ambition. He has always had enough of his own.

BLANCHE: He drives me from Navarre, as you were driven. He drives us from Sicily. He becomes more rapacious, more unforgiving, as he grows older. When he assumed the throne of Aragon, should not the throne of Navarre have reverted to you? This's his last crime against us. He is filled with new hatreds and new conspiracies. Who inspires him? Who keeps him young, when he should be weak and senile?

CHARLES: It was wrong of me to leave you behind in Navarre. I'm glad you're here with me again. We've lost, Blanche.

BLANCHE: Lost? Why?

CHARLES: We've more than the king and queen arrayed against us. I can't fight my own inclination.

BLANCHE: And shall Eleanor's French husband usurp your inheritance?

CHARLES: I've come into a new legacy. The Greeks have left me a fortune.

BLANCHE: What Greeks are these?

CHARLES: Plato and Aristotle. They were philosophers. They speak of a new world. One different from Navarre. A world of reason, learning, and light.

BLANCHE: This light, I think, is the one in my stepmother's eyes.

CHARLES (*holding up her face*): Is this Blanche, my little sister? The shy Blanche? Blanche, who quailed at every loud sound and bold glance? The Blanche I loved?

[38]

BLANCHE: Is this my brother? Is this Charles the prince? I don't think so.

CHARLES: What has time done to us? What has love done to us?

BLANCHE: It has made a woman of me. But something less than a man of you. Is my brother a coward?

CHARLES: Call me that. I am not so much a coward as to be afraid of the word.

BLANCHE: Do they love you in Sicily?

CHARLES: Yes.

BLANCHE: Then stay here.

CHARLES: And bring my father against them? That'd be a poor way to repay their affection.

BLANCHE: Navarre would rise again at your name. This truce serves us. Beaumont still defends himself and commands his forces.

CHARLES: Bloodshed. I don't want a throne at that price.

BLANCHE: You were offered the throne of Naples. Yours without struggle. You refused.

CHARLES: My uncle willed Naples to his bastard. He was kind to us. Should I be less kind to his dying wish? To his memory?

BLANCHE: You're filled with scruples. But they're only excuses. Our father and stepmother, who rule half of Spain, are they so scrupulous?

CHARLES: Let *me* be honest.

BLANCHE: Who is honest in a dishonest world? Only the weak. The cowardly.

CHARLES: Is dishonesty strength?

BLANCHE: Honesty is weakness, because it is quickly crushed. Only the strong can afford to be honest. You are not strong. After, when you have crushed your father. . . .

CHARLES: This's not logic but the embittered will.

BLANCHE: Yes, bitter.

CHARLES: You're implacable.

BLANCHE: I remember what has happened to me. I do not permit myself the weakness of forgetting. It has already cost too much.

CHARLES (*staring at her*): Where in you are the virtues I once perceived and loved? A sisterly compassion. Loyalty.

BLANCHE: I am a better sister to you than Eleanor. And a more loyal one. And if I have compassion, it's to find you so without manly honor and pride.

CHARLES: I'm sorry for my father. You should have been his son.

BLANCHE: Is Navarre small and Sicily weak? You are so filled with pity for them, that you deliver them to the king. That's a strange show of pity. In return for their love, you give them over to tyranny and repression. As, in return for my love, my husband handed me back to my father.

CHARLES: What else?

BLANCHE: Catalonia is strong. Stronger even than Aragon. And sends you a deputation. They do not love the king in Barcelona.

CHARLES: You ask me to rob our father of realms rightfully his?

BLANCHE: As he has robbed you of yours.

CHARLES: Are we a family of thieves?

BLANCHE: When princes steal, it is not called theft.

CHARLES: Does the world find a more magniloquent name?

BLANCHE: I don't read Greek. I'm not a philosopher. But I can find moral reasons enough to steal three Catalonias from my sister and stepmother. And from my stepmother's son, for whom night and day she schemes to destroy you.

CHARLES: You imagine this.

BLANCHE: How much will you suffer? I, who should be Queen of Castile, am your penniless dependent. And you, who should be King of Navarre, cannot even hide yourself in a Sicilian monastery, without the voice of your father and stepmother pursuing you. Do you want peace? They'll never let you at peace.

CHARLES (convinced): No.

BLANCHE: I might believe this of you, were you an Italian. But you are a Spaniard. Is this the portrait of a Spanish prince you present to the world!

CHARLES: I don't wonder that Henry divorced you for witchcraft. I, too, am impotent before you.

BLANCHE: I see you dressed as a king. You do not act as one. (turns to the canvas) And how have they painted you?

CHARLES: As you see.

BLANCHE: A book beside you! A scholar in a velvet suit, with a gold chain at your neck. That's not how our grandfather was painted!

[40]

Charles the Bold . . . For whom you were named. Even our stepmother wields a sword.

CHARLES: She too has witchcraft, but casts a spell of a different sort. And my father is all potency.

(AUSIAS MARCH *enters from right.*)

MARCH: Your Highness, the deputation from Catalonia awaits you.

CHARLES: Here's the world.

MARCH: Take it, my prince.

CHARLES: My sister is Elektra. She'd have me play the rôle of Orestes. And you, Don Ausias, speak to me in a nobler language than any Greek poet. In my sister burns hatred. In you, duty. What burns in the heart of these Catalans?

MARCH: Though I too am from Valencia, they shall speak for themselves.

CHARLES: Withdraw, Blanche. I do not want them to know, when they see how strong you are, how weak I am by contrast.

(BLANCHE *is about to speak, but March, raising his hand, warns her to silence. She withdraws.*)

You, Master March, stay with me.

MARCH: Yes, Your Highness.

(*He goes to the door and admits* NICOLAU VINOT, FRAY JUAN, *and the others of the deputation. The men enter and kneel, save for the Dominican, who remains upright.*)

DEPUTATION: Your Highness.

CHARLES (*to Fray Juan*): You do not kneel to earthly princes?

FRAY JUAN: No, Your Highness.

CHARLES: Why do you kneel to the Heavenly Prince? He reads your heart. He's in less need of your outward show of homage than I am.

(*The Dominican hesitates, then suddenly kneels.*)

I'm grateful for this. You are friends from Catalonia? Welcome. And please rise. (*as they do so*) Who speaks for you?

VINOT: I shall, my lord.

CHARLES: Do you know Master Ausias March? He's the glory of Catalonia. Her greatest poet. It might be the glory of all Spain, did he not write poems so difficult to comprehend, that not ten men in any generation can understand them. He is also a patriot and has served as your unofficial embassy at my court.

VINOT: If he's a patriot as well as a poet, we honor him.

FRAY JUAN: Though he's a pagan poet and in his youthful work sings mostly of love . . .

CHARLES (*to the Dominican*): You've honored him further by reading his youthful poems? The pagan ones? Is not love a commendable subject? Are we not all the creatures of love? Whether it be our love of God? Or love of our country? Or love of one's prince . . .? We add; we always become more than ourselves. Why, were we as clever as our friends the Arabians, with the mathematics of love we might solve all our problems. I suggest this to you, Friar.

FRAY JUAN: I suggest prayer.

CHARLES: The fearful heart's poetry. I honor the prayer of thanksgiving. I despise the prayer of supplication.

VINOT: We come neither to thank nor supplicate.

CHARLES: I'm speaking of God. I'm not God.

VINOT: You are one of those appointed by God. A prince. Our prince, heir to Catalonia, since your father is now our king.

CHARLES: I'm not yet my father's heir.

VINOT: You're his eldest son.

CHARLES: I'm first in line. But last in my father's heart.

VINOT: Your father is not God. He cannot set aside what has been ordained. By the divine right of primogeniture, you succeed to his throne.

CHARLES (*to the Dominican*): Do you sustain this?

VINOT: We come at his prompting.

CHARLES: And who is this friar? Since when do the Dominicans cherish me?

VINOT: None is so powerful in Barcelona as this Dominican, my lord. He leads the people.

CHARLES: Leads them? Or incites them? In all times there're those political priests who devote themselves to the rabble. Who raise mobs. They're not long the friends of princes.

FRAY JUAN: You're no ordinary prince. In your heart's a love of God, however flippant your tongue.

CHARLES: You'd frighten me, as you've frightened others? But with flattery? No flattery is more compelling than to say to a man he's God-fearing. He's afraid of you churchmen then. He is your instrument.

[42]

FRAY JUAN: Let it be so.

CHARLES: I will be no man's instrument. Even one who announces himself as the voice of God.

FRAY JUAN: I'll speak to the people. They shall speak to you.

CHARLES: Since when is the voice of the mob the voice of God?

FRAY JUAN: Since One died on the cross for them, calling Himself the Prince of Peace.

CHARLES (*tensely*): What is this?

FRAY JUAN (*advancing*): You too are a prince of peace. We invite you to Barcelona.

CHARLES: Am I the rabble, that you speak to me with these phrases? Is this man mad?

VINOT: Your father sends you to Majorca, my lord. Then you must stop at Barcelona. We ask, when you come, that you remain there.

CHARLES: For what purpose?

VINOT: That, by your honored presence among us, your succession to the throne may be assured.

CHARLES: Why?

VINOT: So that, when you're king, you'll remember us kindly. And be forever in our debt.

CHARLES: Do you know what you risk if I remain in Barcelona? It'll anger the king.

VINOT: We of Catalonia are not a craven race. We've angered kings before.

CHARLES: My father's anger's lasting. He fears no God. No Dominican. His ambition is ceaseless. He'll never let you rest.

VINOT: That's why we want you.

CHARLES: Do you wish to set me against my father?

VINOT: Are you friends?

CHARLES: This's treason.

VINOT: We do not conspire against the king. We merely wish to make sure that you are king after him.

CHARLES: You think, because my father's old and blind, it may not be long?

VINOT: Your sister's married to a vassal of the King of France. We

[43]

do not wish to see the French on our throne. Be our guest. We shall protect you, as your uncle, our king, protected you before us. That's all we ask. That's all we offer.

CHARLES: That can't be all.

VINOT: You're a liberal prince. We Catalonians are an independent people. When she was our governor, your aunt, Alfonso's wife, ruled us lightly. It's changed now. We shall not long submit to the absolutism of your father.

CHARLES: Then, by my presence, you wish to challenge him?

VINOT: It shall serve as a warning.

CHARLES (*to the Dominican*): You spoke of me as a prince of peace? This might mean war.

FRAY JUAN: Peace with freedom. Not peace with tyranny.

CHARLES: I risked angering my father to force a peaceful issue with Castile. What was the consequence? Five years of civil war in Navarre that cost many more lives than the original war would've taken. It's best that priests and scholars not meddle in affairs of state.

FRAY JUAN: Are you a scholar?

VINOT: Shall not history remember you as the liberal prince who, loving peace, and loving freedom, brought both to a people who asked him to be their champion? Let us champion each other.

CHARLES: History does not long remember princes. During the three years I was my father's prisoner at Monroy, I wrote a Chronicle of the Kings of Navarre. A story of endless, futile dynastic struggle. A history to which I've already added another bloody and meaningless chapter. Do I want to be remembered? This is a new age, my friends, when men in commoner occupations may win easier immortality than princes. I spend my days at translation. I shall give Spain the wisdom of one of the greatest men who ever lived. The *Ethics* of Aristotle. Is this not labor enough for one man? Shall I not, in the reflected light of his fame, be also immortal?

FRAY JUAN: This is not Christian philosophy.

CHARLES: I hear bigotry.

FRAY JUAN: It's not philosophy at all, but monstrous egotism.

CHARLES: Perhaps.

MARCH: There're many kinds of egotism. Your Highness has tried them all but one.

CHARLES: And that?

MARCH: Self-interest. Realism. You're poor. Strike a bargain with the people of Barcelona.

CHARLES: There speaks the poet. All poets are mathematicians. Not only of love. They are realists. They must learn to count the metrical feet in a line.

VINOT: We're not poor in Barcelona.

CHARLES: The world likes to look at kings, but not pay for them. The people of Sicily, who cherish the memory of my mother, grant me a pension of twenty-five thousand florins.

VINOT: We'll better it.

CHARLES: I do not ask it for myself. Many have followed me into exile. I spoiled them at my court, when I was rich, and now I must support them in a befitting style.

MARCH: Painters. Poets. Singers, whose music will echo long in the memory of Spain.

CHARLES: You cannot starve the sweet voice. Or it does not long remain sweet. (to Vinot) In Barcelona, I think, I should soon be able to return to Aristotle? You do not want me because I would be a good king, but a poor one? The world's growing tired of good kings. Good kings make wars, have foreign schemes, collect taxes. Whereas I'd neglect my kingly offices and trouble no one. Men want to be left alone and rule themselves. That's why all these thrones are offered me.

VINOT: We need the appearance of a king. Otherwise the princes of Spain will not leave us in peace.

CHARLES: Is this the liberal prince? The appearance, not the substance of a king? But don't think, my friend, you buy only the shadow. Or that your pension alone has purchased my heart's interest. Or that my father will consent so readily to this gesture.

VINOT: Then let him oppose us.

CHARLES: I could love you as subjects, because you're a proud people. (to March) Though the mob in Barcelona, I suppose, is no different from the mob in Naples. It'll stink as strongly.

MARCH: That is the odor of humanity, my lord.

CHARLES (to the Dominican): You sweeten it, do you not, with incense in your churches?

MARCH: And the fragrant breath of freedom.

CHARLES: Always the poet with his lovely, untrue phrases. I like poetry better when it's metaphysical and I cannot understand it.

MARCH: Do you like Aristotle better in Greek?

CHARLES: No. We shall translate truth into Spanish. I am in your hands. This shall be a different kind of translation. Freedom into Spanish. The word's never been heard there.

VINOT: This's your answer?

CHARLES: When we sail, let us avoid Sardinia, lest I be offered another throne and diverted from my present resolution. Now, thank you, my friends, and leave me. But stay, Master March.

(*The deputation kneels. All but the Dominican*)

Is this pride, Friar? Or piety? Or rheumatism?

FRAY JUAN: You do not make heroic speeches. I'll not make them, either.

CHARLES: A most heroic answer. Very well. When I'm King of Barcelona, you shall never kneel in my presence. As a reminder to me that the mob too produces princes. Its own leaders. (*to March*) Is this not one of those of whom you preached?

MARCH: No. This man's a fanatic.

CHARLES: In these times, there's a very fine distinction between a liberal prince and a fanatic. Give me your hand, Friar. (*He holds out his hand, but the Dominican does not move.*)

FRAY JUAN: I shall serve you.

CHARLES: That's good enough (*Along with this remark he bids the deputation to rise.*)

VINOT: If it be war, you'll lead us?

CHARLES: It'll be peace. I'll win it for you in my own way.

VINOT: How?

CHARLES: By going to my father.

MARCH: By humbling yourself?

CHARLES: Peace is worth it.

MARCH: Who ever won peace by compromise with tyranny?

VINOT: We want peace, Your Highness, but we're prepared to fight for it.

CHARLES: Let me fight for it. Strong speech may accomplish as much as strong methods. But let one mingle strong speech and soft speech, and you confuse your enemy. I shall try it. Now again, leave me to the mercies of Master March.

VINOT: God bless Your Highness.

(*The deputation departs.*)

MARCH: You'll not succeed in this.

CHARLES: Not for long. My father has his own gift of words. A fiercer heart.

MARCH: Then why do you temporize!

CHARLES: I'm that most unhappy man. Who cannot strike at his enemy. Because I'm the son of my enemy!

MARCH: Are we not all sons? Are we not all brothers? If we do have enemies, why should we say that any one has a more natural countenance? I thought you'd dispensed with fine distinctions. Your father's life is no more sacred than any other.

CHARLES: You're not serious?

MARCH: I've never considered my own life sacred. I've often risked it. Why should I consider that of anyone else more sacred? If you're willing to die for a cause, shouldn't you be willing to kill for it?

CHARLES: The friar was right. This's the pagan poet and philosopher.

MARCH: How many have died for Christianity? And kill and torture for it?

CHARLES: What's the cause for which men shall die? Who shall determine it? I do not serve Catalonia without at the same time serving my sister's hate.

MARCH: Do you search for the pure motive? You'll never find it. Nowhere in nature or man. It exists only in the abstract truth of philosophy.

CHARLES: The Gorgon with the petrifying face.

MARCH: That would turn you to stone. Immobile. Inhuman. In a world that cries for your action.

CHARLES: Why do I deceive myself that I am making a decision? This act has long been decided for me.

SCENE FIVE: CHARLES *and* VINOT *anticipate the king's arrival at Barcelona.*

VINOT: You await Beaumont? And the king?

CHARLES: Both. But not together.

VINOT: Was it wise to ask Beaumont here? Barcelona's not Navarre.

CHARLES: Can we make peace with a clenched first behind our back? Beaumont is my fist.

(*The strong, elderly* BEAUMONT *enters. He kneels to Charles.*)

BEAUMONT: Sire, you've come back to Spain.

CHARLES: You mustn't address me as though I were king.

BEAUMONT (*rising*): To me, you're King of Navarre.

CHARLES: My uncle rebuked you for that claim.

BEAUMONT: Your uncle is dead.

CHARLES: And how many others. No, Beaumont, the truce shall last. I've lost Navarre to my sister Eleanor. But this is Vinot. He'll give me Catalonia.

BEAUMONT: Let it be Navarre *and* Catalonia.

CHARLES: My father has committed himself to my brother-in-law. Gaston will never let him go back on his promise. That way we'll never win peace. We must make concessions.

BEAUMONT: What are these?

CHARLES: Let my sister Eleanor, and her ambitious husband, rule in Navarre. But first I'll demand an amnesty for all who've supported me.

BEAUMONT: We do not seek an amnesty.

CHARLES: I seek it.

BEAUMONT: What amnesty is this? There're no materials for amnesty in your father. Do you think he'll forgive even you?

VINOT: Barcelona has greeted the prince in triumph.

BEAUMONT: Of what consequence is that?

CHARLES: My father has heard this noisy welcome and may, in a small fashion, echo it.

BEAUMONT: Have you so little knowledge of him?

CHARLES: You were my tutor, Beaumont, What did you teach me? I've been loyal to your loyalty, your clumsy love, and this has almost destroyed me. I don't mean you've made me into my father's enemy, but into my own. You're a man of honest emotion but rude perception. Such qualities belong to the past.

BEAUMONT: Is this how my prince speaks to me?

CHARLES: I must love you less, Beaumont, for having loved you too much. Without your knowing it, you've made me your agent. It wasn't that you fought for me, but fought against the Agramonts. You couldn't help loving me, my sympathies served you so well. You're not now, and never were, the man to see that.

BEAUMONT: Is this the gratitude of princes?

CHARLES: Do you ask me to be grateful?

BEAUMONT: I ask nothing. Your cause has been my cause. I shall continue to serve you in my heart. And with my sword.

CHARLES: Brave, loyal Beaumont! Were you my tutor? My Constable? My Grand Prior? My friend? My fist? Did you strike for me not once, but again and again? These things you have been and done. But now you must be my pupil. You must learn a new language and different thoughts. We live in different centuries. You belong to the fourteenth, but I belong to the fifteenth. In this century, kings shall be strong and nobles weak. Because when kings are strong, there's peace. And we shall buy peace with words.

BEAUMONT: You'll be a merchant, not a prince.

CHARLES: All the world has its vision of a prince. And the old vision dies slowly. But the new prince is a prince of learning, of knowledge. He is a prince because he knows ancient philosophy, and with his purse encourages new science and modern art in classic forms. He can do these only if peace prevails.

BEAUMONT: These're Italian ideas. You've allowed your love of luxury to soften you in Naples. But in Spain we buy peace a harder way.

CHARLES: No. The time's coming when wars will be fought by ambassadors. And in the council rooms. Our language grows richer. It shall fight our wars for us.

BEAUMONT: And how you shall be tricked! Those're no victories. Words.

CHARLES: In words there're defeats. There're victories, too.

BEAUMONT: You'll learn better. Your father'll teach you.

CHARLES: In your heart, do you own me your king? Then take this as my royal command. My words shall prevail over your inclinations.

I'll purchase you an amnesty in Navarre. You're to live in peace with my sister Eleanor, accepting her as your governor. And you're to join the Agramonts as friends.

BEAUMONT: I can accept these conditions, knowing how short a time they'll last. Your father comes shortly.

CHARLES: The clever ruler would keep you and the Agramonts divided, lest by your union you grow too strong. But there're some kinds of wisdom despised by the wisest man. What's often called realism takes too little account of what's unrealistic in man. His dreams. His ideals. They're real, too.

BEAUMONT: In you there was always a melancholy. I can understand it now.

CHARLES: You're one of those active men, Beaumont, who fancy all men who think must be melancholy. No, it's not that we think, but what you give us to think about, that sometimes makes us sad. But help me in this design for peace. And peace itself shall be your reward.

BEAUMONT: Once before you betrayed me with these words. When we made peace with Castile, against your father's plans. But, loving you, I'll let you betray me again.

CHARLES: You're older than I am. And not all the world's learning, nor the subtlest wit, can take the place of your experience. You're still my tutor, were I clever enough to see it. But I'm determined upon this course.

(*A sound distracts them.*)

VINOT: The king comes.

CHARLES: Remember, Beaumont, we join forces now. Silence is courage! And offer your hand, when I command it.

BEAUMONT: The Marshal may take my hand. But he'll know what's in my heart.

(*The king enters, led by* JOANNA; *and accompanied by his daughter,* ELEANOR; *his tall, broad son-in-law, the* COUNT DE FOIX; DON PEDRO; *and* DE PERALTA.)

CHARLES: Well, are we met so quietly?

GASTON: Barcelona's not quiet, but rings with the cheers that greeted your arrival.

JOANNA: You're to be felicitated, Charles, at such a show of affection.

CHARLES: Madame, I'd forgotten how beautiful you are.

JOANNA: You're kind, Charles. And we're pleased to see you in continuing good health.

CHARLES: Are you truly, Madame? And do you not find me somewhat pale from the mephitic air of Naples? I came close there to catching a fever.

GASTON: Let's hope you catch no fever in Barcelona. Though the noise is contagious.

CHARLES: The contagion of noise is one I've always been well able to resist. You know my taste for solitude.

GASTON: We've always admired it.

CHARLES: I believe you. And so it's his son-in-law now, who presumes to speak for the king? Has the king himself nothing to say to me?

(*John remains silent.*)

JOANNA: Where's Blanche?

CHARLES: Blanche rests. The journey from Sicily has tired her.

GASTON: We hope the journey to Majorca will not tire her as much.

CHARLES: Do you think Blanche plans to go to Majorca without me?

GASTON: Shall you not go there?

CHARLES: Could my father bear to have me so far from him?

GASTON: He orders it.

CHARLES: Well, Gaston, I see you're not only French ambassador at this court, but perhaps, as my sister's husband, you've become heir apparent.

GASTON: I've been delegated to talk to you.

CHARLES: And from my sister Eleanor, no word of greeting? (*to Gaston, as Eleanor is silent*) You're Eleanor's fate. I wonder, had you been Blanche's husband, would Blanche be Eleanor?

JOANNA: Speak softly, Charles.

CHARLES: Ah, you've been delegated a different role, Madame? (*to Gaston*) You and I were friends, Gaston, and hunted together. Now you hunt alone. Why, indeed, should my father consent to the reversion, when time itself reverses us? I'm the creature at whom you aimed your arrow. Had I but known it then, when I rode beside you and you shot the helpless deer.

[51]

GASTON: What would you have done?

CHARLES: I should have turned the arrow in its flight. Don't you know I've a witch for a sister? In fact, two witches. (*turns to Eleanor.*)

GASTON: A devil impels your tongue.

CHARLES: Why yes, I've been told the artist sells his soul to the Devil. It was you who once said I was better fitted for ballades than battles. You were wise, and how well you've profited by your wisdom with a fine French economy. (*to his sister*) They say, Eleanor, that you inherit our father's blindness. And do you know what else they say in Navarre? That she who seeks to lose a brother, well deserves to lose an eye, even the right one. (*as Eleanor angrily turns from him*) It's true! I saw that eye —it's lifeless.

ELEANOR: Of my brother's love for his father, the tongues of Europe wag.

CHARLES: You mean the tongues of women. Women can move more worlds with their tongues than Archimedes' lever.

ELEANOR: My brother still parades his classical learning.

CHARLES (*to Gaston*): And since when, Gaston, have you become so good a son to my father?

GASTON: Since I've myself become a father.

CHARLES: A respectable answer. A respectable excuse. To hide a most disreputable motive.

JOANNA: Those who have virtue enough of their own, need not look for it in others.

CHARLES: Are you as virtuous as you're beautiful, Madame? I would believe it. I cannot afford to believe that beauty ever deceives us.

JOANNA: Are you not the deceiver, with this incessant talk of beauty?

CHARLES: No. (*to John*) Do your eyes fail you, Father, because such loveliness dazzles you? You were never the artist that I am. What blinds the eyes of other men, but sharpens my sight. (*to Joanna*) And where's the boy? I don't see him. My stepbrother Ferdinand? You've not brought him to Barcelona?

JOANNA: He's but a child.

CHARLES: Yet they say he rules the queen. And the queen rules the king. And the king rules Aragon, Navarre, Catalonia. This's a remarkable boy.

JOANNA: We do think so, Charles.

CHARLES: Are all mothers fanatics? My mistress plagues me at all hours to marry her for the sake of my bastard son. But what sort of example has my own father given me, that I should consider anything but my selfish desires where a son's concerned?

JOANNA: Once more I entreat you, speak softly.

CHARLES: Madame, I speak softly. My mission is peace. My mood is humble.

GASTON: We're pleased to hear that.

CHARLES: My mood. But not the mood of Barcelona, which for three days has shouted itself hoarse at my arrival. These people protest that they love me. And love's precious. I am anxious that so much of it should not be wasted.

GASTON: You threaten the king?

CHARLES: With what? With love? Once more I make war on my father with peace. I submit myself utterly to His Majesty and beg him to absolve me of the legend of unfilial disrespect that condemns me in the eyes of all Europe.

GASTON: A subtle threat, so cunning you can't read it at once.

CHARLES: But you're quick-thinking?

GASTON (to John): He brings Barcelona against you, unless you forgive him. He doesn't fear your anger so much as the judgment of men.

CHARLES: Your son-in-law does not know you, Father, as I do. Who knows that no threat could move you, or sway your fierce temper. Do you want my surrender? You have it, with only one condition.

JOANNA: What condition is that?

CHARLES: Peace in Navarre. I see the Marshal of Navarre and the Constable of Navarre in one room. But they stand far from each other.

DON PEDRO: Much separates us.

CHARLES: Why yes, Don Pedro. But if I've stood between you, look, I step back, that you may come together.

DE PERALTA: A step back, my lord? Not a step forward?

CHARLES: A certain suavity, Don Mossen, has always masked the ferocity of your nature. This's no time for you to drop it.

DON PEDRO: We've fought for the king in Navarre. And will abide by the king's decision.

CHARLES: You're a marvel of disinterest, Don Pedro. And I hope you can persuade your cousin to a similar loyalty. I've always suspected, under your enemity, a certain kinship of feeling between us.

DON PEDRO: While you're the king's son, I honor you. When you're no longer the king's son, you are my enemy.

CHARLES: I'm always the king's son. It does not lie with my father to undo the work of God. You know how to qualify your professions. Your words shine like mirrors. No matter what face a man makes in the glass, his reflection comes back at him.

DON PEDRO: Your Highness wrongs me.

CHARLES: Why no, Don Pedro. I make my very best face in your glass. Let us treasure the image. *(to Joanna)* My mistress Brianda stays night and day at her tapestry. She weaves bright, contrasting colors, but when she's finished there's a single, pleasing pattern.

JOANNA: And what does she call this pattern?

CHARLES: She calls it, Madame, "The King's Amnesty". And I would it came true in Navarre. I appeal to my sister Eleanor, who may remain as viceroy in Navarre without further objection from me . . . And I appeal to my stepmother.

JOANNA: Do not address us, Charles. Address your father.

CHARLES: My father's not only blind. He's mute.

JOHN: Not deaf. I hear what you say. And some things you do not say. And I'm glad I cannot see you clearly. For I should see an ungrateful son, who shows his father neither respect nor love. Who raised Navarre in arms against me. Who, by his effeminate charm, seeks to seduce my subjects in Naples and Sicily. And who returns now in vulgar triumph, allied to the rabble of Barcelona, meaning to be their spokesman and champion.

CHARLES: You heard me say this?

JOHN: Do you think yourself so clever? What sort of king should I be, if I took men at their word? Since I'm blind, I see many things I didn't see before.

CHARLES: What blinds you and Eleanor? Selfishness. It's true that selfishness makes clever men stupid.

JOHN: Who has been blind? And who has been stupid? My son

Charles, vaunting his unselfishness to himself. Beaumont's pawn. And now the rabble's pawn in Barcelona. Do you think they love you? What a deep, childish vanity you have! All men are willing to pay you worship while you can serve them. If they're hungry, their bellies. If they're strong, their interests. Or if they are poets at your court, their metrical exercises in idealism. The daydreams of unpractical men. They will gladly sacrifice you for a fine phrase. That's what poets are like. They sacrifice everything for a rhyme.

My son thinks me senile. A woman's tool. He thinks me short-sighted, where he is profound. He runs here and there about the edges of Europe, serving first one faction, then another. He sues at my brother's court, but then flees to Sicily, when strong action is called for. He woos the Sicilians, then, like the moth, flutters to the brighter flame of Barcelona. He seeks to sell me Navarre, as though it's not already my possession. And thinks, perhaps, I'm frightened by the noise of beggars shouting in the streets. He poses one moment as the patron of art. And another, as a scholar. And then, without knowing the meaning of the words, as a liberal humanitarian. It is no wonder he sees mirrors in the words of other men, and enjoys the image he finds there. He thinks the whole universe created to observe his princely progress. The hearts of men are filled only with him. Their words are intended only to praise or condemn him. Their acts, to help or obstruct him. And he says his sister and father are selfish?

CHARLES: This's an excellent portrait, Father. Better than Don Moreno's.

JOHN: And while my son has contemplated the philosophical meaning of the world, and enlarged his already over-extensive vocabulary, I have spent thirty years fighting in Spain. I've been fighting my son in Navarre. Beaumont in Navarre, Henry in Castile. And watching over my rebellious subjects in Sicily and Catalonia. I've faced blindness and heard my daughter Blanche denounce me. I've borne my son's infamy. And all for what purpose? Why, might it not be to see Spain united? One Spain . . . Castile, Aragon, Navarre, Catalonia . . . stretching from sea to sea, presenting a common front to the Moor! One Spain, sweeping southward to drive the infidels from Granada, the Moors from Europe, until Christianity replaces an abhorrent religion that flourishes on our borders. If this has been my design, how has my son helped me, who deems himself advanced and intellectual, and who would forecast the future, and who's noted for his piety? This is Charles of Navarre, the Christian prince. My priestly son.

CHARLES: In my youth, while my mother lived, I said many prayers.

JOHN: I let your mother raise you. And surround you with priests. That was my fault.

CHARLES: My mother was an exalted, mystical lady.

JOHN: My son Charles, too, is exalted. In his own opinion. And flaunts his expensive morality in my face. Who has paid for your morality? Your peace with Castile cost me a year's campaign. Were you not my son, would you be welcomed in Catalonia? I too might play the lenient prince, the do-nothing king, and be loved by the laziest and most vociferous of my subjects. Because I act, you inherit the hatred I accept as the price of my endeavour. And when you act, do you think it'll be any different? And now, if I love the design I have served, to which I've dedicated my life, shall I leave all I have wrought to a weakling? Your most unfilial deed is to have been the kind of son you are to me.

CHARLES: This may be true.

JOHN: Do you wish to make peace with me? Very well. You may live where you will, but you're never again to enter Navarre. Beaumont's to strip himself of whatever he's taken from the Agramonts. And Blanche is to be my hostage until this is done.

CHARLES: I can't ask this of Blanche.

JOHN: She's my daughter!

CHARLES: Yes, more yours than the sweet mother for whom she's named. Even so, she must answer for herself.

JOANNA: Blanche will consent. She enjoys living with those she hates.

CHARLES: That's all too true. (to John) But you'll acknowledge me as your heir?

JOHN: Perhaps. But not now.

CHARLES: I shall remain in Barcelona. And do I see the Marshal of Navarre take the Constable's hand?

JOHN: What meaning's in a handshake? Let it pass.

[56]

CHARLES: My uncle Alfonso too sought to build an empire. But already it crumbles.

JOHN: He went to Italy. We'll build a Spanish empire in Spain. So that peace, when it comes, will be a lasting peace at home.

CHARLES: Is it really peace you want? Can you achieve peace through war? And do you want a strong Spain for her own sake, or only that you may have more power? When Castile is defeated, and Spain is one, shall you be a kinder king? More just? No, I don't believe it.

JOHN: I need render no account to my son. Let him first prove himself worthy of being called my son.

CHARLES: It's only power you want. Some fire burns in you. Some tempest blows in you always. You don't know the meaning of peace. How did you ever have a son as gentle as I am? It was Providence. Were I like you, we should long since have destroyed each other.

JOANNA: Now that a peace is made, don't unmake it.

CHARLES: My father's fortunate to have married two such wonderful women. My mother. And my stepmother. He must needs be a great king to be worthy of them.

JOANNA: Do you not read, in the king's anger, some love for his son?

CHARLES: I must hope for it. For if sons must love their fathers, should not princes love their kings?

JOANNA: They should.

CHARLES: I had thought to speak softly. But you speak so much more softly. And yours is an eloquent beauty. I'm susceptible to beauty, Madame. Beaumont and Barcelona trust in me. But I trust in you. For I'm told that you are the guiding star in my father's untimely night. And though some have said that your marriage was an evil conjunction, we cannot help ourselves, but must steer by such stars as we find.

JOANNA: If you love the king, by so doing you'll love me. And you may be sure of my love for you.

ACT TWO

SCENE ONE: *A company of French musicians has just finished playing.*
CHARLES *listens, while* BRIANDA *works at her tapestry, and* VINOT
stands opposite.

VINOT: You yourself do not play, my lord?

CHARLES: When I was younger, I sang with the viol. And after,
when I wished to remember my youthful dreams.

VINOT: Music recalls them.

CHARLES: I envy youth no longer. Youth is graceful, but it's the
grace of the unformed mind and the ungrown body. (*to the musicians*)
Let us hear you again.

(*They play for the thoughtful prince.*)

VINOT: What language do they sing?

CHARLES: French.

VINOT: They say Charles, the King of France, is insane.

CHARLES: They say that of all kings. They shall probably say that
of Charles, the King of Navarre. A king in France! A king in England!
A king in Castile! How remote they all sound! Do you suppose the
same incessant conspiracies flourish around them? What is bringing
Blanche and Beaumont back from Navarre? I don't like this. My father
crosses me.

VINOT (*with a warning sign that indicates the musicians*): They'll hear
us.

CHARLES: They're musicians. Their ears are deaf to these cruder
sounds.

VINOT: They say that music's the voice of angels.

CHARLES: The voice of what's angelic in man, wherewith he makes
angels. (*to the musicians*) I wish you could play us a song by Ausias
March.

VINOT: Have you not heard, my lord? Master March is dead in
Valencia.

CHARLES: March dead?

VINOT: I thought you'd been told.

CHARLES: I didn't know. March dead?

VINOT: He was old.

CHARLES: Do poets grow old? They say that when kings and princes die, there're portents. Bursting stars and comets in the dark sky. This's my portent. That was Ausias March among the men of our time.

VINOT: You take this too hard.

CHARLES: No. I'm warned. You don't know how I need him.

VINOT: All admired the poet.

CHARLES: The poet has the courage to dream for us in a most unlovely world. He was also my conscience. (*to the players*) That's an end of the song. Some part of the world's beauty, some part of the world's wisdom, is dead. Thank you. Leave us.

(*The players withdraw.*)

VINOT: I believe Blanche and Beaumont come to urge this marriage on you.

CHARLES: I've been married once. God delivered me. Do you wish to put me in chains again?

VINOT: You've no other security.

CHARLES: You distrust my father?

VINOT: Has he declared you his heir?

CHARLES: Not yet.

VINOT: At your marriage, he'd be forced to do so. You could learn his intention. At the same time, by your alliance with Castile, you'd be so strengthened that your father wouldn't dare deny what's rightfully yours.

CHARLES: This marriage is folly. It'd offend my father.

VINOT: Your very existence offends him.

CHARLES: I believe my father plans to marry Ferdinand to this princess.

VINOT: Your stepmother plans it.

CHARLES: Well then, how would they welcome the news that I've entered into secret negotiations with Henry of Castile to marry his sister, when they themselves wish the match for my stepbrother? Why does Henry flaunt them and turn to me?

VINOT: By your marriage to Isabella of Castile, and your succession to your father's throne, you'd unite Castile with Catalonia, Aragon, Navarre. You'd unite Spain.

CHARLES: That's my father's design. And peacefully accomplished. Then why shouldn't he approve the marriage?

VINOT: If he doesn't, my lord, it means that your father doesn't intend you to succeed him. Nor either of your sisters. He'll contrive, in his own way, to be rid of all of you. And leave the throne to your stepbrother. To Ferdinand.

CHARLES: Be rid of us? Even Eleanor?

VINOT: Her husband's French. Can you believe the king ever meant his dominions to pass over to France?

CHARLES: After a fashion, I've kept some forgiveness for my sister Eleanor, thinking that by her action the throne of Navarre was preserved for one of our mother's children.

VINOT: Which is it to be? Which is the better match? Charles and Isabella? Or Ferdinand and Isabella?

CHARLES: You're sure that Henry prefers me?

VINOT: Because you're the legitimate heir. And because Henry hates both your father and stepmother. They've long been his enemies.

CHARLES: Yes. But Blanche hates Henry. He used her ill. She can't forget that. Nor can I. I do not know whether Blanche loved him. Or would have loved him. Or was merely unloved.

VINOT: It was a marriage of state. As this would be.

CHARLES (to BRIANDA): You work at your tapestry, Brianda. But you've heard everything?

BRIANDA: Yes, my lord.

CHARLES: The Princess Isabella is ten years old. And I'm forty. We of the royal blood are not more than human. We're less than human.

BRIANDA (rising tearfully): Yes, my lord.

(She flies from the room.)

CHARLES (staring after her): I was married at eighteen to a French princess, and my wife had all the commonplace vulgarity of the French. At sixteen she was lovely. At twenty-five, unspeakably tiresome. But I lived with her. My first mistress was a lady-in-waiting to my sister Eleanor. Her name was Maria de Armendariz. When she finally married a good man, I gave her a handsome present. She deserved it.

My next was Maria's sister, Graciana. I thought such amiability might run in the family. But I was mistaken. Brianda's my third. She has been with me ever since my wife died. And she's beautiful!

VINOT: Yes.

CHARLES: But not faithful, although she's given me a son. Maria gave me a daughter. So I have children. But none who're legitimate and can succeed me.

VINOT: You're sure your mistress is unfaithful?

CHARLES: Not sure. And what a look of virginal innocence! But you see, I know she's not a virgin. So might she not be false to me? Her beauty torments me, as Ausias March said physical beauty does. You cannot grasp it. It's not truly physical. It exists in the mind. Is she not more beautiful when I close my eyes, than when I gaze upon her? I don't wonder at my father's perpetual restlessness if he cannot see my stepmother's lovely face. Yet he knows less torment than us.

VINOT: I'm not impressed by your stepmother's beauty. And I think her affection toward you is variable.

CHARLES: Do you think that? And if it be true, I wonder is it a sweet inconstancy, or an inconstant sweetness?

VINOT: A better name for it might be maternal ambition.

CHARLES: How consistent is the world's opinion of her. It's good to find some consistency in the world, even though it be only a consistent error.

VINOT: And your opinion of the queen?

CHARLES: She's not only beautiful, she's brave. Brilliant, tenacious, and kind. She speaks honestly. She's faithful to my father, and if she's ambitious for her son, is that wrong? Was not my mother ambitious for me? And was not my mother a good woman?

VINOT: She was.

CHARLES: My stepmother is my enemy. But a good enemy. I trust her. You do not understand, Vinot. I war with women. My sister Blanche. My stepmother. And my own mother within me. Those're unequal odds and offensive to chivalry. I must lose.

VINOT: I think this a man's world.

CHARLES: How can one be a man these days? The courses of princes are prescribed, but a plain man must find his own way.

(BEAUMONT enters with BLANCHE.)

BEAUMONT: Your Highness.

CHARLES: You are both here? Blanche, has my father released you from hostage so soon?

BLANCHE: He sends me with a message.

CHARLES: And you, Beaumont! The peace is five months old. Have you already broken it?

BEAUMONT: Your father breaks it. And your sister Eleanor.

CHARLES: That is your story.

BEAUMONT: All who were loyal to you, suffer in Navarre. The Agramonts deprive us of our towns. To have been a friend of Prince Charles now merits punishment.

CHARLES: The same quarrel.

BEAUMONT: Save that, by your command, we're defenseless.

CHARLES: I forgot I was born in Navarre, but you remind me.

BEAUMONT: Before all, you belong to us.

CHARLES: Your petty quarrel pursues me. We cannot plan great actions, Vinot, while these ignoble squabbles surround us. Our dreams are a century ahead of the reality.

BEAUMONT: I speak only of your friends, who've sacrificed much for you.

CHARLES: You have. We must live in the little world, Vinot. The little world of Navarre. Of the Agramonts, Beaumontais, their perennial war. The greater world of Spain is not yet for us.

VINOT: Let Catalonia join with Navarre. Both love you.

CHARLES: We shall multiply our little quarrels, until even we are impressed by the magnitude they assume. In that way, we shall believe ourselves fighting for important causes. But at bottom, the quarrel's the same, the story's the same. My father distrusts me. The Marshal distrusts the Constable, and the Constable distrusts the Marshal. My stepmother plans for her son. My sister schemes to hold Navarre from me, even after I've given it to her. These great angers arise from our small personal flaws. I must still be loyal to your damnable loyalty, Beaumont. What moves do we make?

BEAUMONT: First, the alliance with Castile. But in secret.

CHARLES: How can we keep it a secret, when it seems so logical, inevitable? My father must guess it.

VINOT: What he guesses, he still does not know.

CHARLES: Does anything happen in Castile, without the Admiral hearing of it? What the Admiral learns, his daughter the queen knows soon after. And surely she holds back nothing from my father.

BEAUMONT: They act together in everything.

BLANCHE: You blind yourself by this fondness for the queen.

CHARLES: I must be fond of someone. I cannot hate my enemy with a whole heart. This way, by sparing the queen, I do not spare my father.

BLANCHE: You depend on self-deception.

CHARLES: Anyone who can't deceive himself is half-paralytic, dangerous to the world. As this marriage is dangerous. Besides, I do not suppose an alliance to Castile will appeal to my sister Blanche. What does she say? An alliance with her former husband? My marriage to Henry's sister?

(*As* BLANCHE *stands bitterly considering*, BEAUMONT *and* VINOT *withdraw at a sign from Charles. He approaches* BLANCHE.)

Yours is not a choice, Blanche, between two loves. But between two hates.

BLANCHE: I must submit to your interest.

CHARLES: It's not my interest. I act mostly in this because your love drives me to it. Beaumont's love. And Barcelona's love, for whatever it may be worth. I'd readily surrender my claim to the throne, had not my father taught me that others pay for my generous gestures. You succeed me. And you'd pay. You'd stand perilously between my father's anger and Eleanor's envy.

BLANCHE: It would be so.

CHARLES: Our stepbrother Ferdinand's eight years old; the Princess Isabella's ten. It would be the perfect match.

BLANCHE: It's not between *two* hates. But *two* in Aragon and *one* in Castile. I hate Henry alone. But in Aragon I hate my father and step-mother. Both.

CHARLES: It'd be two for one? You too are a mathematician. It's the poet in you. The excelling poetry of hate.

BLANCHE: Yes!

CHARLES: Some think kings have a gift whereby all they touch are healed. Had I that, Blanche, I'd cure you of this hate. But our Master March was wrong. There's no magic in kings.

BLANCHE: You're not yet a king, and when you wear a crown, you'll see what miracles can be worked with your royal fingers.

CHARLES: Miracles of love?

BLANCHE: Perhaps.

CHARLES: There're many loves that await a miracle. Your love, Blanche. And the splendid love our Master March had for love itself, and for all our passions. He could work miracles with words. But can any kingly miracle raise him from death and restore the magic of life to him? No, I don't think kings and poets are small gods. They're merely large talkers. A king doesn't speak of himself as "I", but as "we", as though he were two persons, when all the time he must know he's only one. Unless he be my father, who's my stepmother as well. Aye, there's a consummation.

(*He watches as* BLANCHE *turns and leaves. He pauses, considers, then speaks loudly, accenting the last word.*)

And where's my mistress? I await Brianda.

(BRIANDA *enters.*)

My sister came with a message. She forgot to deliver it.

BRIANDA: Beaumont told me the king goes to meet the Catalonian Council at Lerida. He asks that you join him there.

CHARLES: Does he?

BRIANDA: Beaumont begs you not to go.

CHARLES: Fearing the king? But that's Beaumont's habit. He thinks I cannot keep a guilty secret. And what do you think, Brianda?

BRIANDA: Concerning what, my lord?

CHARLES: Can one keep a guilty secret? What can you teach me?

BRIANDA: Nothing, my lord.

CHARLES: I have always loved you. Not as you may be, but as I think you are. You have never deceived me?

BRIANDA: Never, my lord.

CHARLES: Not with Don Moreno? Not with my treasurer?

BRIANDA: With none!

CHARLES: What does it matter? Your deception? Or my self-deception? You're lovely to behold. I treasure the illusion. And while I do not know for certain, the illusion's as good as the truth. (*as Brianda is silent*) I'll go to Lerida. And afterward to Castile. But later I'll return to you.

BRIANDA: Shall it be a long while?

CHARLES: The delays of love are the blemishes in art that make its beauty whole, make the illusions real, furnish the ecstasy by tormenting us with ineffable visions. There's no doubt about it: I do love you.

BRIANDA (*suddenly kneeling before him*): You do, my lord?

CHARLES (*looking down at her*): I do, Brianda. And if you've deceived me, thank you, at least, for having kept your secret.

SCENE TWO: CHARLES VII, *the mad King of France, receives his ambassador.*

THE KING: Who're you?

AMBASSADOR: Your Ambassador to Castile, Sire. I pray that my services have been of value.

THE KING: You're not an agent sent by my son Louis to poison me? I've eaten nothing for three days. My son can't wait until I am dead.

AMBASSADOR: No, Your Majesty. I come from Castile.

THE KING: What do you want?

AMBASSADOR: I entreat Your Majesty to listen to me. My errand's important. The war continues.

THE KING: What war's that?

AMBASSADOR: Between Castile and Aragon.

THE KING: What're they fighting about?

AMBASSADOR: A year ago, Sire, Prince Charles of Navarre sought to marry the sister of the King of Castile and form a political alliance with him. His father learned of this. They met at Lerida. At first the king smiled and was friendly, but then, as they stood talking, he suddenly laid an arm on his son's shoulder and ordered his arrest.

THE KING: The king arrested his son! That was a good idea!

AMBASSADOR: No, Sire, it was a disastrous move. The prince was imprisoned, but since he was a guest in Catalonia, the Council of that country immediately offered to pay ransom for him. When that was refused, Barcelona revolted. The King of Castile joined Catalonia, and John is finally defeated.

THE KING: The king's defeated! I will hear no more!

AMBASSADOR: Sire, I entreat . . .

THE KING: These Spanish princes! Who cares about them? And who can remember one from the other? The king's defeated!

AMBASSADOR: He has fled from Catalonia, Sire, leaving the queen there. The queen has long professed to be a friend of the prince. She moves now to make peace and release him. He's kept at Morella, where the Catalonian troops cannot reach him.

THE KING: The Spanish are always fighting. They're barbarians. The queen will release the prince? What sort of woman's the queen?

AMBASSADOR: I know only by hearsay.

THE KING: Hearsay? Everything's hearsay. History's hearsay. By hearsay, you'll be told I am mad.

AMBASSADOR: They say, Sire, Joanna of Aragon's the most remarkable woman of our century.

THE KING: I knew a woman named Agnes Sorel. She loved me.

AMBASSADOR: Who has not heard of Agnes Sorel?

THE KING: You're sure my son Louis didn't send you? While the prince was in prison, why didn't the king poison him?

AMBASSADOR: He's now in the queen's charge. The king has fled. And your cause in Navarre is lost, Sire, unless France will come to his aid. I urge this course on Your Majesty. An alliance with John against Catalonia and Castile. For a price.

THE KING: Everything's for a price. Listen! You're my ambassador to Castile? Return there!

AMBASSADOR: Yes, Sire.

THE KING: I've had nothing to eat for three days. (*seizing the Ambassador's arm*) And when you reach Castile, send me some olives. A capon stuffed with peppers. A bottle of sherry.

SCENE THREE: A dungeon at Morella. The prince, thinking the gaoler has come, does not turn as a hooded figure enters.

CHARLES: You needn't bring fresh straw, gaoler. I've eaten nothing today.

THE FIGURE: I bring no straw, Your Highness. I bring reassurance and news.

CHARLES (*faces about and waits as his visitor throws back the hood*): Oh, you, Friar. I thought for a moment it might be Vinot beneath that hood. Do you pass through walls and locked doors?

FRAY JUAN: As you see.

CHARLES: And what's your news?

FRAY JUAN: The King of France is dead. He went mad, then starved himself to death, for fear his son Louis would poison him.

CHARLES: Was he mad in so doing?

FRAY JUAN: Quite mad, Your Highness.

CHARLES: The King of France is dead? What concern of mine is that?

FRAY JUAN: It means he cannot come to your father's aid.

CHARLES: Then his son Louis can come in his place. Does my father need aid?

FRAY JUAN: He does. You've heard nothing of the fortunes of war?

CHARLES: Only what my gaolers tell me. Which is little. I've not been curious.

FRAY JUAN: You know that Catalonia rose on your behalf, and Castile joined her?

CHARLES: On her own behalf.

FRAY JUAN: The king's defeated and has fled to Aragon, leaving the queen to continue the war. Frago is captured. And the queen, professing to be your friend, marches here to release you with her own hands.

CHARLES: Does she?

FRAY JUAN: But I've come first.

CHARLES: Are your hands as white? And as beautiful?

FRAY JUAN: You shall return to Barcelona in greater triumph than before. They worship you there.

CHARLES: They might well worship me. Having seen and heard nothing of me this past year. You've made a cult of me? But tell me, how does my mistress, the Dona Brianda?

FRAY JUAN: I've not asked about the health of your mistress.

CHARLES: Before you make me a saint, Friar, remember I've had three mistresses.

FRAY JUAN: Men have sinned more than you. And died saints.

CHARLES: You are a fanatic, aren't you? March said you were, so you must be. March always spoke the truth.

FRAY JUAN: Am I a fanatic?

CHARLES: You are. As the queen is a fanatic. And Brianda. All for a cause they love. What's your cause? Why do you lead the people? Is it that you love them? Or hate them? I know, it's that you hate yourself.

FRAY JUAN: I love God.

CHARLES: You smother God with your kisses. This's disgusting.

FRAY JUAN: I said before, you've learned the speech of pagans, but I accept you, my prince, because you are a Christian at heart.

CHARLES: It's true I'm a Christian. But I am chaste in my religion, as you are unchaste. You love God to excess.

FRAY JUAN: One cannot love God to excess.

CHARLES: Beaumont. Was he also imprisoned?

FRAY JUAN: Yes. But already released.

CHARLES: You say the King of France went mad and refused to eat, fearing poison?

FRAY JUAN: He did.

CHARLES (with a gesture): Do you wish fruit, Friar? For the past week my stepmother has sent me a fresh basket every day.

FRAY JUAN: The queen! You ate none?

CHARLES: You think it might be poisoned? You hold my stepmother in poor esteem. Does she not proclaim herself my friend?

FRAY JUAN: But none believes her.

CHARLES: She's beautiful. Do you not believe that physical beauty's the visible evidence of God? I've always believed it.

FRAY JUAN: You didn't eat the fruit!

CHARLES: The risk was all in your favor. The sooner I am a corpse, the sooner I'll cease to trouble you with my unsaintly opinions. The sooner my actions shall cease to belie the picture of me you give to the people. My father was right. I'm your pawn, as I was Beaumont's pawn, and March's pawn. The Church finds me useful. Princes rule by divine right and must maintain belief in the authority of God. But republics breed atheism . . .

FRAY JUAN: I came to speak to you against the queen.

[69]

CHARLES: Advice? Am I still a prince, if I'm governed by you?

FRAY JUAN: She is anxious to hold your favor. To ride with you to Barcelona, thus maintaining her position and showing to the world her friendship with you. Though, as she approaches, the villages close their gates and toll their bells, as when the enemy's sighted.

CHARLES: My father's cause is fallen so low?

FRAY JUAN: The terms of peace will be harsh.

CHARLES: A harsh peace makes new wars, and hence is no peace at all.

FRAY JUAN: You shall be King of Barcelona, under your father's sovereignty. But while you live, John is never again to re-enter Barcelona.

CHARLES: He's barred from Catalonia, as am I from Navarre?

FRAY JUAN: He shall acknowledge you heir of all his dominions.

CHARLES: Shall he?

FRAY JUAN: I hear them!

(JOANNA *appears, accompanied by* VINOT *and the* MARSHAL OF NAVARRE.)

CHARLES: Welcome, Madame.

JOANNA: I thought to open these doors with my own hands. I find them already open.

CHARLES: The Church has come before you. As it must always come, since we belong to the Kingdom of God before we belong to the Kingdom of Aragon.

JOANNA: Am I greeted with your cynicism?

CHARLES (*kneeling*): My greetings, Madame. My thanks.

(*The queen, with an impulsive gesture, withdraws her hand and turns from him.*)

You withdraw your hand? And turn from me? You're right. I should not kneel at an altar when I've neither thanksgiving nor supplication in my heart, only bitterness. (*He rises.*) You do not enquire after my health, as you did the last time we met. Do you not find me pale from my three years in Monroy? My year in the feverish air of Naples? My year in Frago and here in Morella?

JOANNA: I sought only to keep peace between you and your father.

CHARLES: Most politic! (*to Vinot*) Your face is welcome, Vinot. And yours is familiar, Don Pedro. You still wear the same expression. Have you looked on the Gorgon? Have you turned to stone?

DON PEDRO: Your wit eludes me.

CHARLES: Why, the Gorgon is truth. But where could you find truth in Aragon?

DON PEDRO: Where, indeed, when Prince Charles is not there? Who carries the whole world's truth with him wherever he goes.

CHARLES (to Joanna): There, Madame, is cynicism. (to Vinot) Prepare for our return to Barcelona. The queen'll accompany us.

FRAY JUAN: Do not take her, my lord!

CHARLES: Do I hear the voice of the mob? It disgusts me.

FRAY JUAN: You are easily disgusted.

CHARLES (tensely): You do not know.

VINOT: I'd listen to the Friar, Your Highness.

CHARLES: The queen'll not remain long in Barcelona. She'll return to Aragon to rejoin her husband and son. But doesn't all the world applaud her amazing courage? Will not Barcelona cheer her, as it will cheer me, who has done nothing! I want the world to know what indomitable blood courses in royal veins. The Admiral of Castile's daughter has taught them. Now await me without. I would speak to the queen.

(All retire.)

Madame, I've not thanked you for the luscious fruit you sent me.

(As Joanna is silent) You borrow my father's defense of muteness? I spoke of the fruit.

JOANNA: Yes, Charles.

CHARLES: It's true that even my gaolers gave warning, saying the queen might well wish to poison me. I could not believe it. I've eaten the fruit. I'm told the King of France went mad and would touch nothing, fearing the portion might come from his son. But I am your son, Madame. You'd have nothing to gain from my death? You'd not expect me to emulate such French madness and starve myself? You're silent again?

JOANNA: You've eaten the fruit. And I see you before me.

CHARLES: You do in fact. Though some might say I'm more the shadow than the substance of a prince. What you see before you's a virtuous man. For I said to myself, if there's any virtue in me, if there's any virtue in the world, what poison shall prevail against me? Being a Christian. Loving God. If evil can prevail over virtue by such subtle and deadly means, then I hate this world. I'm better ended. No, let me eat this fruit. And if it is poison, let me spew it forth. Because nature rebels. My nature. More important, the world's nature.

JOANNA: You believe yourself of transcendental significance.

CHARLES: I do, Madame. Having devoted myself to abstract thought. To philosophy. To music, art. All teach us we're transcendental. But what happened, when I ate of your fruit? There're some, Madame, who've delicate stomachs. The least thing upsets them and they retch it forth. And the vomit of a prince smells no better than the vomit of the commonest man. I've a delicate stomach like that. It's well known. And I have retched. Not once, but every day. There, in a corner of my cell. Each day a new basket of fruit from you, and each day I tasted it. I ate. As some men, being over-religious, mortify the flesh, I mortified my spirit. The vomit's still there. Can you smell it? I did not let them clean it, but only told them to cover it with fresh straw daily. For that smell is the smell of Naples. The stench of alleys in Barcelona. The odor of humanity! It was time I grew accustomed to it. (*pauses*) I ate, Madame, because you are beautiful. I couldn't believe that God sets traps such as Joanna in this world. The beautiful face. White throat. Swelling bosom. It's not enough to learn that the vomit of princes hangs as foul on the air as that of any man, that queens are false, that kings are blind, and sisters hate. Beauty too deceived me.

Shall you precede me? We go to Barcelona.

(JOANNA *turns and leaves the dungeon. But* CHARLES *remains and stands alone.*)

SCENE FOUR: CHARLES, *in a brocaded silk robe, sways as though ill. He is in his bedchamber with* FRAY JUAN, BRIANDA, *and* BEAUMONT.

CHARLES: Am I king? I do nothing but place my signature on laws passed by the Council of Catalonia.

FRAY JUAN: They're just laws.

CHARLES: The Emperor Charlemagne couldn't read or write. He was a great man. But if I'd not learned to spell my name, the world would have heard nothing of me.

[72]

FRAY JUAN: You think too much of the world.

CHARLES: Shouldn't I? Since I'm to leave it so soon.

FRAY JUAN: You speak of this always.

CHARLES: Where's Beaumont?

BEAUMONT: Here, my lord.

CHARLES: That's the faithful voice! Will you help me to a chair? (*as Beaumont assists him*) You've a strong arm, Beaumont. I undervalued your simple strength.

BEAUMONT: It might have served you better than philosophy.

CHARLES: What's philosophy but a child's delight in a pattern! A tapestry of thought. It's women's work. Shall you mourn me, Brianda?

BRIANDA: Speak not of death!

CHARLES: I'm a poet, though a very poor one. And the poet's a mathematician. I can count the metrical feet in a line, and know I draw near the end of mine.

BRIANDA: Are you suddenly ill, my lord?

CHARLES: I'm suddenly better. Let me sit and rest. But send for my sister Blanche! Send for her at once.

BRIANDA: Yes, my lord. (*exits.*)

CHARLES: All know I'm dangerously ill. And all keep the secret. Among them Brianda, who's skillful at secrets.

FRAY JUAN (*approaching him fiercely*): You were poisoned. The queen did it.

CHARLES: That was four months ago.

FRAY JUAN: You've hidden it from us.

CHARLES (*with an indifferent turn of his hand*): The queen poisoned the fruit. And this's the fruit of the poison. Her act poisoned me. For I cannot forget it.

BEAUMONT: Why not summon a physician? Is there not a famous Jew in Barcelona?

CHARLES: It's no use. I've had physicians all my life, but have lived longer than most, having youth on my side. Youth alone, of the gluttonous mind, cures us. It has a better stomach for the world's poison.

BEAUMONT: You've not disclaimed philosophy.

CHARLES: Poor Beaumont, how you fear an idea! It's the poison of

[73]

action that kills me. Disillusion. I wonder which's the hardest to bear. The tyranny of kings? The tyranny of idealism?

FRAY JUAN: You were never the skeptic.

CHARLES: There was a deep, genuine idealism in me, though I tried to hide it even from myself. That was my fault.

FRAY JUAN: I must leave you.

(BRIANDA re-enters.)

CHARLES: You can't wait to tell people this news? And shall you return to cut locks from my hair? As relics?

(The Dominican goes out.)

BRIANDA: Your sister comes.

CHARLES: My first physician was an Arab. His name was Muza-al-Korthôbi. My next was a Christian, Brother Bernard. But I think our poet, Master March, was the best doctor of them all. A rare chemist who showed me the alchemy of the seasons and taught me how poetry distils all conflicting sounds into music. The year's madrigal. Summer. Autumn. Grey winter. Spring.

(VINOT enters.)

VINOT: They say you're ill, Your Highness.

CHARLES: A pleurisy. Contracted in my long confinement.

VINOT: Your voice is strong.

CHARLES: Why not? I need no longer save my breath. Only for Blanche. Does she come?

BRIANDA: She comes, my lord.

VINOT: I'm told the queen too is ill. And in her agony, she cries: "Ferdinand, my son, what've I not done for you!"

CHARLES: Does she? From what does she suffer?

VINOT: They've discovered a cancer hidden beneath her breast.

CHARLES: A cancer!

VINOT: Yes, my lord. A hard lump.

CHARLES: In the white slope of that bosom! Her beauty hid that?

VINOT: Do you fear death, my lord?

CHARLES: Why?

VINOT: Your death's a victory for the king.

CHARLES: I cannot postpone it on that account.

VINOT: But you can still win. And defeat the queen and your sister.

CHARLES: How?

VINOT: Marry Brianda, making her son legitimate, that he may succeed you.

BEAUMONT: This could be done, my prince.

CHARLES: What ceaseless conspirators you are!

VINOT: I urge it.

CHARLES: Would you have me in death, Brianda? You've waited so long.

BRIANDA: Yes, my lord.

CHARLES: My son a prince? With my father against him? And my sister Eleanor? Your pawn? And the Friar's pawn? The world's pawn? No, I shall spare him that heavy heritage.

VINOT: I beg you to do it.

CHARLES: And I shall spare my lovely, inoffensive Brianda. If I leave her nothing, she'll mourn me a shorter time.

BEAUMONT: Consider it, my lord.

CHARLES: My son's a child. Let him remain a child. Shall we presume on divinity, that ordains princely births?

(BLANCHE enters.)

BLANCHE: You call me, Charles?

CHARLES (to the others): Leave us alone.

(All withdraw save BRIANDA, who remains tautly at the entrance.)
How old am I, Blanche?

BLANCHE: Forty-one.

CHARLES: It's young to die.

BLANCHE: Why do you say this?

CHARLES: It's so. And listen. You'll succeed me, Blanche. And you're in danger.

BLANCHE: That much I know.

CHARLES: Our father hates you, as you hate him. Do not trust Louis, the new King of France, though he may approach you with smiles. Beware of Eleanor. She too has sons. She may do for them what the queen does for hers.

BLANCHE: I know my fate. I shall not long survive you.

CHARLES: Your one hope is Henry, your former husband. Ask his protection. Offer him Navarre in your will. That will spite Eleanor. But if Henry accepts, do not go near him. You're safe nowhere. Poor Blanche. I'm sorry to leave it thus.

BLANCHE: I was born a princess, as you were born a prince.

CHARLES: It's too late. I can't do better.

BLANCHE: You have done well.

CHARLES: Have you heard? The queen hides a cancer in her breast that'll ravage her beauty.

BLANCHE: Time too will do that.

CHARLES: Yes. Time's a cancer in the breast of beauty. Was that what deceived me? Or was it never beauty at all, since it hid pain and evil? How does God answer this question? How shall we know beauty, if we cannot trust our eyes and our senses?

BLANCHE: It is safer to hate than to love.

CHARLES: You learned this, Blanche.

BLANCHE: But I learned this, too. Those who hate, live in a world that hates them.

CHARLES: Yet you loved me, Blanche, And hardly knew me. Is it true, as March said, that there're some men all love, even though the world scarcely knows them?

BLANCHE: They're loved, Charles, because they themselves love others.

CHARLES: I loved everyone. You. My father. Even the queen.

(*He faints.* BLANCHE *cries out.* BRIANDA *echoes the cry and runs forward, and* BEAUMONT *hastens into the room. He l*; *s* the *rince and carries him to a couch.*)

BLANCHE: Send for a priest!

BRIANDA (*carrying the message*): Send for a priest!

(VINOT *enters.* BLANCHE, *bending over her brother, suddenly covers his face.*)

BLANCHE: My brother is dead.

(*All kneel, save* BLANCHE, *and cross themselves.* BRIANDA *hides her face in her hands.*)

BEAUMONT (*rising*): I beg one memento of him, Madame. His velvet cloak.

BLANCHE: I don't think he'd like to be remembered by it. Yet he loved that cloak. He would want you to have it.

BEAUMONT: Thank you, Madame.

BLANCHE: I wish to be alone with him.

VINOT: Yes, Your Highness.

(*All withdraw.* BLANCHE *stands stiffly, alone. The lights darken. A bell tolls. A sound of voices rises from the streets. The Dominican enters.*)

FRAY JUAN: The prince is dead! (*He goes to the couch and makes the sign of the cross over him.*) Already the people murmur in the streets and bells toll.

BLANCHE: He doesn't hear them.

FRAY JUAN: But the king shall hear them. All Spain.

BLANCHE: He would hate this noise. Shutter the windows!

(*She herself does so. The darkness is increased; a silence falls.* BLANCHE *can restrain her emotions no longer. She cries out.*)

Can you teach me, Friar, to feel grief? Must I die as he died? Cynical? Ashamed of my dreams?

FRAY JUAN (*The Dominican has not heard her. In an access of fanaticism, he has knelt by the couch, kissing the hem of the prince's garment*): He's dead. Barcelona has a saint! (*turns to Blanche*) Think of it! Think of it!

SCENE FIVE: LOUIS XI, *King of France, is dressed in plum velvet. He receives the Ambassador to Castile.*

THE KING: Welcome to France.

AMBASSADOR (*rising*): I thank Your Majesty and pray my services have been of value.

THE KING: What's the news from Spain?

AMBASSADOR: The war continues.

THE KING (*jumps to his feet and paces angrily*): That damnable war! Endless!

AMBASSADOR: The Queen of Aragon's dead, Sire.

THE KING: At last? She was a longer time dying than my dearly beloved father.

AMBASSADOR: Our late king often spoke of his son's affection for him.

THE KING: How did the queen die?

AMBASSADOR: Horribly. Of a cancer in the breast.

[77]

THE KING: She was our only hope. She was a man and woman in one. And the king is blind.

AMBASSADOR: No, Sire. A Jewish doctor has restored his sight. Though he's past seventy, he has married again, to a very young girl, causing a great scandal at the court in Aragon.

THE KING: Well, then there's still some life in the king! We may win the war.

AMBASSADOR: Prince Ferdinand takes the field. He's now engaged to the Princess Isabella, and when they're married, they'll unite all Spain.

THE KING: Except for Catalonia.

AMBASSADOR: You shall crush Barcelona. In the end, it'll yield.

THE KING: This war's gone on seven years! Why was France ever drawn into it?

AMBASSADOR: For a price, Sire.

THE KING: The cost is too great. We'll not show a profit on our Spanish investment. These Spanish are a cruel, a barbarous people.

AMBASSADOR: So your late father was wont to remark.

THE KING: Did he? He was sometimes quite wise, before he went mad.

AMBASSADOR: He was, Sire. But sometimes mistaken. The Spanish are no more cruel, no more barbarous than most. Men fight, Your Majesty, when words are inadequate.

THE KING: You're a diplomat! When are words ever inadequate?

AMBASSADOR: Against tyranny, Sire. Against repression.

THE KING: Our tyranny?

AMBASSADOR: No, Sire. All know you for a liberal prince. But against the King of Aragon, with whom you've wisely allied yourself. For a price.

THE KING: Liberal princes must sometimes do this. Join forces with tyrants. That's realism.

AMBASSADOR: Many call it that, Sire.

THE KING: Is it true that Eleanor of Navarre poisoned her sister Blanche?

AMBASSADOR: All such rumors and suspicions of poison must be considered delicately. They often harm most innocent persons.

THE KING: But if Eleanor didn't poison her sister Blanche, then she didn't do as I told her.

AMBASSADOR: Some say Princess Blanche sickened of hate, as her brother was sickened by poetry in an unpoetic world. But no matter, since all the children of the first Queen of Navarre are dead. For Eleanor herself has passed away.

THE KING: Everything goes to Ferdinand.

AMBASSADOR: His mother did not plan in vain. When his marriage to Isabella is consummated, the union of Spain too shall be consummated. Joanna of Aragon was a great woman.

THE KING: A realist.

AMBASSADOR: Some'd call her that, Sire. All mothers are realists, when they plan for their children.

THE KING: You forget Catalonia.

AMBASSADOR: This rebellion can't last forever.

THE KING: Seven years is a long time.

AMBASSADOR: How short a time in the span of history.

THE KING: What demon's in these Catalans, that they fight like this and won't admit defeat!

AMBASSADOR: Sire, they're possessed by the legend of Prince Charles. You know that miracles are performed at his tomb. He's called a saint. The people of Barcelona claim to see his ghost at night, walking the streets with empty hands, crying for vengeance.

THE KING: A better king to them dead than when alive.

AMBASSADOR: That, Your Majesty, would seem to be the legacy of heroic men. They live in memory and inspire new heroism.

THE KING (*after a thoughtful pause*): As my father'd say, on almost every occasion, the question we must ask ourselves, my friend, is what does all this mean to us?

THE CURTAIN FALLS

EDGE OF THE JUNGLE

EDGE OF THE JUNGLE

A Mystery in Three Acts

THE CHARACTERS

Major Alec McLean, *a District Officer*
Della McLean, *his wife*
Eric Cowan, *a Tax Surveyor*
Jakob Groendyck, *Chief Police Inspector*
E. Azubiki, *his assistant*
Mbonu, *the House-boy*
Akamba, *a Servant*
Dr. Ahmed Saidi, *a Syrian Doctor*
Sekgoma, *a Tribesman*

TIME: The present.
SCENE: An outpost, in a British African colony. All the action takes place in the living-room and study of Major McLean's bungalow.

ACT ONE: *Scene One:* Late evening.

ACT TWO: *Scene One:* Next morning.

ACT THREE: *Scene One:* Afternoon, the same day.
Scene Two: Twilight, the same day.

ACT ONE

The appointments of Major McLean's living-room and study are by no means primitive. He is District Officer of this remote African outpost; as such, he has the highest rank and influence locally. The room has rattan tables and chairs and divans, and mats and electric fans. At left, two doors open to other rooms of the bungalow; at right, a door leads out. At back hangs a map of the world and a photograph of Queen Elizabeth II.

In the centre of the room, a wide desk with chairs around it. This is where Major McLean holds conferences and conducts his official business when the occasion requires. On the desk is a small African fertility figure.

AT RISE: MBONU, the house-boy, enters and crosses to the windows at the rear. He begins to lower the jalousies, shutting out the bright moonlight on the flower-lined verandah and the vista of tropical foliage beyond it. He lights the lamps. Mbonu is 28. He is very dark, and dressed in a trim khaki house-coat, over a long white singlet; this garment causes him to look tall and slim. When he has about finished his task, AKAMBA, the maid-servant, glides into the room. Akamba is also very dark and young and pretty. She is perhaps 18. She wears a traditional tobe (robe), with a skirt of bright-colored stripes, and sandals.

Mbonu turns to stare at her. She takes up a tray on which are two after-dinner demi-tasse cups and some cigarette ends and ashes.

MBONU: Did they sit and talk a long time after dinner, just those two?

AKAMBA (*with a look of bright understanding*): Yes, they did.

MBONU: I think the bwana, Major McLean, would not like it very much.

AKAMBA: He does not know.

MBONU (*as he goes about lighting additional lamps in the room*): I think he does. (*Pauses.*) Mr. Cowan likes the woman too much, and this will make trouble.

AKAMBA: I do not wish to hear or see any trouble.

MBONU (*crosses to a spot near her. Gazes hard at her. Changes his tone*): Akamba, I think I will go to your parents. I will ask them to let me take you as my wife.

AKAMBA: You have one wife already. Is not the saying, spoken by the First Wife: "Second Wife, thou givest annoyance; seeing thee, one curses one's husband"?

MBONU (*grasps her arm*): That is it, Akamba? Or no? Between you and bwana McLean—what happens at night?

AKAMBA (*frees herself*): What should happen?

(*With a somewhat wise smile, she exits left.* MBONU *gazes after her for a time. Then he returns to his duties and approaches the desk to light the green lamp on it. When he has done this, he opens the drawer and takes out a revolver from it. He contemplates it for a long moment: then replaces it. Unbeknown to him,* DELLA MCLEAN *appears in the doorway at left. She is 30, with faded good looks. Her voice is soft and emotional, her gestures are often sympathetic, and there is a hint of courage and strong impulse in everything she does.*

She watches Mbonu for an instant: and is obviously disturbed by what she sees.)

DELLA (*finally*): Why do you have the drawer open, Mbonu?

MBONU (*startled. Hastily shuts the drawer, then turns to face her*): Put away something Bwana left on desk—he told me so.

DELLA: What was that?

MBONU: Paper. With some writing on it . . .

DELLA (*with disbelief*): But you can't read. How do you know it's the right paper?

MBONU: Bwana said always . . . nothing must get lost . . . put away every paper (*gesturing toward the jalousies*) . . . or the wind . . .

DELLA: Yes? Well, never mind . . .

MBONU (*anxious to escape from the room*): Memsahib would excuse me now?

(MBONU *exits right.* DELLA *looks after him with a troubled expression.* ERIC COWAN *enters from left, unseen by her. He is 27 or 28, rather handsome, but something in his manner betrays that he is ill-at-ease; he is*

*involved with Della and has a bad conscience. He is intelligent and sensitive,
which deepens his problem. He has a pronounced stammer at times. A footstep
causes her to become aware of his presence.*)

DELLA (*sees him*): Oh, Eric . . .

ERIC: Startle you?

DELLA: Something's happened I don't like . . .

ERIC: What's that?

DELLA: Just now I came in . . . Mbonu was going through the
drawer where Alec keeps his revolver. He claimed he was putting
something away—but I couldn't believe him. He was too confused.

ERIC (*weighs this*): You've had Mbonu a long time?

DELLA: Ever since we've been here—Five years. We always trusted
him, but now, who knows? Whom can you trust? It might even be
Mbonu? You heard such dreadful things about Kenya—houseboys
who'd been faithful all their lives suddenly took the secret oath and
killed whole families they'd lived with.

ERIC: It could never happen here.

DELLA: It already has—that's where Alec's gone.

ERIC: An outbreak?

DELLA: A herd of cattle's been slaughtered on the Lambert plantation.
And there's some kind of riot. Alec went with two cars of police.

ERIC (*convinced*): This's no place for you.

DELLA (*intensely*): It's not—for many reasons. I've made up my
mind. I'm going to ask Alec to let me return to London *at once.*
If I wait until you go, and then ask him to let me return to London,
he'll think I'm following you. But if I go first, it'll look different. He
may not guess why—

ERIC: Oh?

DELLA: I couldn't sleep, thinking about it. Trying to decide. But
I'm sure it's the right way.

ERIC (*softly*): Yes.

DELLA: I'm going to tell him tonight.

ERIC: Will he let you go?

DELLA (*with bitter irony*): He won't like it.

ERIC: What excuse will you give him?

DELLA: That I'm tired and nervous—ill—and it might be dangerous
here.

ERIC: Will that convince him?

DELLA: Why not? It's the truth—I don't want to lie, if I can help it. I've never liked lying—

ERIC (*thinking of himself*): We're often forced into lies, when we try to be kind.

DELLA (*resentfully*): Should I be kind to him? He's never been very kind to me, or anyone else. It's not his nature.

ERIC (*with reluctant admiration*): No. He's strong. Sometimes you can't be strong and kind at the same time. But, still, he's human.

DELLA: I don't think he'll be human, when I tell him. He'll make a terrible scene. (*Pauses.*) Eric, how do you feel about it?

ERIC: I don't like to see you go. That's why I can understand his feelings, too.

DELLA: I'll be in London when you get there.

ERIC (*dubiously*): Yes—

DELLA: (*searchingly. Anxiously*): How do you feel about that?

ERIC (*frankly*): I've mixed feelings.

DELLA: I'll not be as attractive to you there—there're so many other women. I'm somewhat older than you—

ERIC: That doesn't matter.

DELLA: I really know so little about you.

ERIC: When I say "mixed feelings", I mean: In London, you'll soon meet men—you'll attract them—and will I seem so important to you, then? I haven't all the qualities you admire in a man—

DELLA: Why do you say that?

ERIC: Because you married *him*—and he's many things I'm not.

DELLA (*vehemently*): I don't like those things in him. I hate them.

ERIC: Perhaps you're drawn to them, without realizing it.

DELLA: He thinks I married him only for security.

ERIC: Did you?

DELLA: I did want security—doesn't every woman? But I also wanted to love him—I wanted to be a good wife. I've tried very hard.

ERIC: You don't love him any more?

DELLA: I'm still trying, Eric. And more than ever, since you're here. I want to be faithful to him. But of course he's not faithful to me. He's had one mistress after another, amongst the white women here.

ERIC: What does that mean, you're trying to love him—more than ever—now that I'm here?

DELLA: You know how I feel about you.

ERIC (*pauses*): Would you leave him for me?

DELLA: Not if he really wanted me to stay—Oh, not to save his face —I've remained with him all these years because of that—I didn't want to ruin his career. But if he still valued me for myself, if something was still left of our marriage, I'd stay.

ERIC: He must've prized you, or he wouldn't have married you.

DELLA: For years I've tried to tell myself that. I'm convinced now he thought I'd make an ideal District Commissioner's wife—I know how to pour tea so well—and he cast me for the part.

ERIC: Why didn't you leave him sooner?

DELLA: I hadn't met anyone I cared enough about, to make it worth the while—the struggle, the scandal.

ERIC (*intimidated*): It'd be a scandal?

DELLA: Out here. In London, it'd matter less.

ERIC: You hate him?

DELLA: Yes.

ERIC (*candidly again*): It makes me ask myself whether you're drawn to me for that reason—because I'm not Alec—whether you wouldn't be drawn to any other man out here?

DELLA (*slowly*): It'd be no different in London—we're separate, lonely people, each of us—we're at the edge of the jungle in London as much as here. I'm not a foolish girl, with a lot of dreams. I'm not looking for the perfect man. I'm not waiting for an ideal to appear, but only for another *human being*, someone by whom I'm needed, that I won't be lonely any more.

ERIC (*confesses*): I do need you.

DELLA: I felt it in you, Eric, when I first saw you . . . But you're often so indecisive, so cautious. Can you really love?

ERIC: I do want you!

DELLA: Are you sure?

ERIC (*stirred*): I'd like a chance, just once, to prove I can be reckless too. God knows, I could kill him for the way he's treated you.

DELLA: That'll hardly be necessary.

ERIC: If he refuses to let you go?

DELLA: Nothing'll stop me. I mean to fight for my happiness now.

ERIC: You'll divorce him in London? You'll marry me?

DELLA (*simply*): I promise it.

ERIC: Don't let him talk you down or threaten—he can be very harsh, even violent—

DELLA (*intimidated, despite herself*): Yes—

ERIC: If you must tell him the whole truth about me, do it. I'll be here—you can call me. I can talk to him, too.

DELLA: He'd lose his head completely, if he suspected you. It would only be much worse.

ERIC: You're probably right.

(*Offstage: sound of a jeep.* ERIC *turns toward the noise.* DELLA *goes to the jalousies and peers through them.*)

Is that Alec?

DELLA: It's his jeep.

MBONU (*enters from right*): Bwana comes.

DELLA (*to Mbonu*): Very well. (*to Eric*) Let's not stay—I've something else to tell you.

(*After a moment's hesitation, he follows her off, left.* MBONU *gazes after them thoughtfully. Then* MAJOR MCLEAN *and* MR. E. AZUBIKI *enter from right.*

McLean is 49 or 50, tall and strongly built. He has large features, darkened by tropic sun. His voice is harshly authoritative.

Mr. E. Azubiki, native Deputy Inspector of Police, is 38. He is small and very black, and neatly attired in a white duck-suit. He wears gold-rimmed glasses, and talks in a quiet voice, with a British accent—acquired at the Oka School in Nigeria.)

MBONU: Good evening, Bwana.

MCLEAN (*merely an acknowledgment of Mbonu's presence*): Yes.

(MBONU *exits left.* MCLEAN *takes off his sun-helmet. Refers to day's work.*)

MCLEAN: Nasty. Very nasty.

E. AZUBIKI (*apologetically*): Yes, Major. The tribesmen behaved in a very foolish, very rebellious manner.

MCLEAN: This may be only the beginning for us. Take action early and head it off—we'll have to do that. Sit down a moment, Azubiki.

I want to talk to you before Groendyck gets here. I'm afraid things are going to get worse. Riots and cattle raids. We're likely to have the same sort of trouble here they had some years ago in Kenya—something like the Mau-Mau. Or lately in Mozambique.

E. AZUBIKI: It is possible, yes.

MCLEAN (*sits at desk*): E. Azubiki. What's the "E" for?

E. AZUBIKI (*surprised, sits opposite*): "Edward". It's my Christian name—I took it when I entered school, in my 16th year. I was baptized on that occasion.

MCLEAN (*makes a note on pad on desk*): I had to write out your name the other day and didn't know what the initial stood for—just E. Azubiki. (*Looks up from pad.*) Groendyck's term—his civil-service contract—as Inspector of Police expires very shortly. If he retires, someone else'll be appointed—

E. AZUBIKI (*interested, but trying not to show it*): Does Mr. Groendyck plan to retire? I know nothing of it.

MCLEAN: You don't, naturally. Groendyck himself doesn't.

E. AZUBIKI: Oh?

MCLEAN: Why do you wear those glasses? Are you near-sighted?

E. AZUBIKI (*takes them off*): No. My eyes are good. (*Holds them up for McLean to notice.*) These glasses are plain. I see very well. I wear the glasses to look like an intellectual, an educated man.

MCLEAN: Lots of natives do that? Wear glasses like yours—?

E.. ZUBIKI: Some do, yes.

MCLEAN: You've always seemed pretty sharp to me—not at all near-sighted.

E. AZUBIKI (*politely*): You are very kind, Major McLean.

MCLEAN (*who needs this information*): You went to a missionary college?

E. AZUBIKI (*proudly*): At Oka, in Nigeria.

MCLEAN: An odd background for your present work. And how did you enter the service? Did you take an examination?

E. AZUBIKI: Yes. I passed it very well. After I had studied philosophy and theology, I became interested in the question of right and wrong, so I decided to become a policeman.

MCLEAN: I don't see the exact connection.

E. AZUBIKI (*with deep sincerity*): A policeman is a philosopher—he

seeks to learn the truth. To me, police work is a form of theology—
because, when we learn about people, we learn about God.

MCLEAN (*with superior amusement*): A very novel approach. May I
ask if you've discovered anything of importance—about man and God?

E. AZUBIKI (*slowly shakes head*): The mystery is very profound. Why
does He let us act as we do?

MCLEAN (*speaking for himself*): Perhaps there is no God—or perhaps
He doesn't care.

E. AZUBIKI: I cannot believe that. But what they taught us at Oka
doesn't always seem adequate. Man is a wicked creature. But why was
he made so?

MCLEAN: And how long have you been in the service?

E. AZUBIKI: Eleven years—

MCLEAN: And you've worked with Groendyck all that time,
haven't you?

E. AZUBIKI: Yes. I admire his abilities greatly.

MCLEAN: He's a good police officer. Very shrewd. I've nothing
against him. This's something else—a political matter. Don't you think
a native as Chief Police Inspector would be a good thing—would please
the tribes?

E. AZUBIKI (*amazed*): A *native*—as Inspector of Police?

MCLEAN: Yes. How would your people like it?

E. AZUBIKI: If I may say so, the appointment of a black native would
have a very beneficial effect. It would be a very great advance!

MCLEAN: That's what I think. It'd be a very bold, but very clever,
move. What if I should name you?

E. AZUBIKI: I am hardly prepared for this—

MCLEAN: It's not yet definite. The question is, can you handle things,
if there're more outbreaks? Can you prevent our having anything here
like the Mau-Mau?

E. AZUBIKI: It must be done by tact, not force. To use force is very
foolish. Everything is better done with tact—here, in Africa.

MCLEAN: The whole policy of the Colonial Office is toward self-
government by the natives. So it might be a good idea to try some here.

E. AZUBIKI: It would be wonderful!

MCLEAN: When Groendyck gets here, I'll speak to him. It's something he won't like.

E. AZUBIKI: Ordinarily, I would not like to usurp his place. But this would mean so much not only to me but to my people—

MCLEAN: Social progress?

E. AZUBIKI (*almost breathlessly*): It is certainly that. It will make you a very popular man throughout the district.

MCLEAN: With the blacks. Not with the whites. They'll cry bloody murder and send fifty protests to Freetown and London.

E. AZUBIKI (*appreciates*): It will be difficult for you—

MCLEAN: That won't stop me. I've authority to name you—

(*Offstage: the sound of a jeep. Both men turn to listen to it. Enter* MBONU, *from left.*)

MBONU: Bwana, Mr. Groendyck is here.

MCLEAN (*to Mbonu*): Is he? (MBONU *exits left, after this announcement. Azubiki rises from his chair.*) Say nothing of this yet, Azubiki. First let me talk to Groendyck and tell him—

E. AZUBIKI: Shall I not leave? It would be more proper.

MCLEAN: Better. You'll hear from me—maybe tomorrow. Fact is, I've already sent in my recommendation.

E. AZUBIKI: It is an act of confidence. A mark of respect for the black man.

(JAKOB GROENDYCK, *the Inspector of Police, enters from right. He is 52 and vigorous. His keen glance suggests that he is very astute; but he is moody, and sometimes saturnine. He has a slight touch of a Dutch accent in his speech.*)

GROENDYCK: I dropped off Brady at his place. Roberts is on the trail of some of them.

MCLEAN: Good!

GROENDYCK: I think we can round up some of the instigators. The boys on Lambert's plantation recognized several faces in the crowd.

MCLEAN: I thought they didn't.

GROENDYCK: On second thought, they did. We finally convinced them—

MCLEAN: Keep at it.

GROENDYCK (*advancing into the room*): If you're coming my way, Azubiki, I can take you in the jeep.

E. AZUBIKI (*almost humbly*): No, thank you, Mr. Groendyck. I will walk.

D   [91]

MCLEAN: I wish you'd stay a moment, Groendyck. I've something to discuss with you.

GROENDYCK: All right.

E. AZUBIKI (*leaving*): Thank you both very much. (*to Groendyck*) Please believe always, Mr. Groendyck, I have only deep respect for you. (MR. E. AZUBIKI *exits*).

GROENDYCK (*looking after him. Frowns. Puzzled*): What's that?

MCLEAN: He's an unusually clever man, little Azubiki.

GROENDYCK (*still gazing after him*): Yes, sometimes; but can you trust him? Can you trust any of them these days?

MCLEAN: You're suspicious of him, too?

GROENDYCK: Of anyone who's black.

MCLEAN: Isn't he loyal?

GROENDYCK: I've nothing against Azubiki personally. He's a decent enough fellow and does his job well, better than I ever expected any black would. But he'll stick with his own people. If we're going to have trouble along those lines, he can't be depended on.

MCLEAN: Is that your opinion?

GROENDYCK: It is. What happened today—those riots—are nothing to what'll follow. We're in for real disturbances. And that brings me to another thing. You weren't armed today, out there at Lambert's. And I think you should always carry a weapon, from now on. And, in the house, too, you should always have one at hand—

MCLEAN (*opens drawer, takes out revolver, displays it to Groendyck, then lays it on top of desk*): I've this—in here.

GROENDYCK: As District Officer, you're a natural target—you and your wife. Take precautions—both of you.

MCLEAN: The best prevention is to quiet the unrest. To take steps immediately. Not all brush fires are started or put out in the same way. What happened in Kenya and Ghana needn't happen here—We must win over as many as we can—

GROENDYCK (*with no inkling*): How?

MCLEAN: By the right gestures—

GROENDYCK: What sort? I wish I knew—

MCLEAN: A few concessions are called for, to begin with.

GROENDYCK: I agree. We should make some.

MCLEAN: I've one in mind, and unfortunately it concerns you.

[92]

GROENDYCK: Me?

MCLEAN: Your appointment expires shortly.

GROENDYCK (*tensing*): In two months.

MCLEAN: You've done an excellent job here, but I'm afraid I can't recommend renewal.

GROENDYCK: You can't? Why not?

MCLEAN: It's nothing personal. I'll give you the highest references, and you can surely get a post elsewhere in the colony, or else back in Johannesburg. But I've someone in view to replace you—

GROENDYCK (*amazed*): Replace me? I've had this job fifteen years, long before you came out here. This's my life, my whole career. I've never heard of any complaints about my work—

MCLEAN: No complaints. It's purely a matter of political expediency.

GROENDYCK: But I've my home here—And a son at school in England! I can't afford to pull up suddenly, to move out, to be without income. I've put in fifteen years of my life here, I've always done my best—

MCLEAN: I don't enjoy doing this. I've no choice.

GROENDYCK: Be frank with me—What's it all about?

MCLEAN: There's a spirit of revolt to be headed off. (*Rises. Gestures toward map on wall.*) This isn't just local unrest—it isn't only in Africa that the colored races are rising against us; it's happening all over the world. One answer is steps toward self-government, and that's what I'm proposing here—

GROENDYCK (*grasping it*): And you're going to replace me by—?

MCLEAN: A black Inspector of Police, yes. The whole constabulary's black—or will be soon.

GROENDYCK: Are you insane? You won't be allowed to do it. The whites here will never stand for it.

MCLEAN (*a bit ironically*): I expect a lot of criticism. But I've a free hand with minor appointments. And, in certain quarters, I'll be praised for imaginative liberalism. After all, you're an Afrikaner—and bigoted —at least, they say you are.

GROENDYCK (*after a stunned moment*): Who's it going to be? Azubiki—

MCLEAN (*very directly*): It is.

GROENDYCK: Azubiki—that little black man—is to take my place? Mine?

MCLEAN: I've decided on it.

GROENDYCK (*genuinely appalled*): Have you any idea how his mind works? How devious and irrational he is?

MCLEAN (*calmly*): He's been very successful on all his cases.

GROENDYCK: Under my direction. He's sensible half the time, and crackbrained the other half, like all these people.

MCLEAN (*undeterred*): I'll take a chance—on his record. Only a moment ago, you yourself spoke well of him.

GROENDYCK: A Black. Azubiki? You'll get a hundred protests.

MCLEAN: I'm prepared for that.

GROENDYCK (*feeling his humiliation*): Does Azubiki know of this? Have you told him?

MCLEAN: Just now.

GROENDYCK: And anyone else?

MCLEAN: I've sent in a formal recommendation. It's not been acted on, but I'm sure it will be.

GROENDYCK: And I'm to be thrown out—made the scapegoat—and replaced by a Black? What happens to me, after all these years . . . how'm I to provide for my wife, and go on educating my son . . . you don't care at all about that?

MCLEAN: It's hard on you. But I can't consider the problems of one man, you or myself. I'm entrusted with the safety of this whole district. You can go elsewhere and be used to good advantage. You're still a young man.

GROENDYCK (*bitterly*): Fifty-two.

MCLEAN: Even so.

GROENDYCK: If you'd let me stay three years longer, I'd have some of my pension rights, and my son'd be finished with his school, at least—

MCLEAN: Three years? Impossible.

GROENDYCK (*urgently*): Why?

MCLEAN: This race situation isn't going to stay quiet for three years. It's likely to blow up any moment. But a black chief of police might help us keep order.

GROENDYCK: Put the police in his hands? You're committing suicide.

MCLEAN (*curtly*): I don't think so.

GROENDYCK: You'll see!

MCLEAN (*unimpressed*): Will I?

GROENDYCK: You'll have a massacre here. A black massacre.

MCLEAN (*still unimpressed*): Shall we? I'll take that chance. (*rising*) Jakob, I'm sorry. I'm acting merely as an official with unpleasant responsibilities, not in any personal spirit at all. You still have two months to get ready and to look around . . .

GROENDYCK: Two months?

MCLEAN: I'll be glad to write any letters you need and make enquiries on your behalf.

GROENDYCK (*bitterly again*): Very kind of you—But wait—

MCLEAN (*brusquely*): For what? Don't try to stir up any trouble amongst the whites—Don't talk about it too much—

GROENDYCK: Is that an order?

MCLEAN: If you don't act properly, you'll get no reference. Clear?

GROENDYCK (*staring at him*): I'm not going to take this quietly. You're District Officer here, but you aren't God.

MCLEAN: I'm asserting my authority as far as it goes—and no farther.

GROENDYCK (*as he goes out*): We'll see how far!

(MCLEAN *is left alone for a moment; then he calls.*)

MCLEAN (*as* MBONU *enters*): Mbonu!

(MCLEAN *studies a chess-board on which are black and white pieces. He moves one.*)

MCLEAN: Tell the memsahib I want to see her.

(MBONU *exits.* MCLEAN *takes up the revolver on his desk, puts it down.* DELLA *enters from left.*)

Della, I want to talk to you—

DELLA (*quietly*): Yes.

MCLEAN: There was a riot today at Lambert's, over grazing rights. Part of their herd was slashed. So things may be kicking up.

DELLA: I know.

MCLEAN: Groendyck thinks you should take precautions—as my wife. We're natural targets. I just wanted to remind you that this revolver's kept here—in the desk drawer. And, perhaps, if you want to carry one when you go out, I can buy a smaller one for you.

DELLA (*after a moment*): No, Alec, I don't care to carry a weapon.

MCLEAN: Then don't go out alone. Take Mbonu with you.

DELLA: Can I trust Mbonu?

MCLEAN: He's been with us five years.

DELLA: I found him looking at that revolver only an hour ago, when I came in here.

MCLEAN (*alerted*): Did you? What was he doing?

DELLA: The drawer was open—he said he was putting away some papers for you. The revolver was there, so I tried not to excite him.

MCLEAN: I never told him to touch any papers on my desk!

DELLA: I didn't suppose you had. So I don't think I want to take Mbonu with me, when I go out.

MCLEAN: Don't get the wind up that fast. He was probably just looking for loose coins. Servants always snoop.

DELLA: Alec, I'm nervous about things here. It's become dangerous, hasn't it? And I'm tired and ill.

MCLEAN (*gazing at her*): What's wrong?

DELLA: I'm too tense. I'd like to go back to England for a time, for a bit of a change. As soon as I can.

MCLEAN: Oh?

DELLA: In fact, almost as soon as I can pack.

MCLEAN: It's quite impossible.

DELLA: Why?

MCLEAN: Because you're my wife, and I'm District Officer. If you went, it'd look as though it were because of the Lambert affair—as though you were scared, or I was scared for you. It'd start a panic amongst all the white women in the district.

DELLA: Not if you explain if properly.

MCLEAN: I can't. We're expected to set the example—

DELLA: But it's not the Lambert affair—I'm ill, as I've just told you—and nervous, and tense—

MCLEAN (*sharply catching up her word*): Tense?

DELLA: Very tense. I wasn't meant to live in a place like this all my life. In all this heat, and isolation . . . I need a change, Alec.

MCLEAN: I dare say. You'd enjoy a few months in London, wouldn't you, while I'm out here with the Blacks taking pot-shots at me?

[96]

Nothing doing. I'm staying here, because it's my duty. And you're staying here, because it's yours, too.

DELLA: Do I have that duty?

MCLEAN: I rather think so. You married me, because you wanted me to provide for you—hardly because you loved me. I've gone through with my share of it, and I expect you to fulfill yours. Equal shares—that's the size of it.

DELLA: It wasn't a business transaction—

MCLEAN: Every marriage is.

DELLA: Isn't it something more?

MCLEAN (approaches her): Not between us. Ours wasn't a marriage made in Heaven, Della. It was made in a registry office, and it was recorded there just like any other legal contract. And that's what it's been.

DELLA: You don't talk at all like a human being. You never feel sympathy or compassion for me. Never! My happiness, my health, my life mean nothing to you—you're only concerned about what'll best serve your career—

MCLEAN: You can put it that way. You cheated me, when you married me, because you didn't love me.

DELLA: I meant to. But how can anyone love you, when they get to know you?

MCLEAN: Ah, is that it? I'm not lovable—like Eric Cowan, perhaps? (grasps her) And just why do you want to go to London now, in such a hurry? Is it because Mr. Cowan's going there next month, and you want to be there before he arrives? Then what'll happen, between you two?

DELLA: What makes you think that?

MCLEAN: What makes me think you're going off to whore it in London with Eric Cowan? Just that I know you, and how your mind works. You hope to use him to get away from me?

DELLA: No!

MCLEAN: I think you do. But he has nothing to offer you—He's a pencil-pusher, only half a man . . . A timid little clerk in the Tax Office.

DELLA: He's someone who needs me, Alec. Can you understand how important that is to me? Can you let me have that chance not to be lonely any more? A chance to start again, after the mistake I made?

MCLEAN: The mistake of marrying me?

DELLA: I know now I shouldn't have, and it wasn't fair to you, either. But I meant well, believe me I did. And I've been the best wife I could to you—

MCLEAN: Not as I see it, you haven't. Why do you deny yourself to me?

DELLA: My God, when I think of all the other women you touch!

MCLEAN: You're cold. I need something more in a woman than you've ever given me!

DELLA: Why should we stay together? We don't love each other. Let me go—

MCLEAN: No. I've a future. I'm not going to have people say my wife left me.

DELLA: I *will* leave you.

MCLEAN: You won't. You've no money. On your own, you can't travel twenty miles from here. If Cowan tries to take you away, I'll kill him! I won't let any man help himself to my wife . . . make a laughing-stock of me . . .

DELLA: As usual, you're thinking of yourself . . .

MCLEAN: Why should I think of you or Eric Cowan, who lives in my house and makes love to my wife behind my back . . .

DELLA: He hasn't, really. Nothing, nothing has happened between us.

MCLEAN: Maybe that's true, maybe not. But your little affair with him is over from this moment on. In the morning I'll throw him out of my house.

DELLA: That'll cause a scandal.

MCLEAN (*viciously*): I'll take good care of Cowan's reputation— He'll be sorry he ever dared look at you.

DELLA: What will you say about him?

MCLEAN: An official report to end his career.

DELLA: It'll be lies—!

MCLEAN: But I'll do it.

DELLA: You'll ruin his life.

MCLEAN: I'll do my very best!

DELLA: You've no pity. No kindness, no honesty.

MCLEAN: I play the game my own way.

DELLA: It's not a game, Alec! It's our lives. I'll never let you do it. I'll make a public scandal that'll really hurt you—I'll tell the truth about you—What a brute you are.

MCLEAN (*approaches her swiftly, slaps her sharply, stingingly*): Shut up. Go to your room! I'll tend to Cowan in the morning.

(*After a moment, she retreats, one hand pressed to her cheek, which has been bruised by his slap. He stands a moment, glaring after her. Then he moves about, almost automatically, turning out the lamps. From far off comes the sound of singing and drums—a village ceremony. The room is progressively dimmed, and at last is in utter darkness. Suddenly there is a noise offstage, as if tin has been struck. McLean's voice is heard:*)

Who's that? What's that?

(*Curious or alarmed, he opens the door at right and steps outside in the moonlight to look around—but we cannot see him do this: the door opens inward and hides his egress from us. Meanwhile, we cannot make out what is happening in the dim room: only the faintest bit of moonlight filters through the jalousies. But the shadow or silhouette of someone moves about in the room, near the desk. Once again McLean's voice is heard—apparently outside:*)

Is that you, Mbonu? Who is it?

(*MCLEAN seemingly re-enters the room and crosses it. The singing and drums grow louder, as does the shrill noise of night insects. Suddenly there is a shot, a gasp, and the sound of a falling body. We are still unable to make out what has occurred. After an instant, AKAMBA steals in, bearing a dim lamp. She beholds the sprawled form of the Major and recoils from it, then quickly she crosses to the desk and snatches up the little wooden idol, and hastens out, leaving the room in darkness again. The ceremonial singing and the chorus of insects—crickets and cicadas—reach a climax, cut off by a woman's horrified scream; in it are fear and hysteria.*)

ACT TWO

SCENE ONE: The scene is the same; the next morning. The jalousies have been raised, and the tropical garden is vivid in the hot African sunlight. MBONU, *undergoing a verbal examination, stands between* GROENDYCK *and* E. AZUBIKI. *McLean's revolver, partially wrapped in a handkerchief, lies on the desk. On the floor white tape in the shape of an "X" marks where McLean had fallen.*

GROENDYCK (*leaning forward in his chair, behind the desk*): You've been here five years? In all that time, did you have any trouble with Major McLean?

MBONU (*shakes head*): No, Bwana; no trouble.

GROENDYCK: You heard the shot very clearly. You rushed in here. Major McLean lay dead over there. Where was the revolver? How far from him?

MBONU (*points*): There . . .

GROENDYCK (*to Azubiki*): Exactly how far does it measure?

E. AZUBIKI: About five and one-half feet.

GROENDYCK (*to Mbonu*): And the bwana was dead when you found him?

MBONU (*gravely*): Bwana was dead. (*points to a spot near the door at left*) There . . .

GROENDYCK: You also heard the memsahib scream?

MBONU: Auck! (*Puts hands to his ears, as if to shut out the remembered sound.*)

GROENDYCK: It was after the shot, and before you ran into this room?

(*Mbonu simply nods.*)
And how did she act?

MBONU (*eloquently*): Very much.

GROENDYCK: Very much what?

MBONU: Very much loud.

GROENDYCK (*to E. Azubiki*): She was hysterical?

E. AZUBIKI: Constable Brady says that's how she was when they found her. (*to Mbonu*) But before the shot, before the bwana was killed, was there any noise in the room . . . here?

MBONU (*nods*): Ehe, very much.

E. AZUBIKI: What kind of noise, Brother?

MBONU: Talk. Much talk.

E. AZUBIKI: Between whom?

MBONU: Bwana, memsahib. (*Puts hands to ears again, to indicate the talk was loud and angry.*)

E. AZUBIKI: They had a quarrel? They were angry?

MBONU: Ehe. Very much.

E. AZUBIKI: About what?

(*Mbonu shrugs.*)

GROENDYCK: He probably doesn't know.

E. AZUBIKI: Mbonu understands English better than he speaks it. (*to Mbonu*) Was this quarrel, this angry noise, just before the shot?

MBONU: Noise; then gun.

E. AZUBIKI: And you heard everything, Brother? Where were you?

(*Mbonu points left.*)

In the next room?

(*Mbonu nods.*)

Was the fight about money?

(*Mbonu shrugs.*)

About the husband—the bwana was not a good husband—or about the wife—the memsahib was not a good wife?

(*Mbonu nods.*)

Which? The husband or the wife?

MBONU: Not good wife.

E. AZUBIKI: Oh? With another man?

MBONU: Maybe. Bwana—(*he points left toward Cowan's room*)

E. AZUBIKI: The white man who is here? Mr. Cowan?

MBONU: Ehe, that one.

E. AZUBIKI: And the loud words were about this?

MBONU: Ehe, very loud. Very bad.

E. AZUBIKI: Was there silence before the shot?

(*Mbonu thinks a moment, as though trying to recall, and then nods.*)

Do you think the memsahib was still in this room with the bwana?

(*Mbonu shakes his head indecisively, and then shrugs—he does not know.*)

E. AZUBIKI: Was the other bwana here?

(*Again, a headshake and a shrug.*)

GROENDYCK (*suddenly interrupting*): You were in the next room all the time? You were listening? Why?

(*Mbonu shakes his head again, as if to imply that he does not know or cannot say.*)

After the lights were put out, what happened?

MBONU (*points toward garden*): Noise. Bwana call my name. (*points to self*) But no answer—

GROENDYCK: Why?

MBONU: Too late! Bwana comes back into house—(*claps hands suddenly, to give effect of a shot*) Dead—!

GROENDYCK (*sharply*): How do we know you're telling the truth? Maybe you shot Major McLean yourself?

MBONU (*startled*): Auck, not me! No, not Mbonu!

(DR. SAIDI *enters from left, a tall thin Syrian of 48, with a tufted chin. His manner is superior, his smile cynical. His hands are delicate and graceful, and he is fond of speaking with suave humor; his dark eyes moving from listener to listener, as he does so. At this moment, he carries his black leather bag—he has been examining the corpse—and he stops wordless and motionless, to watch the exchange between* GROENDYCK *and* MBONU. *As we shall learn, he is a Mohammedan, but has a special—and somewhat distorted— sense of values all his own.*)

GROENDYCK (*finally*): What sort of noise did the Major hear outside?

MBONU (*unable to explain*): Noise—

GROENDYCK (*ironically*): That helps a great deal. (*stares fixedly at Mbonu for a long time, then speaks to E. Azubiki*) I think that's it for now. He's to stay in the bungalow. We can question him again—I'm sure he'll have more to tell us, after a while.

E. AZUBIKI (*to Mbonu*): You hear? Thank you, Brother. Stay near— but not in the next room—don't try to listen to anyone else.

(MBONU *backs out, nodding his head vigorously, frightened.*)

GROENDYCK: He very well might have done it, perhaps with the help of someone else, outside. This's a political murder, obviously.

E. AZUBIKI: Obviously? A political murder?

GROENDYCK (*referring to the dead man*): He was the District Officer. Many people in the tribes hated him. (*turns to Dr. Saidi*) Did you extract the bullet, Dr. Saidi?

DR. SAIDI (*who speaks English with a foreign intonation*): Not yet. I'll do it this afternoon. Do you need an official report on the cause of death?

GROENDYCK (*nods*): As soon as possible. He was shot from very close, wasn't he?

DR. SAIDI: To judge from the powder burns. Altogether, the Major is most unsightly. But dead people are—when they've bullets in them. In this heat, keep plenty of ice on him.

GROENDYCK: When you were summoned last night, did you notice anything significant?

DR. SAIDI: Much excitement. I treated Mrs. McLean for hysteria. Mr. Cowan was helpful. Everyone was shocked, it seemed, but I don't think anyone was very fond of the Major or was mourning him.

E. AZUBIKI (*sadly*): He was a human being.

DR. SAIDI (*with a touch of mockery*): What, really, Mr. Azubiki, did you learn at your missionary college to prepare you for a case like this?

E. AZUBIKI: That is very similar to a question that Major McLean himself asked me, only yesterday. A study of theology is really quite appropriate. When a murder is committed, one faces the problems of life and death, crime and punishment, sin and redemption.

DR. SAIDI: Oh? You take it as seriously as that?

E. AZUBIKI (*earnestly*): To me every crime raises the deepest question of all—the existence of evil in the universe, apparently with God's sanction.

DR. SAIDI (*still lightly*): Do you expect to solve that?

E. AZUBIKI: Mustn't a man, in order to know what to believe?

GROENDYCK (*matter-of-factly*): Let's not solve the problems of the universe—let's try to answer just one problem—who killed Major McLean?

E. AZUBIKI: Is it not all *one* question? (*Pauses.*) You speak of a political murder. Was it that? Mbonu says there was a quarrel between the Major and his wife.

(SAIDI *takes up the chess set, holds it, studies it.*)

GROENDYCK: Can you believe what he says? Or any of these people? It might be his way of shifting our suspicion—it's simple— he's clever enough for that.

E. AZUBIKI: It might also be true.

GROENDYCK: Yes. But even if they did quarrel, as all husbands and wives do, it doesn't follow that she murdered him with his own revolver. Mrs. McLean's a soft, gentle woman. I'm sure she loved her husband.

E. AZUBIKI: If this is a crime caused by hate, it will not be difficult to solve—because it is easy to understand the working of hate. But if it is a murder caused by passion, it will be hard—because passion is a mysterious thing.

DR. SAIDI: Passion makes monsters of us—sometimes.

(*Hands chess board to* AZUBIKI *who stares at it, carries it to desk.*)

E. AZUBIKI (*thoughfully*): Sometimes.

DR. SAIDI: In every woman there's a tiger with long nails who can spring out in the night.

GROENDYCK: I think you're going off on the wrong track. We must pursue it, of course—because we must solve this, and quickly. But everything points to a political murder, an act of revenge. Probably by a secret society here, like that of the Mau-Mau.

DR. SAIDI (*preparing to leave*): The Blacks're becoming so civilized that they have to organize to commit murder—like the rest of us? I'll be back to probe for the bullet. And you want the report?

GROENDYCK: Please.

DR. SAIDI: Very well.

(*Exits right*).

GROENDYCK (*after a moment's silence*): We might as well be frank, Azubiki. This killing definitely ends any chance you ever had of taking my place when I leave. If the Blacks have murdered the District Officer, there's no possibility the whites here would permit a native to head the police. I'll probably be staying on now—

E. AZUBIKI (*quietly considering this*): I appreciate that.

GROENDYCK: I've nothing against you—I want you to realize that— the idea of appointing you in my place wasn't yours, I'm sure—it was McLean's. He didn't see how crazy it is. Here five years, he still didn't know enough about Africa. The point is, the murderer has to be caught, or neither of us'll go on having jobs—so we must work together.

E. AZUBIKI: We must perform our duty.

GROENDYCK: Let's talk to the house-girl.

E. AZUBIKI: Shall I call her?

(GROENDYCK *nods. Azubiki goes to the door at left*).

Akamba!

(AZUBIKI *walks back to centre-stage.* AKAMBA *enters, in response to his call.*)

Come in, Sister.

GROENDYCK (*to her*): You're the house-girl here? Don't be nervous, but answer truthfully. What do you know about what happened last night, when the Major was shot?

AKAMBA (*shakes her head, as Mbonu did*): Nothing.

GROENDYCK: Where were you?

AKAMBA (*looks at them pleadingly*): Sleep.

GROENDYCK: Oh? But where were you asleep?

AKAMBA (*points left, toward her room*): There—

GROENDYCK: In this house?

AKAMBA: Yes, Bwana. But I was not in this world—I was in the other world.

E. AZUBIKI (*interpreting*): She means that she was dreaming.

GROENDYCK: Before you went to sleep, or after you woke up— what did you hear, what did you see?

AKAMBA: Nothing.

GROENDYCK: You're sure?

AKAMBA: Very sure.

GROENDYCK: You never heard any loud words between the bwana and the memsahib?

AKAMBA (*shakes her head*): No.

GROENDYCK (*emphatically*): Never?

AKAMBA: No.

GROENDYCK (*again with emphasis*): You're positive?

AKAMBA (*to Azubiki*): "Positive?"

E. AZUBIKI: You're sure that you never saw Mrs. McLean and the bwana angry at each other?

AKAMBA: No.

GROENDYCK (*to Azubiki*): It's what I thought. The boy was probably lying.

E. AZUBIKI (*to Groendyck*): Permit me to speak to her, please. (*to Akamba*) The memsahib and the bwana were happy together?

AKAMBA: No.

GROENDYCK: Never?

AKAMBA (*shaking her head*): Never happy.

E. AZUBIKI: Why not?

(*Akamba shrugs, as Mbonu did.*)

GROENDYCK: How do you know they weren't happy?

AKAMBA: Smile. Laugh. (*Shakes her head, to suggest she never saw them do this.*)

E. AZUBIKI: With the other bwana, Mr. Cowan, did the memsahib ever smile or laugh?

AKAMBA (*progressively more frank*): Don't know. Maybe sometimes. Yes.

E. AZUBIKI: And did this make the Commissioner angry—ever?

AKAMBA: Perhaps yes.

GROENDYCK: Everything's perhaps, maybe, yes *and* no. You never get anywhere with them.

E. AZUBIKI (*explaining*): My people have a very nice regard for the truth. Whatever *is* "yes or no" in this world? Who ever is really guilty in this world, and who ever is really innocent?

GROENDYCK (*smiles. Shakes his head*): You may've gone to school at Oka. But you still talk like a tribesman.

E. AZUBIKI: I learned part of this at Oka too, We are all guilty— that is Christian doctrine. But if we're born guilty, it seems to me that we cannot be blamed for it—so are we not innocent, too?

GROENDYCK (*after staring at him almost goodnaturedly*): Save those questions for Sunday.

E. AZUBIKI (*humbly*): I ask myself this question every day.

GROENDYCK: Good for you. But let's get on with it—we've a job to do. The girl says she was asleep. Maybe she was, maybe she wasn't. Let's talk to Cowan and Mrs. McLean. So far, I think the quarrel's something the houseboy made up—a false lead.

E. AZUBIKI (*quietly persistent*): I should like to follow it, all the same.

GROENDYCK: When we've heard their stories, we can call back the house-servants and check. We should talk to the responsible witnesses first.

E. AZUBIKI (*to Akamba*): Thank you, Sister. You will wait elsewhere now—but you must not leave the bungalow. And please ask Mr. Cowan to come in?

AKAMBA: The bwana?

(*Exits left.*)

GROENDYCK: I've been questioning these people of yours for fifteen years. I can never get anywhere with them. When you really want to know what they're thinking or what they know, you have to make a leap in the dark.

E. AZUBIKI (*almost reverently*): To seek the truth is always to make a leap into the dark—

GROENDYCK (*still amused, but slightly impatient*): Try being logical, for a change. (*Pause.*) When Cowan comes in, we'll be talking to a rational man, at least. And in *my* language.

E. AZUBIKI (*quietly again*): Are no lies told in English?

GROENDYCK (*rising from his chair*): Yes, but sometimes you can see through them.

E. AZUBIKI (*softly repetitive*): Not always. Some of your people lie to themselves in very complicated ways . . . and to see through those deceptions is often very difficult, indeed. My people have, by contrast, very simple fantasies and illusions.

(*Enter* COWAN, *from left. He is trying to hide his apprehension.*)

GROENDYCK: Mr. Cowan, please sit down.

COWAN: Thank you.

GROENDYCK (*seating himself again*): This horrible business has raised questions which we must answer.

COWAN: I realize that.

GROENDYCK: We must ask about some very personal matters—and we hope you'll be frank with us.

COWAN: I'll do my best.

GROENDYCK: You're a tax surveyor?

COWAN: Yes. I've been here a month for a complete audit of the District finances.

GROENDYCK: Was there some special reason for your coming? A complaint or suspicion?

COWAN: No, it's routine. I'm one of a group from England, and we've each been assigned to a District.

GROENDYCK: How far advanced is your work here?

COWAN: I'm about half finished.

GROENDYCK: Is everything in order? Financially?

COWAN: As far as I can see.

GROENDYCK: No irregularities of any kind?

COWAN: None that I know of.

GROENDYCK: And Major McLean invited you to stay here—in this house—as his guest?

COWAN: I had to be someone's guest—there're so few facilities for visitors.

GROENDYCK: What can you tell us about last night?

COWAN: Very little. I was in my room; I heard a shot, a scream. I rushed in—I found Major McLean lying on the floor, already dead and very bloody—Mbonu had reached here before me—I sent him for the doctor—the Syrian doctor—what's his name?

E. AZUBIKI: Dr. Saidi.

COWAN: I don't think he's a very good doctor, but I don't suppose there was anything much he could do. He gave Mrs. McLean a sedative . . . she was hysterical.

GROENDYCK: You heard no sounds of anyone else in the house— intruders.

COWAN: I can't say so—no—though obviously there must've been one or more.

E. AZUBIKI: Obviously?

COWAN: I assume this killing's an act of vengeance or warning by native terrorists.

GROENDYCK: You knew that Major McLean anticipated something of the kind—and, in fact, that I warned him of it only yesterday afternoon?

COWAN: No, I didn't see him all yesterday—but Mrs. McLean had spoken to me of how dangerous the situation has become.

GROENDYCK: You knew of the riot at Lamberts'?

COWAN: Yes, though not in detail.

E. AZUBIKI: Could we ask if you heard any loud voices—any quarrelling—in here, in the period just before the shot?

COWAN (*after a moment*): None.

GROENDYCK: No controversy—no dispute—between Mrs. McLean and her husband?

COWAN: No. Their relations were always very amicable.

E. AZUBIKI: Always?

COWAN: I'm an outsider. But from what I could see, in a month's residence.

E. AZUBIKI: Your own relationship with Major McLean was good?

COWAN: Very good. Why not?

GROENDYCK: You were investigating the finances of the District, under his administration.

COWAN: We had no dispute. He interfered in no way. He voiced no objection to anything I was doing here.

GROENDYCK: I gather that your relationship with Mrs. McLean was —and is—equally good?

COWAN: She has been a charming hostess.

E. AZUBIKI: She's also an attractive woman, Mr. Cowan. Were your relations with her ever more than formal and correct?

COWAN (*hesitates*): I assure you I regarded Mrs. McLean as my hostess, nothing more—and she's far too fine a woman ever to encourage anything else. She was, I'm sure, a perfect wife to the Major.

GROENDYCK: The servants say there was trouble between them. That they quarrelled—in fact, had been arguing very bitterly just before the shooting.

COWAN (*hesitates again*): I know nothing about it. One would hardly describe Mrs. McLean as the sort of person who would quarrel *loudly* with anyone.

GROENDYCK: He did have a violent temper. At times he was rude and arbitrary. Even to me.

COWAN: I've heard that said of him. But I never saw any signs of it myself.

GROENDYCK: The servants suggest that the quarrel last night was about you, about your relations—your intimacy—with Mrs. McLean.

COWAN: That's a lie. Untrue!

GROENDYCK: They say Major McLean was objecting to his wife's interest in you, or your interest in her—or perhaps it's a mutual interest?

COWAN: There's none—has been none—

GROENDYCK: You understand we must investigate that report very thoroughly—since the allegation has been made by the servants. It might provide a motive for a domestic murder, instead of a political one.

COWAN: I can assure you the servants are mistaken, or are lying—perhaps for reasons of their own. The fact is, Mrs. McLean distrusted Mbonu, the houseboy. She remarked on it to me only yesterday evening, an hour before the shooting. She surprised him acting suspiciously.

E. AZUBIKI: In what way?

COWAN (*excitedly*): I think you should ask her about the details, when you can—when she has recovered from her shock and's able to speak to you. But from what she said, she came into this room and found him going through a drawer in the Major's desk—where he kept his revolver—the same one used in the killing.

GROENDYCK (*indicates the weapon on the desk*): This?

COWAN: That must be it, yes. You might find his fingerprints on it.

GROENDYCK (*standing at desk*): We'll have to send the weapon away —we've no one here who's an expert. It'll be done—as soon as possible.

E. AZUBIKI: We've not definitely established this is the weapon— that it was fired, that the bullet came from it. That must also be determined by a ballistics expert.

GROENDYCK (*folds the edges of the handkerchief over the weapon, to cover it*): No one should handle it, until the fingerprints have been taken; they'll be our best clue.

E. AZUBIKI (*to Cowan*): You're implicating the houseboy? If the Major was in this room, how could Mbonu come in and take the weapon from the desk drawer? The Major would have seen him and prevented him. At least, there would have been a struggle. None was heard. The Major was a very strong man.

COWAN: I didn't say it was Mbonu—it might've been any native.

E. AZUBIKI: If anyone else of my people came here to murder the Commissioner, how did he get in?

GROENDYCK (*logically. Enacts this*): First Mrs. McLean left. Then, apparently, McLean heard a noise and went out to investigate—Mbonu

himself says that. While the Major was out there, the door was open—
it was dark—someone could've slipped in and gotten to his desk.

COWAN: It wouldn't have been necessary for anyone to come in
that door. There're two others, in other parts of the bungalow.

E. AZUBIKI (*still quietly*): It is very true that my people are not
rational, as you have said, Mr. Groendyck. But I do not think any of
them would plan to enter a strange house in the dark, steal a revolver
from a drawer where it might no longer be, and shoot a man with it—
all in the space of a few minutes' time. No, this does not strike me as
even an irrational plan. May I suggest again that it would be much
easier for someone already in the house, and very familiar with it, to do
that? (*to Cowan*) Including *you*.

COWAN: Maybe Mbonu stole the revolver earlier?

E. AZUBIKI: Does Mrs. McLean say that?

COWAN: I don't know. You must ask her. I understood her to say
that Mbonu was going through the drawer where the revolver was.
I don't know whether he touched it, or took it up.

GROENDYCK: I saw the revolver at a later time. McLean himself
showed it to me.

E. AZUBIKI (*to Cowan*): Let me ask something else, if I may? How
is it Major McLean himself put out the lights in here—he didn't leave
it for the houseboy?

COWAN: No, it was his custom to put out the lamps at night. He
was always afraid of someone forgetting to turn down the wicks, and a
lamp overheating or being knocked over in the dark and starting a fire.

E. AZUBIKI: Mr. Cowan, *you* knew where the Commissioner kept
his revolver?

COWAN: Only after Mrs. McLean mentioned it to me.

E. AZUBIKI: A short time before the shooting?

COWAN: That's true.

E. AZUBIKI (*enacts this*): If Major McLean went out into the garden—
distracted by some noise—*you* could have entered the room and found
the revolver without trouble in the dark? Waited by the other door,
and shot him as he crossed the room?

COWAN (*after a long moment*): Possibly. But I didn't do it—I had no
reason to.

E. AZUBIKI: None? You say the servants are lying—

COWAN: Even if I had a reason, I'm not sure that I would've had the courage—

E. AZUBIKI: You are right about *that*—To commit murder requires moral courage of a special kind. I have often thought so.

GROENDYCK: A kind of courage, yes. But *moral* courage?

E. AZUBIKI: A man does not kill another unless he is very certain that he has a good right to do so. He feels virtuous in doing it. Even the thief who robs another has this feeling that he is entitled to the privilege of doing what he does.

GROENDYCK: Where McLean was concerned, lots of people probably had a motive. What we have to look for is the facts.

E. AZUBIKI: The facts? But, in the present instance, there are no facts. Everything is darkness—this murder took place in the darkness—

(GROENDYCK *gives his assistant a somewhat baffled and impatient glance—though he is, of course, accustomed to these mystical flights.*)

COWAN (*breaking in*): If you knew me, you'd hardly think it likely I could commit a murder.

GROENDYCK (*flatly*): If the most likely people always committed murders, the police wouldn't have a serious problem of detection. But the fact is, anyone can do it. It's a simple thing to press a trigger—

COWAN (*softly*): No, it must be very difficult—

E. AZUBIKI (*seriously*): I should imagine it to be very simple and difficult at the same time.

GROENDYCK: Let's stick to the point. There was a purported quarrel here, Cowan, between Mrs. McLean and her husband. Were you the subject of that quarrel?

COWAN: I don't see why I should've been.

GROENDYCK: You do have a high opinion of Mrs. McLean?

COWAN: I respect her very much.

E. AZUBIKI: Let me ask—If you felt that her husband had been cruel to her, would you have been outraged?

COWAN: I'm outraged by cruelty wherever I encounter it.

E. AZUBIKI: And where Mrs. McLean is concerned, you would be even more so?

COWAN: She's a very fine woman and deserves only the best. But I've no knowledge that her husband was ever cruel to her.

E. AZUBIKI: She never told you so?

COWAN: She did not.

E. AZUBIKI (*hesitates. Then, to Groendyck*): I have nothing more to ask—just now.

GROENDYCK (*after a moment. To Cowan*): Thank you, Mr. Cowan. Would you be kind enough to ask Mrs. McLean to come in—if she's well enough?

COWAN (*rising*): Please don't press her too hard—she's under very great strain.

GROENDYCK: We'll know what to do.

GROENDYCK (*to Azubiki; after Cowan exits, left*): What do you think of him?

E. AZUBIKI: He is an honest man. But even an honest man does not always tell the truth.

GROENDYCK: He just doesn't seem the sort to kill anyone.

E. AZUBIKI (*after a slight pause*): At the missionary college we had a teacher who talked always of his love for God—he was fanatical; but it soon became clear to me that our teacher did not love God at all and was frightened by it. So he talked loudly against everyone else who didn't love God, to cover up his own lack of faith.

GROENDYCK: I don't follow you.

E. AZUBIKI: You say that Mr. Cowan does not seem like a killer. He does not, indeed. But perhaps he blames himself for it. He might, for that very reason, have driven himself to murder Major McLean. To prove to himself that he is a man capable of killing for love of a woman —In him, there might be a failure of love which desperately frightens him.

GROENDYCK: I don't think people are as complicated as you make them out to be.

E. AZUBIKI: There is nothing complicated, Mr. Groendyck, in what I've just said—it's very simple. Otherwise, I would not be capable of thinking or expressing it—for I myself am only half-educated.

GROENDYCK (*turning in the direction Cowan has gone*): Cowan talks as though he's very well educated. My son's going to attend Oxford—

E. AZUBIKI: You have great love for your son.

GROENDYCK: A man's son is more important to him than anything else—even than his wife. A son is his immortality—

[114]

E. AZUBIKI: My people also feel that way. But I have no son, unfortunately.

(DELLA *enters, left. She wears the same dress as on the preceding night. Signs of strain and shock mark her features and bearing, yet she carries herself well. The two men rise to greet her, and silently she takes a chair near the desk.*)

GROENDYCK: Mrs. McLean, you must excuse us for intruding upon your grief so soon—even before your husband's buried—but I think you'll appreciate our problem.

DELLA: I understand.

GROENDYCK: I wish I could've spoken to you last night—But of course, we couldn't in your shocked state.

DELLA: I must ask you to excuse me for that.

GROENDYCK: We'd like to know everything—all the details—that led up to your husband's death, and everything of significance that followed.

DELLA (*slowly*): Alec and I were in this room talking—then I left him; he stayed behind a moment to put out the lamps. The room was in darkness—I'm sure of that, because I looked back from the hall—I was about to return here to say something else that had just occurred to me—suddenly I heard the shot.

GROENDYCK: Can you tell us anything else of importance?

DELLA: I'm not sure—

GROENDYCK: Is anything missing? Has anything been stolen?

DELLA: I've not had time to look.

GROENDYCK: According to the constable, you made some reference last night, and so did the others, to a sound in the garden just before the shooting.

DELLA: I heard it—quite clearly. A noise as if someone were moving about. Alec went out to investigate and called out Mbonu's name, but got no answer—Then he came back into the room and crossed it—

GROENDYCK: How can you be so sure of all this, when it was so dark?

DELLA: In one's own house, one knows where people are, when they move about in the darkness—It's almost a second sense.

E. AZUBIKI: Amongst my people, it would be simple to locate anyone in the dark, by his breathing, the least sound—

GROENDYCK (*to Della*): Your husband called out "Mbonu". Was it a question, or was it an identification?

DELLA: A question. I don't think Mbonu was in the garden; I believe he was in the house, because when I screamed he reached my side almost at once.

GROENDYCK: We've partially searched the garden. We've found no marks—no signs of any sort.

DELLA: May I ask if you looked by the poinciana bush, the one next to the house? Where the tin roof-drain is?

GROENDYCK: I'm not sure—Why?

DELLA: The sound seemed to come from there—as if someone had knocked against the tin by accident.

GROENDYCK (*to Azubiki*): We should look there—Under the drain? The ground might be damp there. We could get a footprint?

E. AZUBIKI: Yes.

(GROENDYCK *goes out, right. After an instant,* AZUBIKI *follows him. As soon as the room is clear, Della's aspect changes. She glances about, finds she is unobserved, and then moves rapidly to the desk, where she grabs up the weapon. With the handkerchief which has partially covered it, she cleans the revolver's exterior thoroughly—obviously to remove any telltale fingerprints from it. She is breathing quickly, almost in panic. She has barely completed her task and is back in her chair, when* GROENDYCK *and* AZUBIKI *re-enter from the garden.*)

E. AZUBIKI (*to Della*): The ground's dry—the bush has not been broken or disturbed in any way.

GROENDYCK: No trace there—

DELLA (*after a moment—to compose herself*): I'm quite certain I heard that sound of the tin being struck—

GROENDYCK: Maybe so. You say you think Mbonu was in the house, not the garden—because, after you screamed, he reached you so quickly?

DELLA: Yes.

GROENDYCK: But of course the murderer was in the house when the shooting occurred.

DELLA (*with feigned surprise*): The murderer?

GROENDYCK: Yes. Mbonu might've been in the garden. When

your husband went out, Mbonu might've slipped back in, taken up the revolver from the desk, and shot the Major a moment later.

E. AZUBIKI: Why should Mbonu have troubled to do all that—gone into the garden, slipped back into the house? He was already in the house. He could come and go as he wished, at all times?

GROENDYCK (*to Della*): He knew where Major McLean kept his revolver?

DELLA (*almost dubiously—as though not sure what she should say*): I think so.

GROENDYCK: Mr. Cowan told us that you came into this room only a short time before the killing, and found Mbonu standing over the desk, with the drawer open—the drawer where the revolver was.

DELLA (*finally*): Yes. Mbonu's actions were suspicious. And I was frightened. But I don't think he did the killing. I don't believe that my husband was murdered, at all.

GROENDYCK (*confused—momentarily taken aback*): What then? An accident?

E. AZUBIKI (*suddenly. Welcoming this explanation*): He might have taken up the weapon, when he heard the noise in the garden—he was nervous, because of the riot at Lamberts'—and later the gun might have gone off in his hand as he came back in and crossed the room.

GROENDYCK: Who'd believe that? Why would he walk with the revolver pointed toward himself? He'd hardly do a thing like that. He was too well coordinated, too careful. (*to Della*) Just what were you going to say, Mrs. McLean?

DELLA: Not that it was an accident. As you say, he was too careful. I'm convinced that my husband killed himself.

GROENDYCK (*again taken aback*): Oh?

E. AZUBIKI (*quietly*): What makes you think that?

DELLA: We had a long conversation, just before the shooting, and I know that his mood was dark, even desperate.

E. AZUBIKI: Did he speak of suicide?

DELLA (*slowly*): He didn't use the word—or words. But he said he couldn't go on—not the way things were. Of course, I didn't guess that he would—or I wouldn't have—

E. AZUBIKI (*softly*): Wouldn't have—what?

[117]

DELLA: Gone out of the room—at that moment.

E. AZUBIKI: And why was your husband so unhappy—desperately unhappy?

DELLA (*lowering her head*): I was about to leave him, to go back to England.

E. AZUBIKI: Was he also angry, when you talked to him?

DELLA: Yes. He became very angry.

E. AZUBIKI: Just why were you leaving him, Mrs. McLean? Why was he so angry and unhappy?

DELLA (*looking away from them*): It's a delicate matter to discuss—very personal.

GROENDYCK: We appreciate that—but of course this is an urgent matter, too.

DELLA (*at last, as if with great reluctance*): My husband was sexually impotent.

GROENDYCK (*with hushed voice*): Oh?

E. AZUBIKI (*after a moment*): And for this reason—because he could no longer be a real husband to you—you were about to leave him?

DELLA: Partly. At least, he supposed it was the reason—Perhaps I was wrong. He was bitterly opposed to my going.

GROENDYCK (*after another moment*): Let me ask you this—were there any other complicating factors? Was Mr. Cowan one of them?

DELLA: Mr. Cowan? In what way?

GROENDYCK: Was your husband, being impotent, jealous of Mr. Cowan? Did he have any suspicions concerning him?

DELLA (*after a pause*): Perhaps so. But they were groundless.

GROENDYCK: Completely so?

DELLA: So far as my relations here with Mr. Cowan are concerned, yes. My husband did not voice any such suspicions, and I didn't mention Mr. Cowan's name in the course of our conversation. But possibly Alec had some such thought in his mind. The mere presence of another man in the house doubtless upset him.

GROENDYCK: Just how well do you know Mr. Cowan?

DELLA: Very well. But not actually very well. He's only been out here a few weeks; but everything I've seen of him has made him seem to be a gentleman.

E. AZUBIKI: Still, he's a stranger to you? There might be sides of his nature, aspects of his life in London, of which you know nothing?

DELLA (*slowly*): That's true.

GROENDYCK: Did your husband ever issue any threats against him? Not last night, but any other time?

DELLA (*firmly*): No, none at all.

E. AZUBIKI: Does Mr. Cowan have a romantic interest in you?

DELLA (*with great reluctance*): This's hardly a time to discuss anything of that sort.

GROENDYCK: I'm afraid we must discuss it.

DELLA: While I was Alec's wife, I couldn't allow myself to consider any other men—

GROENDYCK: Even though your husband was impotent?

DELLA: That wasn't as important to me as it was to him.

E. AZUBIKI: But you were planning to leave him? Was it because of Mr. Cowan?

DELLA: No. It was simply because I was tired and ill, and lonely here. I felt isolated from my husband, not only because of his physical shortcoming but because his personality was often forbidding.

GROENDYCK (*after hesitance*): And this's all you can tell us, Mrs. McLean?

DELLA (*rising, as though she were dismissing them, and not they her*): I've perhaps already told you too much.

(*She leaves them, left, of her own accord.* GROENDYCK *gazes after her, then turns to* AZUBIKI.)

E. AZUBIKI: An accident?

GROENDYCK: Highly unlikely. The gun has a safety-catch.

E. AZUBIKI: He might have released it.

GROENDYCK: But he wouldn't walk with the barrel pointed toward himself.

E. AZUBIKI (*with a little sigh*): It is most unlikely.

GROENDYCK: And I don't believe it was suicide, despite what the woman says.

E. AZUBIKI (*after consideration*): What sort of man commits suicide?

GROENDYCK: Not McLean's kind.

E. AZUBIKI: A man who loved power, as Major McLean did, might kill himself if he lost his sexual power, which is so important to a man—

because, as you said, it is his hope of physical immortality. And his deepest pride.

GROENDYCK: Can you believe that McLean turned out the lights and killed himself in the dark?

E. AZUBIKI: Why not? He was going into darkness . . . Eternally. (*Weighing this.*) But was McLean that sort? He was too practical. He wasn't given to dramatic gestures. (*another pause*) But we never really know what our fellow-men are capable of—what strength lies in them —what gesture they might perform.

GROENDYCK: He was shot at very close range—the gun might've dropped from his hand.

E. AZUBIKI: We can tell from the fingerprints.

GROENDYCK: Did Brady handle it?

E. AZUBIKI: Not at all. He assured me he obeyed your instructions never to touch a weapon—he left it exactly where it was.

GROENDYCK (*after a moment*): I'm glad he remembered . . .

E. AZUBIKI: Why do we not send the weapon away at once?

GROENDYCK: Don't let anyone touch it—so far it's our only clue.

E. AZUBIKI: Should I not lock it away?

GROENDYCK (*who has been thinking*): What? Where? I'll find a place. (*reverts to the new question*) Was it suicide? It never occurred to me before. (*shakes his head*) That explanation's very convenient for everyone, including you.

AZUBIKI: Me, Mr. Groendyck?

GROENDYCK: Or me. I'd a motive, too—a good one, as you know. But I had no access to the gun.

(*A momentary pause.*)

E. AZUBIKI: Is it true? Was Major McLean really not a proper husband? He seemed very vigorous to me.

GROENDYCK: He certainly did. Quite virile. Very much a man.

E. AZUBIKI: We might ask Dr. Saidi—

GROENDYCK (*catches sight of Akamba on terrace*): Too late now— Though I'm not sure.

E. AZUBIKI: What do you think? Was McLean faithful to his wife?

GROENDYCK: I doubt it. But Mrs. McLean might not be the only one who can tell us whether he was a proper lover.

E. AZUBIKI (*smiles at this*): Do you mean to canvass all the wives in the district and ask if any of them committed adultery with Alec McLean lately?

GROENDYCK (*serious*): It may not be necessary to look so far.

E. AZUBIKI (*comprehending*): Oh—?

GROENDYCK: In this very house.

(AKAMBA *enters, from left.*)

AKAMBA: Memsahib says now it is luncheon—can she ask you to eat, Bwana?

GROENDYCK (*rising from desk*): Yes, I should think so. But is there some place, first, to wash my hands?

AKAMBA (*points*): Yes, Bwana. Little room—this way—I show you.

GROENDYCK: No, thanks. I can find it myself.

(*Exits left, in direction* AKAMBA *has indicated. As he does so,* MBONU *enters from right. He exchanges a meaningful—but enigmatic—glance with her.* AZUBIKI *observes them and looks thoughtfully from one to the other. After an instant's hesitation,* AKAMBA *also exits left, hurriedly.* MBONU *comes to the centre of the room.*)

E. AZUBIKI (*in a very altered tone of voice—sharp, authoritative*): Mbonu, listen to me! What do you really know about this?

(MBONU *shakes his head. Azubiki suddenly grasps Mbonu's wrist.*) Something?

MBONU (*cowering*): No, not anything—

E. AZUBIKI: Was it the white man, or the white woman?

(MBONU *shakes his head and moans, as though his wrist hurts him; but actually he is merely frightened.*)

Did you see Mr. Groendyck here that night?

MBONU: No, never saw him—

E. AZUBIKI: Did *you* do it?

MBONU (*still bent over and held by the wrist*): No, not me!

E. AZUBIKI: Are you telling me the truth?

MBONU: Not me! No—

E. AZUBIKI:

(*Suddenly releases Mbonu's wrist; but with a quick motion, he tears open the houseboy's khaki jacket, baring blue tattoo marks on his chest.*)

Those are the marks, Mbonu—You have been to the Gri-gri Bush—?

(MBONU, *awed, simply nods his head.*)

If you do not tell me the truth, I will take you back to the Bush Master—And he will curse you—

MBONU (*shrinking back and touching his breast emphatically*): Not me— No, no!

E. AZUBIKI (*seems to draw himself up. We see now that this little black metaphysician—but for his experience at the missionary college—might have been a native witch-doctor*): Or would you like to go before the Old Woman with the Wand—?

MBONU (*falls to his knees, beseeches*): No, no—

E. AZUBIKI (*fiercely*): First, the sharp bamboos on your legs—! Against your shins! To the bone—And then she will call upon the Devil to beat you, beat you—until you speak the truth—The Devil will beat you until you cry out—or die!

(MBONU *prostrates himself in fear. Moans loudly.*)

What do you know?

(*All the fierceness seems to go out of* AZUBIKI. *He stands back and regards the prostrate* MBONU *for a long moment. Then he speaks to him in a different voice—his former soft tone.*)

Very well. Stand up.

(MBONU *slowly rises. Waits awed, submissively.*)

Now I will tell you something. Major McLean was about to make me, a *black* man, Chief Inspector of Police.

MBONU (*stirred*): A black man?

E. AZUBIKI: Yes, me. Mr. E. Azubiki. And this would be a great honor for our people. It would have meant great progress—But if a black man killed Major McLean, it will not happen—So you must help me—we must find out who killed the Major. Mr. Groendyck would like it to be a black man, but I think it was a white man—am I right?

MBONU (*shakes his head*): Know nothing—

E. AZUBIKI: Tell me more about Akamba. Did the Major sleep with her?

MBONU: Maybe so.

E. AZUBIKI: Did he like her?

MBONU: I think yes—Sometimes—

E. AZUBIKI: And you also like her?

MBONU: Akamba my number two wife, maybe . . .

E. AZUBIKI (*suddenly. With fierceness again*): Is that why you killed Major McLean—because you like Akamba, and he was sleeping with her? This made you jealous!

MBONU (*simply*): If Mbonu do it—Run away—No one find me.

E. AZUBIKI: You could do that. So you've probably told me the truth. Mbonu, you will help me? We will prove it is a white person who did this, and I will be Chief Inspector of Police! That will be a mark of respect for the black man.

MBONU (*nods approval*): Ehe, very good!

(*The two men move left, about to exit.*)

ACT THREE

SCENE ONE: *Two hours later, in the afternoon.* DELLA *enters the room from left, closely followed by* COWAN. *Her stress and emotion are ill-concealed, and he is also disturbed.*

DELLA: Even now, when there's a murder to investigate, those men must lie down and sleep.

COWAN: No, they're with the Syrian doctor—

DELLA: It's not Groendyck I fear, but the black one—the way his eyes stare at me, sometimes.

COWAN (*brusquely. Turning to her*): "Fear?" Of what are you afraid, Della?

DELLA: Of being accused of killing Alec.

COWAN: Why should you be?

DELLA: The servants must've heard our quarrel—

COWAN: Yes. I was asked about it too. But it's not you they suspect —it's me.

DELLA: I told them *your* name was never mentioned in the quarrel.

COWAN: Did you?

DELLA: I wanted to protect you.

COWAN: I see—Thank you.

DELLA: I told them something more, Eric. I told them Alec was sexually impotent, and I was leaving him for that reason.

COWAN (*taken aback*): You told them that?

DELLA: I thought if I seemed candid, very open and incautious about some things, they'd believe I was that way altogether. And I told them I was certain Alec had killed himself, because I was leaving him; because he was less than a man—

COWAN (*quickly*): Suicide?

DELLA: The black man—what's his name?

COWAN: Azubiki—

DELLA: He wanted to believe me—I could see that. For a while he seemed convinced. But a moment later, he didn't. His eyes're very disturbing.

[125]

COWAN (*eagerly*): Suicide? If they can't rule out the possibility, it might mean no finding at the inquest. That was clever of you, Della. Very clever! (*He is unaware that she is studying him.*) And what do you think? Could it possibly be true? Might Alec have done it—Killed himself?

DELLA: No. Never. He wasn't the kind—

COWAN (*gazing at her, almost dubiously*): And you know that? But you made up the story about his being impotent—You lied—and you lied very, very well.

DELLA: Yes, I did. For both our sakes—

COWAN (*staring at her. Softly*): Both?

DELLA: I did something else, Eric. I tricked them—they went out into the garden, to look for something, a foot mark—and while they were out, I wiped off the fingerprints—

COWAN: From the revolver—? Good God, why?

DELLA: So there'd be no proof against anyone—

COWAN: But you destroyed the whole story you built up—

DELLA: In what way?

COWAN: About the suicide. If there're no fingerprints on the handle, Alec couldn't have killed himself. His prints would have to be there— If the handle's completely clean, it means he was murdered by someone who wiped it off later to protect himself—

DELLA: I should have thought of that—

COWAN (*incredulous*): Why didn't you? Whose prints *were* on the handle?

DELLA: I don't know—

COWAN Whom were you protecting?

DELLA (*gazes at him*): You—

COWAN: Me? Did you think I killed—

DELLA: I don't know, Eric. But I was afraid—You said that you wished you loved me enough to kill him—Perhaps I even hoped you had—

COWAN: Are you serious—? You've been thinking I killed Alec? That I'm capable of murder?

DELLA: Was I wrong?

COWAN: What kind of woman are you? You even wanted me to— you even hoped I would—

DELLA: You said you loved me—

COWAN: Is that your conception of love? Of what it does to a man?

DELLA: Alec threatened to ruin you—involve you in a terrible scandal—

COWAN (*bitterly*): But I'm already involved—We both are, now—

DELLA: Does it matter? We'll have each other.

COWAN (*unconvinced*): After this?

DELLA: If you didn't kill him—we've no reason to blame ourselves for his death.

COWAN (*irresolutely*): Perhaps not. (*staring at her*) Only, Della, who are you? Do I really know you? You thought I murdered him, and you tried to cover it up? To hide it from them—from the police? You were willing to join me, to become an accessory? I never guessed you could lie so diabolically well. You slander your husband, dead only a few hours, to protect the man you want as a lover, and to protect yourself. (*recoiling from her*) How do I know you didn't do it yourself, Della? You might have—you're quite *capable* of it—

DELLA (*gazing at him*): Yes, I am—

COWAN: Whose fingerprints *did* you wipe off the handle—did you think they were mine, or did you know they were your own? And you never stopped to think that you destroyed the suicide story by doing it? Is that possible? Are you so clever and so stupid at the same time? Or did you know exactly what you were doing? Did you wipe off that handle because you had to? Not to save me but yourself?

DELLA: *I* loved you enough to kill him.

COWAN: Is that what happened? (*pleads*) You can tell me the truth, Della. I'll never reveal it.

DELLA: I am capable of all the things you say—lying, killing, for love—for a chance at happiness. I thought you were my chance.

COWAN: How did I let myself get involved, be caught up in this?

DELLA: With me?

COWAN: With everything—

DELLA: With love?

COWAN: I loved you—and perhaps I still do.

DELLA: Don't you know—any more?

COWAN: I don't know anything—what to think, feel. Give me time —I'm confused.

DELLA (*staring at him—understanding him*): That's the whole trouble with you! You *want* to think—you can't just listen to your heart.

COWAN: We have to use our reason—

DELLA: You're the one who's impotent—(*touches her left breast. Turns away*) Perhaps I'm not worth loving—never was—

(COWAN, *lost in his own perplexity, does not reply—though she waits for him to do so.* AZUBIKI *enters quietly, from left. He observes them for a moment, himself unseen. Then* DELLA *catches sight of him, and says in a weak voice:*)

I thought you were sleeping.

E. AZUBIKI (*politely*): No, Mrs. McLean. I have not been sleeping, not at all. I have been talking to the servants.

COWAN (*anxious to leave*): Perhaps I should excuse myself?

(AZUBIKI *merely turns to look at him.* DELLA *says nothing.* COWAN, *after an awkward moment, withdraws.*)

DELLA (*finally*): May I ask what you learned from them?

E. AZUBIKI: Actually, I spoke only to the girl—

DELLA: Akamba?

E. AZUBIKI: Yes, Akamba. Mrs. McLean, may I ask a delicate question?

DELLA: Anything at all.

E. AZUBIKI: Did you ever wonder if your husband was faithful to you?

DELLA (*pauses*): I knew something of his proclivities—

E. AZUBIKI (*slightly puzzled*): "Proclivities"—?

DELLA: His tomcatting.

E. AZUBIKI: So you knew that sometimes he slept with the girl in this house, with Akamba—?

DELLA (*betrays an instinctive repulsion*): With Akamba! No—(*then, with sudden decision*) Yes! Yes, I did.

E. AZUBIKI: And were you aware that the latest incident took place just the other night?

(DELLA *stands silent, her face turned away from him, with great emotional strain.*)

E. AZUBIKI: And so I do not think that Major McLean, your husband, committed suicide. He was not sexually impotent. The girl has told me so—

DELLA (*finally*): Oh, yes, I knew of it—I've known it a long time. And that's why I did it—

E. AZUBIKI (*quickly*): Did what?

DELLA: Lied to you—about my husband's impotence. And that's why I wiped off the gun—so there'd be no fingerprints—

E. AZUBIKI (*startled*): When did you do this?

DELLA: While you and Mr. Groendyck were out in the garden this morning. (*rapidly*) It occurred to me—somehow—that Akamba might have killed him—my husband. And if so, I wanted to save her, if I could. I felt sorry for her—he treated her so badly—I couldn't blame her—How could anyone?

E. AZUBIKI: So it was Akamba?

DELLA: I don't accuse her. I can't—

E. AZUBIKI: Then why—?

DELLA: It was a momentary assumption on my part—Probably a most mistaken one—It just came to me then—a sudden emotional act.

E. AZUBIKI: And with that assumption—that mere supposition— you acted very generously—you even risked a charge of complicity? At very least, you *condoned* and abetted your husband's murder—? Or murderer?

DELLA (*faintly*): I did. That's true.

E. AZUBIKI: For the sake of a wronged girl. One of my people— You've risked your own freedom to help a rival—

DELLA: I've never considered her a "rival"—

E. AZUBIKI (*quietly*): Mrs. McLean, did you love your husband?

DELLA: I suppose not.

E. AZUBIKI: So you did not care with whom else he slept? And yet you felt sorry for this girl?

DELLA: I knew him so well!

E. AZUBIKI: And, to help her, you made up the story of his physical short-coming, provided a motive for his suicide—but, at the same time, erased what might be Akamba's fingerprints from the weapon?

DELLA (*hesitantly*): Yes—

E. AZUBIKI: But if there were no fingerprints on the handle, how were we to believe that your husband's death was self-inflicted?

DELLA: I realized that too late! I acted impulsively!

E. AZUBIKI: But it wasn't an impulsive act when you tricked us into going out into the garden. That was carefully planned. Were you really trying to help Akamba?

DELLA (*confused*): Yes—

E. AZUBIKI: Still, we might never have known how it happened—why there are no fingerprints on the weapon. Why do you tell me now that you did it?

DELLA: Because you'd have known at once, when you dusted the revolver, that someone was interfering.

E. AZUBIKI: You tried to help her—in a very foolish way? Do you know anything else about her?

DELLA: No. I no longer think she did it. I've no reason to think her any more guilty than anyone else.

E. AZUBIKI: Nor any less guilty?

DELLA (*apparently with sincere doubt*): I don't know—if he was sleeping with her—and he mistreated her—

E. AZUBIKI: Then she'd have a motive, too?

DELLA (*slowly*): She might.

E. AZUBIKI (*after a long pause*): Excuse me now, please. I must go to Mr. Groendyck, who is with Dr. Saidi. I must report to him what I've just learned from you.

DELLA (*dully*): Yes, of course.

(AZUBIKI *goes out of the room left.* DELLA *is alone. She paces restlessly, then sits on divan and buries her face in her hands.* AKAMBA *enters, right.* DELLA *looks up and is surprised to see her, for the girl is coming from outside the bungalow.*)

Akamba? Where've you been?

AKAMBA: To the village, to my father, about Mbonu—he wishes to take me for his second wife. I would ask my father to say no.

DELLA: Weren't you inside, talking to the police—to Mr. Azubiki?

AKAMBA (*shakes head*): Not now—

DELLA (*rises quickly from divan*): You haven't spoken to him since this morning?

AKAMBA (*shakes head again*): No.

DELLA (*urgently*): Akamba, listen—listen carefully—tell me! Was Alec—was the Commissioner—in love with you?

AKAMBA (*seemingly astonished*): With me, Memsahib?

DELLA: Don't be afraid to tell me now—Did he ever sleep with you?

[130]

AKAMBA (*draws back*): No—

DELLA: Did he ever try?

AKAMBA: No, Memsahib. No!

DELLA (*trembling*): You're lying, aren't you? My husband crept in bed with you at night. You laughed at me, the two of you—

AKAMBA (*desperately*): No, Memsahib! No.

DELLA: How do I know if you're telling the truth? A black girl a rival in my own house!

AKAMBA: No man ever touches me, Memsahib. You can see this for yourself—

DELLA (*staring at her*): You're still a virgin?

AKAMBA (*proudly*): Memsahib, yes—

DELLA: Did you tell that to Mr. Azubiki?

AKAMBA: No, never—

DELLA: And he didn't ask you about the Major—? Whether he slept with you—? Only the other night—?

AKAMBA: No, never—

DELLA (*comprehending that she has been tricked*): Then he—

(GROENDYCK *and* AZUBIKI *enter, left.* AKAMBA, *seeing them, tremulously withdraws from the room.*)

DELLA (*to Azubiki*): Why did you lie to me? You never spoke to Akamba—she told you nothing about Alec—?

E. AZUBIKI (*quietly*): But you lied to me, so I lied to you, and by our two lies we learned the truth.

DELLA (*looks away, as she tries frantically to decide what she shall say next*): No, you didn't learn the truth. Not really.

E. AZUBIKI: About the revolver, at least. That you cleaned it off.

DELLA (*at last*): But not *why* I did it. It wasn't to protect Akamba— I never suspected Alec of having anything to do with her—and I had no right to implicate her—

E. AZUBIKI: Oh?

DELLA (*with seeming contrition*): I said that in a moment of anger— because of what *you* told me—that Alec was betraying me with my own servant. But that's not why I cleaned off the gun—Akamba had nothing to do with it. I'm sure she's quite innocent—

GROENDYCK: Just a moment. Whom were you trying to protect?

DELLA: Eric Cowan—

E. AZUBIKI: And you're willing to confess that now?

DELLA: Because I know now that he, too, is innocent.

GROENDYCK: How do you know that?

DELLA (*softly*): He's told me so.

GROENDYCK: And that's enough for you—merely that he tells you he's innocent—?

DELLA: I can't explain, or perhaps you couldn't understand—But I think he'd have been proud to tell me that he wasn't.

GROENDYCK (*after a glance at E. Azubiki*): No, I don't think I could understand that. But let's start over—What made you suspect him in the first place?

DELLA (*quietly*): Alec *was* jealous of him, and Alec *did* make threats against him—he'd send in a report to end his career—And I thought he was in love with me and wanted to see me free of Alec—

E. AZUBIKI (*also quietly, with great tact*): But now you know he does not love you that much?

DELLA: Not enough to've killed anyone for me—Does it sound insane, when I say that? But there was a time when I thought he might have—I knew how I felt; *I* might've killed Alec—to save him, to save his future—

E. AZUBIKI: Cowan's future?

DELLA (*passionately*): Ours—A dream we had.

E. AZUBIKI: You didn't kill your husband?

DELLA: No—With what? I had no weapon—

E. AZUBIKI: So you wiped off the revolver, thinking Cowan's fingerprints might be on it—? But now you think they weren't, because he has told you so?

DELLA: Yes—

E. AZUBIKI: And by wiping clean the handle of that revolver, you've made it almost impossible for us to prove who committed the murder—

DELLA: I did a foolish, foolish thing. I'm very sorry about it—and I'm telling the truth, even though I may be held responsible for what I did—(*suddenly, with a surge of emotion, she begs:*) Excuse me, please.

(*They watch silently as she goes off.* GROENDYCK *purses his lips.*)

GROENDYCK (*finally*): As Mbonu would say—This woman lies very much.

[132]

E. AZUBIKI: They're the lies of an unhappy woman who will not admit the truth to herself.

GROENDYCK: What truth?

E. AZUBIKI: That she hated her husband and could have killed him gladly—and that the man she loves does not love her enough—or as much as she does him.

GROENDYCK (*looks again in direction Della has gone*): Does she love Cowan? Does she believe him innocent? Is she trying to protect him? She speaks of her faith in him, and then gives us a perfect motive for his having done it—McLean threatened to wreck his career. It almost looks as though she really wants to hang him—she's put us on his track and helped us to build up a case against him. Or did she do it herself— and is she rather desperately, but clumsily, trying to throw suspicion on everyone else, one after another? What kind of woman is she?

E. AZUBIKI: Very interesting. How strangely God made us.

GROENDYCK (*shakes his head. Looks at Azubiki*): You yourself have done a bit of lying—

E. AZUBIKI (*with the hint of a smile*): Merely to save me the trouble of going all about the district asking most embarrassing questions.

SCENE TWO: Twilight. The same room. AZUBIKI, *alone on the stage, is measuring the distance from the desk to the place where McLean's body was found—near the door, left.* COWAN *enters from the other door at left and watches him for a moment. The white man's manner is very nervous.*

COWAN (*finally*): Excuse me, Mr. Azubiki—

E. AZUBIKI (*looks up. Stands up from his task. Politely*): Yes, Mr. Cowan?

COWAN: Is Groendyck here? I've something to tell him—something very important.

E. AZUBIKI: No, Mr. Groendyck has gone on an errand. Perhaps you can inform me? I am the Deputy Inspector—

COWAN (*hesitantly*): It's about the question you asked me this morning—about the District finances—

E. AZUBIKI: Yes?

COWAN: I've just discovered a very serious shortage—

E. AZUBIKI: In the tax collections?

COWAN: Yes, a large sum is missing. I can't give you the exact amount, but several thousand pounds—McLean must've had something to do with it.

E. AZUBIKI: And why do you think it is important for Mr. Groendyck to hear this at once?

COWAN: Because it's possible, isn't it, that McLean committed suicide? I mean, he might have—if he had a reason. The shortage—couldn't that be the reason?

E. AZUBIKI: Ah yes. I see. (*Pauses.*) You've heard, I suppose, that Mrs. McLean wiped all the fingerprints from the weapon?

COWAN: Yes, she told me. But, of course, the Major's prints must've been on the revolver, even if no one else's were—because he handled it all the time.

E. AZUBIKI: And you know too, I presume, that Mrs. McLean also suggested the possibility of suicide and gave us a false pretext for it?

COWAN: That's why I came to you without delay.

E. AZUBIKI: May I ask a question, Mr. Cowan? You discovered this shortage—when?

COWAN: Just now. A few minutes ago—

E. AZUBIKI: Despite all the events of last night and today, you are still carrying on your work, your audit—?

COWAN (*unconvincingly*): There were certain totals I just hadn't glanced at—they were already compiled but I hadn't analyzed them—

E. AZUBIKI: Mr. Cowan, may I—an African—say this to you? Your calm, on a tragic occasion like this, is a good example of something—(*Pauses.*) The phlegmatic English temperament? Or a certain insensitivity? Only, you have not until now seemed phlegmatic or insensitive—

COWAN (*inadequately*): It was almost by accident. I—

E. AZUBIKI: I'm sure you have no wish to slander a dead man—especially if nothing can be accomplished by it—?

COWAN (*challenged*): Slander—?

E. AZUBIKI: There is incontrovertible proof that Major McLean did not kill himself.

COWAN (*taken aback*): There is?

E. AZUBIKI: Dr. Saidi has just given it to me. You saw me measuring the room for that reason. The autopsy shows that death was instantaneous—If Major McLean sat at this desk and shot himself, he could not have staggered so far—could never have risen from the desk. And in a standing position, he could not have shot himself at the angle the bullet entered his body—

COWAN: Oh?

E. AZUBIKI: So now—in defense of Major McLean; since he is unable to protect his name, and is still unburied—may I ask is your story true?

COWAN (slowly): No, it's not.

(Enter DR. SAIDI, left. He has the extracted bullet—wrapped in gun-cotton —in his hand. He is unobserved and stands listening to the conversation.)

E. AZUBIKI (to Cowan): You learned that Mrs. McLean's suicide story had failed . . . But suicide would be a convenient explanation, so you were trying to recreate it? Have you altered the tax records to make it seem McLean was a thief? You don't answer. (Pause.) Were you trying to protect yourself—or Mrs. McLean—?

COWAN: I don't see why she should be suspected—of killing her own husband. She'd be the last person in the world—

DR. SAIDI (with a quiet, almost resigned voice): Who's more likely to murder a man than his wife—? She knows him best and has the greatest provocation.

COWAN: I'm serious, Doctor Saidi.

DR. SAIDI (with a wry smile): So am I, Mr. Cowan.

COWAN (to E. Azubiki): Isn't this clearly an act of vengeance—a murder committed by a native who harbored a grudge against the Commissioner?

E. AZUBIKI: Dear sir, this isn't clearly any kind of murder. Though Mr. Groendyck is inclined to agree with you. He has already received several threatening letters.

COWAN: From whites or Blacks?

E. AZUBIKI: Perhaps both. They're unsigned. Like you, Mr. Groendyck is anxious to charge this killing to one of my people. We are supposed to be savages.

COWAN: You're educated, of course—but most of your people are simple and primitive.

[135]

E. AZUBIKI (*with quiet dignity*): We have a culture thousands of years old—perhaps older than yours—and it works very well for us. We are different from you, but I do not think we are inferior.

DR. SAIDI (*ironically to Azubiki*): In one way you have a very superior culture. You have plural marriages (*indicates himself*) like Moslems. (*to Cowan*) Because there're usually more women than men. Isn't it barbarous to condemn a woman to spinsterhood? So a man here has as many wives as he can provide for. That's civilized behavior.

COWAN (*to Saidi*): Do you practise polygamy?

DR. SAIDI (*holds up his hand. Shakes his head*): Not I. I can support more than one wife, but I find even one insupportable.

E. AZUBIKI (*with a show of his natural dignity*): Excuse me, Doctor— Did you find the bullet?

DR. SAIDI (*smiles*): Here it is. From the left atrium.

E. AZUBIKI (*takes it*): We must compare it with other bullets from the same weapon—a ballistics expert is needed. (*Puts it in his jacket pocket.*)

DR. SAIDI: When'll Groendyck get back? I've my official report ready for him.

E. AZUBIKI: He had a telephone call from one of our constables and left at once—it had to do with the Lambert riot.

COWAN: Could there be any connexion between the riot yesterday and this murder?

E. AZUBIKI: Some would like to think so.

DR. SAIDI (*lightly*): As a doctor, I often wonder murder is taken that seriously. It's surprising that we doctors aren't hanged for the murders we commit—with the best of intentions.

E. AZUBIKI: It is chiefly a matter of intention, is it not? That makes all the difference.

DR. SAIDI: Murder's a crime only if there's a great difference between being *here* and being *there*. . . . But we don't know that. My dear friend, you went to school at Oka—you became a Christian there.

E. AZUBIKI: Yes.

DR. SAIDI: As a Christian, you were told the dead enter into God's love and dwell in Paradise. So, to send a man to Paradise—with a well-placed bullet—is an act of kindness, for which he might be grateful.

E. AZUBIKI: The murderer usurps the rôle of God—that is presumptuous, and a crime.

(DELLA *enters, left. She stands to one side, not immediately observed, and listens.*)

DR. SAIDI: It might depend on the circumstances. (*catches sight of her*) Ah, Mrs. McLean. Permit me to tell you that I have finished my examination. So now the burial may proceed; here or elsewhere.

DELLA: I've cabled to my husband's brother in Surrey— I'll do as Alec's family wishes—

DR. SAIDI: A man in Freetown does embalming... But for England, why not cremation?

DELLA (*faintly*): Oh?

(COWAN *crosses to her. Takes her by the arm.*)

COWAN: Perhaps we should go outside?

(*Silently she lets him lead her on to the terrace. Crossing the room, she drops her handkerchief.*)

DR. SAIDI (*his eyes follow them. He sees the fallen handkerchief, picks it up, sniffs the scent of perfume. Then, to Azubiki*): Might not this murder have been inspired by love?

(*Passes handkerchief to* AZUBIKI)

AZUBIKI: To kill for love? That would be the very destruction of love.

DR. SAIDI: The great romantic illusion. A Western one. Whomever we love must be innocent. Once I saw an American film—A lady came into a room. Her lover was standing over the fallen body of his rival and had a smoking weapon in his hand. She cried out, "Darling, I *know* you didn't do it. I shall *never* believe you did, because I love you!"

E. AZUBIKI (*attentively*): Yes, I've seen this.

DR. SAIDI (*continues*): How ridiculous! Is the lady presumed to be intelligent? (*Turns to gaze at pair on terrace.*) If two people deem each other capable of murder, they no longer love each other? What an oversimplified concept of human nature such Westerners have! Perhaps you learned it from those films.

E. AZUBIKI: I still don't agree—!

DR. SAIDI: Everyone's capable of murder.

AZUBIKI: Is everyone? I wonder.

DR. SAIDI (*to him*): If Mrs. McLean killed a man in defense of her virtue, or killed a native robber prowling through this bungalow, you'd think little of it afterwards. And everyone would praise her. She's quite capable of doing that, isn't she? So why shouldn't she or any of us be capable of killing a man who may be stealing not a trivial possession but our happiness, our very hope of life? I should consider myself less than human, if, in such a situation, I couldn't feel indignant enough to save myself by any necessary means.

E. AZUBIKI: But you are not saving yourself—when you murder, you are transgressing against human and divine law, and you will be punished for it.

DR. SAIDI: Divine law—? (*shrugs*) I know nothing of it. Human law? As a doctor, I am lucky—I can kill a man by prescribing the wrong remedy to him, and no one ever even suspects.

E. AZUBIKI (*very quietly*): Another doctor might.

DR. SAIDI (*smiles again. Seats himself by chess board. Moves a piece*): I'm the only doctor in the district.

E. AZUBIKI: After this, I shall investigate carefully when I see a death certificate signed by you.

DR. SAIDI: You don't trust my conscience to police me?

E. AZUBIKI (*with half-serious emphasis*): I'm not sure you have any conscience.

DR. SAIDI: To save myself, of course, I would lie. As someone in this house has probably been doing—A tragic situation like this only intensifies and heightens the whole maze of lies in which we ordinarily live, the whole network of deceptions—the false stories we tell ourselves and others—

E. AZUBIKI: You are very right.

(*Offstage: sound of a jeep. The two men turn to listen to it. AZUBIKI, nearest the jalousies, opens them to look out.*)

DR. SAIDI (*moves another chess piece*): Perhaps it's Groendyck.

(GROENDYCK *enters, right—accompanied by* SEKGOMA, *a tall, muscular Black. His right wrist is manacled and connected to Groendyck's left wrist.*)

GROENDYCK: I'm back—and I've brought a prize witness. This's Sekgoma. (*to Azubiki*) Get Mbonu, will you?

E. AZUBIKI: Yes, sir.

(*Exits, left.*)

GROENDYCK (*to the others*): One of my constables—Roberts—was tracking down the Lambert rioters—the instigators of the trouble there—and caught up with this one, who finally told us some very interesting things.

(AZUBIKI *re-enters, followed by* MBONU. *When the houseboy sees the captive Sekgoma, he quails; then stands indecisively, as though not knowing what his next move should be.*)

GROENDYCK (*continues*): Azubiki, free me, will you? (*Azubiki does so, and manacles both of Sekgoma's wrists.*)

All right, Sekgoma. Two nights ago there was a meeting, wasn't there? A secret society was formed—?

SEKGOMA (*reluctantly*): That is true, Bwana.

GROENDYCK: A blood oath was sworn, to imitate the Mau-Mau—

SEKGOMA: Yes—

GROENDYCK: You know Mbonu.

SEKGOMA (*reluctantly*): He belongs to my tribe.

GROENDYCK: At the meeting—Was Mbonu there?

MBONU (*desperately*): No, not me—

GROENDYCK (*to Sekgoma*): Was he?

MBONU: No, not me—(*to Sekgoma*) Not me.

GROENDYCK (*to Sekgoma*): Was he? Tell what you told me and Constable Roberts—

SEKGOMA (*slowly, with great reluctance*): Mbonu was there—

GROENDYCK: He took the oath—?

MBONU (*shrilly*): No!

SEKGOMA (*concedes*): He took the oath—

MBONU: No—

SEKGOMA: He swore—with the rest—with all of us—

GROENDYCK: It was an oath against the white man—

MBONU (*insistently, desperately*): No, I did not—I did not swear—

GROENDYCK (*sudenly grasping hold of Mbonu, and forcing the frightened Black roughly to his knees, much as Azubiki did before*): You were there, weren't you—?

MBONU: Yes—

GROENDYCK: And you took the oath, didn't you?

(DELLA *and* COWAN *re-enter. They stand and stare at the interrogation.*)

MBONU: No—yes—

SEKGOMA: It was not an oath against you—against the whites—but only against your cattle, not to kill anyone—

GROENDYCK (*relentlessly*): To murder the District Officer, the Commissioner, first. And then, perhaps, all the white residents.

SEKGOMA: No, not that—Not yet.

GROENDYCK (*to Azubiki*): Your people were plotting a rebellion, bloody riots—terrorism. Mbonu joined the group, took an oath to kill, was the first to act—

DELLA (*to Mbonu*): After five years with us in our house—

COWAN (*to her*): You saw him at the desk—You suspected him—

MBONU: I killed no one—Never, never.

E. AZUBIKI (*quietly*): But why was Mbonu chosen? He has no cattle to graze?

GROENDYCK: He was the most nearly placed to the Commissioner —in his own household. So he was the best one to do it.

E. AZUBIKI (*shakes his head*): *Did* Mbonu commit this murder?

GROENDYCK: You still doubt it?

E. AZUBIKI: It looks bad. I concede he might have done it. But isn't it possible that everyone else in this room, including Dr. Saidi, might have done it, too?

DR. SAIDI (*sardonically surprised*): I?

E. AZUBIKI (*to him*): How true that each of us is born evil—that, as you said, the impulse to kill is universal—

DR. SAIDI: I convinced you of it—?

E. AZUBIKI (*solemnly*): It is Christian dogma, Dr. Saidi. We're born with original sin. But Christianity also tells us that we must learn to overcome our evil impulses . . .

(*A crash of breaking glass as a rock bounces into the room. Groendyck picks it up, examines it. The others, startled, stare at him.*)

GROENDYCK (*to Sekgoma*): From your friends?

SEKGOMA: I don't know—

GROENDYCK: I'm sure of it. (*to Azubiki*) You see, it *is* your people. They hate us and will make trouble. We'll need someone here who's not afraid of them. (*Defiantly tosses aside the rock.*) I want to settle this affair of Alec McLean at once. (*impatiently*) Our question is: Who killed him? (*with an accusing glance at Mbonu*).

E. AZUBIKI: The mystery of *who* will be answered when we ask *why* it was done. What makes people act so wickedly? It would seem that God sanctions it.

DR. SAIDI (*smiling, but speaking sharply*): You're romantic and sentimental. You live on the edge of the jungle, and you can see all life there thrives only by the killing of other life. And man himself's scarcely out of the jungle—

E. AZUBIKI (*troubled*): Perhaps. But has not man a divine soul? Is not the spark of God in him—? Is he not different from the murderous beasts which prey upon one another?

DR. SAIDI: Hardly. In fact, man's the only one who ever kills wantonly.

E. AZUBIKI: I'm sure this was not a wanton act, but premeditated— which is even more terrible. This was *evil*, but did it seem so to the murderer? Probably not. There are few impulses which men recognize as evil—all seem to grow out of good intentions.

GROENDYCK (*to him*): What were you going to say about Mbonu?

E. AZUBIKI (*to Groendyck, directly*): I have a vision of something very frightening. (*Turns to include the others in his gaze.*)

GROENDYCK: From the beginning I suspected Mbonu—

E. AZUBIKI (*to him*): One of my people, who cannot talk for himself, has been accused. So may I speak for him? May I, a humble man, try to expose the truth in my own way?

GROENDYCK: By mysticism?

E. AZUBIKI (*to him*): I shall try to be logical, as you are. (*Pauses.*) Why do we hate someone enough to kill him? While he lives, we cannot attain what we most passionately love. Money, perhaps. Or power. Or a woman. Whatever he wants most obsessively. As Dr. Saidi says, murder grows out of *love*. (*turns to Mbonu*) How does Mbonu profit by the death of the Commissioner?

DR. SAIDI: The houseboy? I'd say he's lost his easy and comfortable post here—

E. AZUBIKI (*gratefully*): Yes. He does not profit that way . . . Or is Mbonu a misguided patriot? Does he *love* his people that much?

GROENDYCK: He took the oath—

E. AZUBIKI: He was drunk . . . the enthusiasm of such a meeting is contagious. But that meant little or nothing the next day, when he was sober again—

COWAN: He was jealous—?

E. AZUBIKI (*to him*): Jealous enough to kill? When Akamba offers to prove that she has retained her virtue—? It hardly seems enough.

(*He hands the folded handkerchief to* DELLA. *Suddenly faces* AKAMBA, *who has apeared in the doorway. To her:*)

The Commissioner had a little wood-carving on his desk. It's gone.

(AKAMBA, *taken aback, lowers her head.*)

GROENDYCK: A wood-carving? What kind?

E. AZUBIKI (*to him*): A fetich. A fertility symbol—for someone who might want to find a mate, or have many children. (*to Akamba*) You took it, when the Major was killed . . . To make you more fruitful some day?

(AKAMBA, *abashed, stands with head lowered in silent assent.* AZUBIKI *whirls to confront Cowan.*)

But you, Mr. Cowan, were you not jealous?

MBONU (*points at Cowan, cries out*): The Bwana—! He is the one—!

E. AZUBIKI (*to him*): Did you and Mrs. McLean love each other so much? No, watching you, I cannot believe it. You are not a lover; you will never be one. If you accuse Mbonu of a crime of passion, it is almost with envy that you speak of it—

COWAN: I'm not a savage, which he is—

E. AZUBIKI: You call my people savages, but you are only an anemic Englishman. You are good, but ignobly good—good from fear, without courage. To me you are not a man in God's heroic image—

COWAN (*angrily*): You forget who you are!

E. AZUBIKI: You came to me with a false story about a shortage in taxes—because figures, numbers, are more alive to you than human beings—that seemed to you the way.

COWAN (*ignores Azubiki. Shows his humiliation by his silence; then turns to Della—apologizes*): I've been a fool. You didn't need my help at all—you're so much stronger than I am.

(DELLA *does not reply. She has been listening to* AZUBIKI *with rigid posture and glazed eyes.*)

E. AZUBIKI: One observes this balance in nature—as if by God's plan—that a weak man turns to a strong woman, and she is ready to lend him her strength. But here that has been perverted somehow—

(*Pause.*) It is also possible that Major McLean committed suicide. (*to Cowan*) You wanted us to believe that. When you came to me with *your* story, I told another falsehood—(*to Dr. Saidi*) that your medical examination showed that suicide was impossible—and Mr. Cowan, not being a doctor, believed me, too, and confessed that he was lying.

GROENDYCK (*to Azubiki*): A lie is a favorite device of yours—!

E. AZUBIKI: The lies of others seem to be a challenge to my own ingenuity. Please believe me, Mr. Groendyck, I lie only to liars—

(*Moving behind the desk and standing near it,* DELLA *surreptitiously takes up the revolver lying on it—and hides it in a fold of her gown.*)

E. AZUBIKI: Still I think I know an even better reason for believing this is not an instance of suicide—why it could not possibly be—

GROENDYKE: What is that?

E. AZUBIKI (*holds up his hand*): I will come to it. First I would like to consider Mrs. McLean.

(DELLA *seems hardly to hear him. She is still behind the desk and is standing as rigidly as before, her features almost expressionless, her emotion frozen or restrained.*)

E. AZUBIKI (*continues*): No one has acted in such a guilty fashion as she has. (*Azubiki's voice rises—it grows sharp and intense, as though summing up a charge against her.*) She wished herself free of the Major. She had decided to return to England, and this made him angry. (*speaks more directly to Della*) But your husband couldn't stop you, could he? If you had no money, you could get it from friends—or even Mr. Cowan—

GROENDYCK: I've never really suspected Mrs. McLean. I'm quite sure I know who did it—

E. AZUBIKI: And so, by now, am I.

COWAN: Who?

E. AZUBIKI: Most murders are solved easily—but this seems to have been carefully done. It was planned, most likely, by someone experienced in such matters. I am trying to accept Mr. Groendyck's criticism and be logical. Who knows the most about such things—who is the best acquainted with the methods of murder?

DR. SAIDI (*sharply, brightly*): I'd say a policeman.

E. AZUBIKI (*to Saidi*): But you speak in jest? You are, as always, ironical?

GROENDYCK: It's a rather bad joke.

E. AZUBIKI (*to Saidi again*): In what way would the police benefit from Major McLean's death?

DR. SAIDI: It would provide them with employment—

(AZUBIKI *catches sight of the revolver hidden by* DELLA—*he moves suddenly and grapples with her; as he grasps her wrist, a shot is fired and goes wild, and* AZUBIKI *wrests the weapon from her. She sinks into the chair behind the desk, burying her face in her hands, gasping, hysterically in tears— her long restraint broken.*)

E. AZUBIKI (*looks about anxiously*): Is anyone hurt—?

GROENDYCK: No—Anyone?

DR. SAIDI: No—

E. AZUBIKI (*to her. Harshly*): Whom were to trying to kill?

DELLA (*raises her face, but does not speak directly to him*): No one—! (*exits quickly to terrace.*)

E. AZUBIKI (*stirred*): She meant to kill herself? Later, in her room? Or in the garden—? (*turns to Cowan*) Why do you not go to her? You see, she *does* need your help—no one is strong enough, no one can be all alone.

DR. SAIDI (*as Cowan remains fixed*): Let me—

COWAN (*suddenly*): No—(*he follows Della off.*)

E. AZUBIKI (*he still holds the weapon. He indicates it, with a sudden change of tone in his voice*): It is dangerous, I think, to leave a loaded weapon lie about so—There is probably a murderer in this room.

GROENDYCK: I agree. It was very careless—

E. AZUBIKI (*turns to Dr. Saidi*): You are witty, Dr. Saidi—and cynical. You said a murder would provide the police with employment. Perhaps you have phrased it perfectly—it could all have been a matter of "employment". (*once more addresses the others*) If the murderer signed his name to his work, should we not hasten to read it?

GROENDYCK: Signed his name—?

E. AZUBIKI: On this bullet. A ballistics expert can compare it with the others in the weapon.

GROENDYCK: Yes—

E. AZUBIKI: But, so far, no steps have been taken to have that test made. Again trying to be logical, Mr. Groendyck, I have asked myself why—

GROENDYCK (*moves toward him*): The gun has fingerprints on it—put it down.

E. AZUBIKI: Mrs. McLean wiped them off.

GROENDYCK (*emphatically*): She mightn't have—not all of them.

E. AZUBIKI (*somewhat excitedly*): Let's get some bullets to send to Freetown!—(*Fires first shot into woodwork.*)

GROENDYCK: What're you doing? Give me the gun—!

E. AZUBIKI (*disregards him*): One will not be enough—(*Fires again.*)

DR. SAIDI: It might ricochet—

E. AZUBIKI: The wood is soft—(*Fires third shot.*)

GROENDYCK (*shouts*): Give me the gun—! Give it to me—

(E. AZUBIKI *fires once more; then turns and points the revolver at* GROENDYCK, *who is advancing toward him.*)

GROENDYCK (*stopping short*): Put it down—it's loaded.

E. AZUBIKI (*still pointing weapon at him. Speaking quietly, yet intensely*): No, it's not—I've fired four bullets, and Mrs. McLean fired one. Let me show you there are no more—(*He raises the revolver as though to aim at Groendyck.*)

GROENDYCK (*believing the pointed weapon will go off at him*): Put it down—for God's sake. It's still loaded. (*He ducks grotesquely and falls to his knees.*)

E. AZUBIKI (*instead of pulling the trigger, suddenly opens the revolver and cries aloud*): As I thought—a bullet's in here! The sixth bullet—! (*snaps it closed again and points at the fallen Groendyck*) So please stand up, Mr. Groendyck, and raise your hands above you—

(GROENDYCK *silently obeys. His face shows him to be experiencing panic and rage. The others are startled, watchful.*)

E. AZUBIKI (*almost triumphantly*): I was certain Major McLean had not committed suicide—because no shots were fired from his revolver —and only one person here knew it was still fully loaded—

(AZUBIKI *reaches in pocket, hands keys to Saidi.*)

Dr. Saidi, take the handcuffs off Sekgoma, please, and put them on Mr. Groendyck.

(SAIDI *hesitates.* AZUBIKI *speaks commandingly:*)

Do as I say! Isn't it clear what happened? This revolver had all its bullets in it; it was never used, at all.

[145]

(SAIDI *suddenly comprehends and acts to free* SEKGOMA *and manacle* GROENDYCK, *instead.* AZUBIKI *then directs:*)

Good! Now I'm sure we'll find Mr. Groendyck's weapon has one of its bullets missing. Look for it, please.

(SAIDI *obeys. Holds it up.*)

E. AZUBIKI (*tensely*): Open it and see—

SAIDI (*doing so*): You're right—it's been fired once!

E. AZUBIKI: And it's the same make?

SAIDI: Yes—

E. AZUBIKI: And we keep no registration numbers here. So no one would have guessed that Major McLean was not killed by his own revolver—the one kept in the drawer—but by Mr. Groendyck's.

(*Attracted by the sound of firing,* DELLA *has returned.*)

DELLA (*to Groendyck*): Why did you do it?

E. AZUBIKI (*to Groendyck*): You quarreled with Major McLean— When it was dark, you returned. The Major heard you in the garden and went out to look, but you slipped in the other door. When he crossed the room, you were waiting for him (*points near the door*) over there—and shot him.

COWAN: The two revolvers—? What's the significance of that?

E. AZUBIKI (*still to Groendyck*): When you came again the next morning, you saw that the Major had carried his revolver and dropped it. You immediately suggested it was the murder weapon, told no one to touch it—Instead of sending this one to Freetown for testing, you would have sent your own—no one would ever have known the difference.

COWAN: He couldn't have planned it that way.

E. AZUBIKI (*to Cowan*): He didn't. (*to Groendyck again*) But on the spur of the moment you realized you could say this was the murder weapon.

COWAN: Why?

AZUBIKI: To narrow suspicion to the occupants of this house. To absolve himself. (*to Groendyck*) And—most clever of all—you were casual about the gun—(*points to desk*) You left it there all day, as if your life did not *depend* upon it. That bit of acting, for a time, deceived even me.

GROENDYCK: This's pure fantasy. Azubiki's a liar—you've all heard him admit how often he lies—(*to Azubiki*) You all lie, and you're all crazy, all you black bastards!

E. AZUBIKI: It will be very simple to prove—when we match

[146]

the bullet which killed the Commissioner with the others in Mr. Groendyck's revolver—

GROENDYCK (*protests*): I put in fifteen years of my life here—

DR. SAIDI (*to Azubiki*): What led you to this, Inspector?

E. AZUBIKI: You did. No love is so strong, so important, as that of a father for his son. I looked around. I saw no one here loved deeply enough ever to hate and to kill, except this man—

GROENDYCK (*bitterly, tauntingly*): You were never so clever on any case before—

E. AZUBIKI: You did this for your son, at school in England— Because you love him? I feel sorry for you—But when Mrs. McLean suggested that her husband had killed himself, you refused to accept her story—you were not content to escape punishment—you wanted to discredit my people, to hold on to your job. You were willing to put the blame on Mbonu, to let him die for your crime?

GROENDYCK: He would've escaped—into the jungle. I would've let him—I would've seen he was never caught.

E. AZUBIKI (*with rising anger*): You would have let him live like a hunted animal in the bush, in the dark forest—to perish there.

GROENDYCK: Let's go to Freetown—Let's get it over with—

E. AZUBIKI (*distressed at the thought*): I cannot take him—

COWAN (*to Azubiki*): You must—Who else is there to do it?

E. AZUBIKI (*seeking help with his moral burden*): You must come with me, Mr. Cowan. And you, Dr. Saidi—

DR. SAIDI: Yes.

COWAN: Very well.

E. AZUBIKI: Sekgoma, Mbonu—You must come with us, too. I must talk to you about the riots—

(SEKGOMA *and* MBONU *take places alongside* GROENDYCK, *almost respectfully, as if to escort him out.*)

GROENDYCK (*defiantly*): You're all glad I killed him. But you'll never admit it to anyone—even yourselves. Someone had to do it—he made us all suffer! I am the hand of the law here, and so I *executed* him.

AZUBIKI: You should have waited for God to do it.

GROENDYCK (*after a long stare at him*): God often takes too long.

(*Bowing his head,* GROENDYCK *walks out, right, toward the jeep. He is accompanied by* SEKGOMA *and* MBONU.)

DELLA: How can I thank you, Mr. Azubiki?

E. AZUBIKI (*gazes at her solemnly*): How grateful we are for others' guilt—

(DELLA *slowly returns his stare, then winces.*)

DELLA (*at last*): That's true.

E. AZUBIKI: What will become of you? You are still looking for love.

DELLA: Love—?

E. AZUBIKI: Don't ask for it. Give it. To everyone. To the whole world—To all of God's Creation. Because all of God's Creation feels pain and needs love.

DELLA: Is that enough?

E. AZUBIKI: That love is not possessive. It asks nothing. And, so, it is the most welcome love of all. Believe me, it will make you precious to everyone.

(DELLA *remains silent—Looks at him a long time. Glances at* COWAN, *glances back at* AZUBIKI; *she goes to her room, with no final glance at* COWAN. AKAMBA *turns and follows her.*)

(COWAN *has watched* DELLA'S *withdrawal. He stares after her for a moment, bites his lip.*) COWAN (*finally. To Azubiki*): I'm going out to the jeep.

(COWAN *exits. Only* SAIDI *and* AZUBIKI *are left.*)

DR. SAIDI: You're a clever little man, Azubiki—very clever and very foolish. You ask questions much too big for you.

E. AZUBIKI: As you said, as you said . . . This was done for love. (*shakes head*) What is God's meaning in all this? (*Looks upward in his infinite perplexity.*) I have solved the murder—but I still have no clue—

MISS LUCY IN TOWN

PREFATORY NOTE

A ballad opera is one that tells its story by setting new words to the popular music of the day. A classic example, of course, is John Gay's *Beggars' Opera*, which contains some fifty-odd songs to carry on its action.

Miss Lucy in Town is a work in this form, that has its setting in eighteenth-century England, shortly after the period described by Gay, and that draws its material almost wholly from the early writings of Henry Fielding.

No Cossack has ever pillaged farther or more high-handedly than I have in composing this work, searching through some sixteen hundred closely printed pages of Fielding's collected pieces for the theatre. The text of *Miss Lucy* is compounded of incidental songs, parts of plots, characters, and satiric flights from about twenty-three of Fielding's stage productions. The chief sources have been two one-act plays, *A Virgin Unmasked: or An Old Man Taught Wisdom*, and *Miss Lucy in Town*, a sequel to the former; *The Welsh Opera* (later called *The Grub-street Opera*, to appease the feelings of sensitive Welshmen*); *Rape Upon Rape*, or *The Justice Caught in His Own Trap* (afterwards more politely re-titled *The Coffee-house Politician*); *Pasquin*; *The Lottery*; *The Author's Farce*; and *The Historical Register of 1736*. Other important sources have been *Don Quixote in England*; *Love in Several Masques*; *The Intriguing Chambermaid*; *Tumbledown Dick*, or *Phaeton in the Suds*; and *The Wedding Day*.

Most of these works were presented by Fielding, at his own theatre, and by his own company, in the ten years between the young author's twentieth and thirtieth birthdays. They won him considerable fame and success as a playwright, until his excursion into the new field of political satire brought Walpole's wrath upon his head. The result was the Licensing Act of 1737 which, under the guise of condemning immorality, closed his playhouse. Thus he was driven from the drama at a time when he was just beginning to learn how to write plays. Those, at least, were his own words. He went on, as we know, to write immortal comic novels: *Joseph Andrews* and *Tom Jones*.

Until recently, few people remembered that Fielding ever wrote for the theater. But not long ago I was presented with a rival, a musical adaptation of some of this same material, which fared well as *Lock Up Your Daughters*. My handling of it, however, is far different.

* * *

What accounts for the virtual disappearance of Fielding's other compositions? It is truly extraordinary, when one considers that the theatre took some of his best years, that his output was so prodigious, and that he was, in the opinion of many, the most virile comic genius that English literature has produced.

Since that is so, I ought to explain why I have taken such liberties with Fielding's work as is evidenced in this present piece. The truth is, Fielding has quite disappeared from our stage because the best of him is too widely dispersed. His remarkable wit does not shine forth from any single, sustained play. I have devoted myself in this opera to a restoration of what appealed to me as the fresh and superlatively good parts of Fielding's theatrical humour. The richness of the material, and my zeal in this endeavour, will account for the length of my piece, the prodigality with which I have introduced the songs, and —not least—my desire to intrude as little from my own pen as possible. (But I could not resist the temptation of including a few lyrics of my own. To exculpate Fielding, I might identify them as Mr. Zorobable's two songs with Mrs. Midnight, and his duet with Lucy; Lord Formal's song with Mrs. Midnight, two of Mr. Ballad's songs—Airs XXVIII and XXIX—and—with music—the Couturière's ballet.) To the character named Fielding, I have assigned the lines he gave several of the playwrights in his farces, particularly Mr. Trapwit of *Pasquin*, the narrator of the *Historical Register:* and Mr. Luckless and his friend Witmore of *The Author's Farce* (this last piece a supposedly auto-biographical one, relating the young playwright's difficulties in starting his career). I have also given to my Mr. Fielding an idea or two lifted from his various prefaces. Sometimes I have transferred lines from one character to another, or combined several characters in one. I am not certain that the workings of this method will be altogether clear to any reader, but he may rest assured that the consequence is an opera still mostly from Fielding's hand.

Should this opera prove too long for the stage, there are modern Mr. Marplays, "poetical tailors", who will know how to cut it with ease. I saw no reason, however, for depriving the reader who, if interested, need not confine himself to a mere two hours of entertainment, of the pleasure of continuing with me through this rediscovered Fielding whose farce to my mind is as delightful, as topical, as pointed and vigorous as though it were written yesterday.

I had two other purposes. One was to present, if possible, a panoramic picture of London as seen through Fielding's eyes. The second was to share with my collaborator his commendable "design", which was "to divert the town and draw full houses".

P. F.

MISS LUCY IN TOWN

A Ballad Opera in Three Acts, Eight Scenes

PRINCIPAL PERSONS

Mr. Goodwill, *a country squire*
Lucy, *his daughter*
Blister, *an apothecary* ⎫
Coupee, *a dancing master* ⎬ *suitors to Lucy*
Wormwood, *a lawyer* ⎭
Mr. Thomas, *a footman*
William, *a groom*
Robin, *a butler*
Mrs. Midnight ⎫
            ⎬ *ladies of the town*
Tawdry   ⎭
Mr. Zorobable, *a moneylender*
Lord Formal
Mr. Ballad, *an English singer*
Signor Cantileno, *an Italian singer*
Mr. Marplay, *a theatre manager*
Marplay Jr, *his son: a tragedy writer*
Mr. Fielding, *a comedy writer*
First Player (and Prompter)
Second Player
Mr. Bookweight, *a bookseller*
Justice Squeezum
Mr. Quiver, *his clerk*
Mr. Staff, *a constable*
First Watch
Mr. Sotmore, *a friend to Ballad*

Also: Servant to Mrs. Midnight; Jeweller, Lottery seller; Couturière; Mask-maker, Manequins; Second Watch; Players in Mr. Marplay's Troupe, *et al.*

SYNOPSIS OF SCENES

ACT ONE: *Scene One:* In the West Country.
Scene Two: At Mrs. Midnight's, in London.
ACT TWO: *Scene One:* At the Playhouse.
Scene Two: At the Couturière's.
Scene Three: A street.
ACT THREE: *Scene One:* At Justice Squeezum's.
Scene Two: In gaol.
Scene Three: At Mrs. Midnight's.

Air LVI

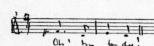

Does my lady wish a mask? I've a very pretty
mask, for my lady.
Does my lady wish a gown? I've a very pretty
gown, for my lady.
Does my lady wish the town? We've a very
pretty
town, for my lady.
I think this town is very fair,
And better far than country air!
Oh, my lady!

PROLOGUE

(Originally spoken by MR. MACKLIN)

Gentlemen and Ladies,

We must beg your indulgence, and humbly hope you'll not be offended
    At an accident that has happened tonight, which was not in the
    least intended,

I assure you: if you please, your money shall be return'd. But Mr.
    ——, today,

Who performs a principal part in the play,

Unfortunately has sent word, 'twill be impossible, having so long a
    part,

To speak to the Prologue, he hasn't had time to get it by heart.

I have been with the author, to know what's to be done,

For, till the Prologue's spoke, Sir, says I, we can't go on.

"Pshaw! rot the Prologue," says he, "then begin without it."

I told him 'twas impossible, you'd make such a rout about it:

Besides, 'twould be quite unprecedented,—and I dare say

Such an attempt, Sir, would make them damn the play.

"Ha! damn my play!" the frightened bard replies;

"Dear ——, you must go on, then, and apologize."

Apologize! not I: pray, Sir, excuse me.

"'Zounds! something must be done: pr'ythee, don't refuse me:

"'Prythee, go on: tell them, to damn my play will be a damn'd hard
    case.

"Come, do: you've a good long dismal, merry-begging face."

Sir, your humble servant: you're very merry. "Yes," says he, "I've
    been drinking

To raise my spirits; for, by Jupiter! I found them sinking."

So away he went to see the play; O! there he sits:

Smoke him, smoke the Author—! (FIELDING *is disclosed in the audience.*)

Isn't he finely situated for a damning—Whihee! Yell—yell!

As Falstaff says: would it were bed-time, Hal, and all were well!
(FIELDING *exits from audience.*)
But to the Prologue.—What shall I say? Why, faith, in my sense,
I take plain truth to be the best defence.
I think, then, it was horrid stuff; and in my humble apprehension,
Had it been spoke, not worthy your attention.
A vast deal about critics,—and good nature,—and the poor Author's
fear;
And something about a third night,—hoping we'd still be here.
(*Steps forward.*)
  To you, the critic jury of the pit,
  Our culprit Author does his cause submit:
  With justice, nay, with candour, judge his wit:
  Give him, at least, a patient quiet hearing:
  If guilty, damn him; if not guilty, clear him.
Accept, though, Fielding, from a heart sincere,
A gift commended by its being rare,
Unfeigned applause!
  In early youth, we know, you first began
To combat with the follies of the town
And raise the sinking honour of the stage
To robust eminence, in this, our age.
  Long have I seen, with sorrow and surprise,
Unhelp'd, unheeded, thy strong genius rise
To form our manners and amend our laws
And aid, with artful hand, the public cause.

ACT ONE

SCENE ONE: The West Country. A hall. SQUIRE GOODWILL, *solus.*

GOODWILL: Where are all the fellows I keep in this place? Thomas, my footman? Robin, my butler? William, my groom? (*calls*) Thomas!
(*To him,* THOMAS.)
THOMAS: Yes, Squire Goodwill. Good morning to you, Sir!
GOODWILL: Where are the others? Are you my footman or not?
THOMAS: Sir, it is my pleasure to be your footman.
GOODWILL: Robin!
(*To them,* ROBIN.)
ROBIN: Good morning, Squire Goodwill! You trumpet early.
GOODWILL: My butler has the manners of a Prime Minister. And like a Prime Minister, he sleeps long and late. Call William.
(*To them,* WILLIAM.)
WILLIAM: Here, Sir, is William.
GOODWILL: Look ye now, fellows. Today we shall go hunting. But first I must marry off my daughter.
THOMAS: Why, Sir, you will have a busy morning.
GOODWILL: My mind is made up. Why should I not take an hour from hunting to marry off my daughter?
WILLIAM: Certainly it is worth an hour of your time, Sir.
GOODWILL: I should gladly spend much more time than that.
ROBIN: But the sun is up. And this is the hour for the fox and hare.

Air I: *There was a Jovial Beggar*
(ROBIN, then SQUIRE GOODWILL, then OMNES)

The dusky night rides down the sky,
And ushers in the morn:
The hounds all join in jovial cry,
The huntsman winds his horn:
And a hunting we will go.

[159]

The wife around her husband throws
    Her arms, and begs his stay;
My dear it rains, and hails, and snows,
    You will not hunt today.
        But a hunting we will go.

A brushing fox in yonder wood
    Secure to find we seek;
For why, I carry'd, sound and good,
    A cartload there last week.
        And a hunting we will go.

Away he goes, he flies the rout,
    Their steeds all spur and switch;
Some are thrown in, and some thrown out,
    And some thrown in a ditch:
        But a hunting we will go.

At length, his strength to faintness worn,
    Poor Reynard ceases flight;
Then hungry homeward we return,
    To feast away the night:
        Then a drinking we will go.

GOODWILL: Well, hark ye, to me it is surprising that out of the multitudes who feel a pleasure in making money, few or none take any satisfaction in giving it away.

THOMAS: To give away money . . . That must certainly be a satisfaction, Sir.

GOODWILL: It should be a vast delight to reward merit, and I do not believe it so difficult to find.

THOMAS: You shall not have so far to look . . .

GOODWILL: That is what I think.

THOMAS (aside): And so think I, Squire Goodwill.

GOODWILL: At present I am worth a good ten thousand pounds, and an only daughter, both of which I have determin'd to give to the most worthy of my poor relations.

THOMAS: Your poor relations, Sir!

GOODWILL: I have summoned them. I believe in giving away my

money, but at the same time I think it is a good idea to keep it in the family.

THOMAS (*aside*): Here's mischief! But my Lucy is clever.

GOODWILL: The girl I have bred up under my own eyes; she has seen nothing, knows nothing, and consequently has no mind but mine. Between the affection of an innocent and dutiful child, and the grateful return I may expect from my son-in-law, I shall certainly be the happiest man on earth.

THOMAS (*aside*): Were he to call me his son-in-law, I should be the happiest man on earth.

GOODWILL: Here she comes. Leave me alone with her. And then we shall be off on the hunt.

(*Exeunt all save* THOMAS *and* GOODWILL. *To them,* Lucy. *She nods to* THOMAS *behind* GOODWILL's *back, and he gestures for her to meet him off-stage. She signals her assent, and he leaves.*)

LUCY: Did you send for me, Papa?

GOODWILL: Yes, come hither, Child. I have sent for you to mention an affair which you, I believe, have not yet thought of.

LUCY: I hope it is not to send me to a boarding-school, Papa.

GOODWILL: I hope my indulgence to you has been such, that you now have reason to regard me as the best of fathers. I am sure I have never deny'd you anything but for your own good.

LUCY: I am afraid you are angry with me, Papa.

GOODWILL: Do not be frightened, my dear child, you have done nothing to offend me. But answer me one question——What does my little dear think of a husband?

LUCY: A husband, Papa! O la!

GOODWILL: Come, it is a question a girl in her sixteenth year may answer. Should you like to have a husband, Lucy?

LUCY: Am I to have a coach?

GOODWILL: No, no: what has that to do with a husband?

LUCY: I have been told by several of our neighbours, that I was to have a coach when I was marry'd.

GOODWILL: Lock up a girl as you will, I find you cannot keep her from evil counsellors.—I tell you, Child, you must have no coach with a husband.

LUCY: Then let me have a coach without a husband.

GOODWILL: What, had you rather have a coach than a husband?

LUCY: Hum—I don't know that.—But, if you will get me a coach and footman, let me alone, I'll warrant I'll get me a husband.

GOODWILL: The girl is out of her wits, sure. Hussy! who put these thoughts in your head? You shall have a good sober husband, that will teach you better things.

LUCY: Ay, but I won't though, if I can help it; for Miss Jenny Flant-it says a sober husband is the worst sort of husband in the world.

GOODWILL: I have a mind to sound the girl's inclinations. Come hither, Lucy; tell me now, of all the men you ever saw, whom should you like best for a husband?

LUCY: O fie, Papa, I must not tell.

GOODWILL: Yes, you may to your father.

LUCY: No, Miss Jenny says I must not tell my mind to any man whatever. She never tells a word of truth to her father.

GOODWILL: You must not regard Miss Jenny. Tell me the truth, or I shall be angry.

LUCY: Why then, of all the men I ever saw in my whole life-time, I like Mr. Thomas, our footman, the best, a hundred thousand times.

GOODWILL: A footman? O fie!

LUCY: A footman! He looks a thousand times more like a gentleman than either Squire Western or Squire Jones, and talks more like one, aye, and smells more like one too. His head is so prettily drest, done all down the top with sugar, like a frosted cake, with three little curls on each side, that you may see his ears as plain! and then his hair is done up behind just like a fine lady's, with a little hat, and a pair of charming white stockings, as neat and fine as any white-legg'd fowl; and he always carries a big swinging stick in his hand, as big as himself, that he would knock any dog down with, who was to offer to bite me. Icod, I should have had him before now, but that folks told me I should have a man with a coach.

GOODWILL: I am amazed! I abhor the mercenary temper in the girl. What, child, would you have any one with a coach!

LUCY: Yes indeed, I would.

(*To them*, BLISTER.)

BLISTER: Mr. Goodwill, your humble servant. I have rid twelve long miles in little more than an hour. I am glad to see you so well; I was afraid by your message . . .

GOODWILL: That I had wanted your advice, I suppose; truly, coz, I sent for you on a better account.—Lucy, this is a relation of yours you have not seen a great while, my cousin Blister, the apothecary.

LUCY: O la! I hope that great huge man is not to be my husband.

BLISTER: My cousin is well grown, and looks healthy. What apothecary do you employ? He deals in good drugs, I warrant him.

GOODWILL: Plain wholesome food and exercise are what she deals in. Leave us a little, my dear Lucy, I must talk with your cousin.

LUCY: Yes, Papa, with all my heart.—I hope I shall never see that great thing again. (*Exits.*)

GOODWILL: I believe you begin to wonder at my message, and will, perhaps, more, when you know the occasion of it. In short, without preface, I begin to find myself going out of the world, and my daughter very eager to come into it. I have therefore resolved to see her settled without further delay. I have determined to marry her to one of my relations, so that the fruits of my labour should not go out of the family. I have sent to several of my kinsmen, of whom she shall take her choice; and as you are the first here, if you like my proposal, you shall make the first application.

BLISTER: With all my heart, cousin; and I am very much obliged to you. Your daughter seems an agreeable young woman, and I have no aversion to marriage. But pray why do you think yourself going out of the world? Proper care might continue you in it a considerable while. Let me feel your pulse. (*Taking it.*)

GOODWILL: To oblige you; though I am in very good health.

BLISTER: A little feverish—I would advise you to lose a little blood and take an emulsion, with a gentle emitic and cathartic.

GOODWILL: No, no, I will send my daughter to you; but pray keep your physic to yourself, dear cousin. (*Exits.*)

BLISTER: This man is near seventy, and I have heard, never took any physic in his life; and yet he looks as well as if he had been under a doctor's hands all his life-time. 'Tis strange; but if I marry his daughter, the sooner he dies, the better. It is an odd whim of his to marry her in this manner; but he is very rich, and so, so much the better.—

[163]

What a strange creature she is! No matter, her fortune is never the worse.

(*To him:* LUCY.) Oh, here comes my mistress: what a pox shall I say to her? I never made love in my life.

LUCY: Papa has sent me hither; but if it was not for fear of a boarding-school, I am sure I would not have come: but they say I shall be whipt there, and a husband can't whip me, let me do what I will; that's one good thing.

BLISTER: Won't you please to sit down, cousin?

LUCY: Yes, thank you, Sir.—(*aside*) Since I must stay with you, I may as well sit down as not.

BLISTER: Pray, cousin, how do you find yourself?

LUCY: Find myself?

BLISTER: Yes, how do you do? Let me feel your pulse. How do you sleep o'nights?

LUCY: How? why, upon my back, generally.

BLISTER: But I mean, do you sleep without interruption? Are you restless?

LUCY: I tumble and toss a good deal sometimes.

BLISTER: Hum! Pray how long do you usually sleep?

LUCY: About ten or eleven hours.

BLISTER: Is your stomach good? Do you eat with an appetite? How often do you find in any day an inclination to eat?

LUCY: Why, a good many times; but I don't eat a great deal, unless it be at breakfast, dinner, and supper, and afternoon's lunchion.

BLISTER: Hum! I find that you have at present no absolute need of an apothecary.

LUCY: I am glad to hear that!

Air VI: *We've cheated the Parson: &c.*

When tender young virgins look pale and complain,
You may send for a dozen great doctors in vain;
All give their opinion, and pocket their fees;
Each writes her a cure, though all miss her disease;
    Powders, drops,
    Juleps, slops,
A cargo of poison from physical shops.

Though they physic to death the unhappy poor maid,
What's that to the doctor—since he must be paid?
Would you know how you may manage her right?
My Thomas shall bring me a nostrum tonight:
    Never vary,
    Nor miscarry,
If the lover be but the apothecary.

I wish he was gone with all my heart.

BLISTER: I suppose, cousin, your father has mentioned to you the affair I am come upon; may I hope you will comply with him, in making me the happiest man upon earth?

LUCY: You need not ask me; you know I must do what he bids me.

BLISTER: May I then hope you will make me your husband?

LUCY: I must do what he'll have me.

BLISTER: What makes you cry, Miss? Pray tell me what is the matter?

LUCY: No, you will be angry with me, if I tell you.

BLISTER: I angry! it is not in my power, I can't be angry with you; I am to be afraid of your anger, not you of mine; I must not be angry with you, whatever you do.

LUCY: What must you not be angry, let me do what I will?

BLISTER: No, my dear.

LUCY: Why then, by goles, I will tell you—I hate you, and can't abide you.

BLISTER: What have I done to deserve your hate?

LUCY: You have done nothing; but you are such a great ugly thing, I can't bear to look at you; and if Papa were to lock me up for a twelvemonth, I should hate you still.

BLISTER: Did you not tell me just now, you would make me your husband?

LUCY: Yes, so I will for all that.

BLISTER: Well, my dear, if you can't abide me I can't help that, nor you can't help it; and if you will not tell your father, I assure you I will not; besides, my dear, as for liking me, do not give yourself any trouble about that, it is the very best reason for marrying me; no lady now marries anyone but whom she hates; hating one another is the chief end of matrimony. It is what most couples do before they are married, and all after it. I suppose you imagine we are to be fond, and hug one another as long as we live.

LUCY: Why, an't we?

BLISTER: Ha, ha, ha! an't we? no! (*aside*) How ignorant she is!—Marrying is nothing but living in the same house together, and going by the same name; while I am following my business, you will be following your pleasure; so that we shall rarely meet at meals, and then we are to sit at opposite ends of the table, and make faces at each other.

LUCY: I shall like that prodigiously.—Ah, but there is one thing though—an't we to lie together?

BLISTER: A fortnight, no longer.

LUCY: A fortnight! That's a long time: but it will be over.

BLISTER: Ay, and then you may have anyone else.

LUCY: May I? then I'll have Mr. Thomas, by goles! why, this is pure; la! they told me other stories. I thought when I had married, I must never have liked anyone but my husband, and that if I should he would kill me; but I thought one thing through with myself, that I could like another man without letting him know it, and then a fig for him.

BLISTER: Well, then, Miss, may I depend upon you?

LUCY: And may I depend upon you?

BLISTER: Yes, my dear.

LUCY: Ah, but don't call me so; I hate you should call me so.

BLISTER: Oh, Child, all marry'd people call one another My dear, let 'em hate one another as much as they will.

LUCY: Do they? Well then, my dear—Hum, I think there is not any great matter in the word, neither.

BLISTER: Why, amongst your fine gentry, there is scarce any meaning in anything they say. Well, I'll go to your papa, and tell him we have agreed upon matters, and have the wedding instantly.

LUCY: The sooner, the better.

BLISTER: Your servant, my pretty dear. (*Exits.*)

LUCY: Your servant, my dear. Nasty, greasy, ugly fellow. Well, marriage is a charming thing though, I long to be married more than ever I did for any thing in my life.

Air VII: *Bessy Bell*

La! what swinging lies some people will tell!
I thought when another I'd wedded,
I must have bid poor Mr. Thomas farewell,
And none but my husband have bedded.
But I find I'm deceived, for as Michaelmas day
Is still the fore-runner of Lammas,
So wedding another is but the right way
To come at my dear Mr. Thomas.

(*To her:* COUPEE.)

Heyday! what fine gentleman is this?

COUPEE: Cousin, your most obedient and devoted humble servant.
I have not the honour to be known to you, cousin; but your father
has been so kind as to give me admission to your fair hands.

LUCY: O Gemini Cancer! what a fine charming man this is!

COUPEE: My name, Madam, is Coupee, and I have the honour to
be a dancing-master.

LUCY: And are you come to teach me to dance?

COUPEE: Yes, my dear, I am come to teach you a very pretty
dance; did you never learn to dance?

LUCY: No, Sir, not I; only Mr. Thomas taught me one, two, three.

COUPEE: That is a very great fault in your education, and it will be
a great happiness for you to amend it by having a dancing-master for
your husband.

LUCY: Yes, Sir, but I am not to have a dancing-master; my papa
says I am to have a nasty stinking apothecary.

COUPEE: Your papa says! What signifies what your papa says?

LUCY: Why, must I not mind what my papa says?

COUPEE: No, no, you are to follow your own inclinations. (*aside*) I
think if she has any eyes, I may venture to trust 'em.—Your father is a
very comical, queer old fellow, a very odd kind of silly fellow, and
you ought to laugh at him. I ask your pardon though for my freedom.

LUCY: You need not ask my pardon, for I am not at all angry;
for, between you and I, I think him odd. I hope you won't tell him
what I say.

COUPEE: I tell him! I hate him for his barbarous usage of you;

to lock up a young lady of beauty, wit, and spirit, without ever suffering her to learn how to dance! Why, Madam, not learning to dance is absolute ruin to a young lady. I suppose he took care enough you should learn to read.

LUCY: Yes, I can read very well, and spell too.

COUPEE: Ay, there it is. All parents take care to instruct their children in low mechanical things, while the genteel sciences are neglected. Forgive me, Madam, at least, if I throw myself at your feet, and vow never to rise till lifted up with the elevating fire of your smiles.

LUCY (*aside*): Lard, Sir! I don't know what to say to these fine things.—He's a pure man.

COUPEE: Shall I hope you will think of me?

LUCY (*aside*): I shall think of you more than I will let you know.

COUPEE: Will you not answer me?

LUCY: La! you make me blush so, I know not what to say.

COUPEE: Ay, that is from not having learnt to dance; a dancing-master would have cur'd you of that. Let me teach you what to say, that I may hope you will condescend to make me your husband.

LUCY: No, I won't say that . . . I can never marry you, Sir, because you are a gentleman whom I could never hate. And the apothecary says no woman marries any man she does not hate.

COUPEE: Ha, ha, ha! Such mean fellows as those every fine lady must hate; but when they marry fine gentlemen, they love them as long as they live.

LUCY: O but I would not have you think I love you. I assure you I can't love you: I have been told I must not tell any man I love him. I don't love you; indeed I don't.

COUPEE: But may I not hope you will?

LUCY: Lard, Sir, I can't help what you hope; it is equal to me what you hope. (*aside*) Miss Jenny says I must always give myself airs to a man I like. It's a pure thing to give one's self airs.

COUPEE: Is that your last word? (*He makes to leave.*) Adieu, then.

LUCY: O stay!—La, Sir! you're so hasty.—Must I tell you the first time I see you? Miss Jenny Flant-it has been courted these two years by half a dozen men, and nobody knows which she'll have yet: and must not I be courted as well? I will be courted, indeed so I shall.

COUPEE: Ay, Madam. I will court you after we are married.

LUCY: But will you indeed?

COUPEE: Yes, I shall; but if I did not, there are others enough that would.

LUCY (aside): That is what my cousin Blister said.—But I did not think married women had ever been courted, though.

COUPEE: That's all owing to your not learning how to dance. Why, there are an abundance of women who marry for no other reason; as there are men who never court any but married women.

LUCY And you shall teach me to dance?

COUPEE: One kiss, my dearest angel! And then one, two, three, and away.

LUCY (aside): Oh, dear sweet man! He's as handsome as an angel, and as fine as a lord. He is handsomer than Mr. Thomas, and icod, almost as well drest. I see now why my father would never let me learn to dance. For by goles, if all dancing-masters be such fine men as this I wonder every woman does not dance away with one.

COUPEE: And so, what are you thinking?

LUCY: Well, then, I don't care if I do marry you. But hold: there is one thing, but that does not much signify.

COUPEE: What is it, my dear?

LUCY: Only I promis'd the apothecary just now; that's all.

COUPEE: We shall dance, and forget that. This way, my dear—

COUPEE and LUCY

Air LIV

COUPEE: When modesty sues for a favour,
        What answers the politic lass?

LUCY: That she mightily likes his behaviour,
        And thinks in her heart he's an ass;
        And thinks in her heart he's an ass.

COUPEE: But when bolder impudence rushes,
        And manfully seizes her charms?

LUCY: Lard! you're rude, Sir, she cries, then she blushes,
        And folds the brisk youth in her arms;
        And folds the brisk youth, &c.

(Dancing lesson here: with music and pantomime.)

(To them, BLISTER)

BLISTER: Heyday! what do I see? my mistress in another man's arms? Sir, will you do me the favour to tell me what business you have with that lady?

COUPEE: Pray, Sir, be so good as to tell me what business you have to ask?

BLISTER: Sir!

COUPEE: Sir!

BLISTER: Sir, this lady is my mistress.

COUPEE: I beg to be excused for that, Sir.

BLISTER: Damnation!

COUPEE: Hell and confusion! *(They draw;* LUCY *runs out.)*

BLISTER: For Heaven's sake, what's the matter? I am afraid we are both disorder'd. Pray, Sir, give me leave to feel your pulse: I fear you are light-headed.

COUPEE: What is it to you, Sir, what I am?

BLISTER: I have a great mind to break my sword about your head, you dog!

COUPEE: I have a great mind to run you through the body, you rascal!

(To them, GOODWILL.)

GOODWILL: Heyday! what are you fencing here, gentlemen?

COUPEE: Do not stop us!

GOODWILL: I hope there is no anger between you! You are nearer relations than you imagine to each other. Mr. Coupee, you was sent out of England young; and you, Mr. Blister, have liv'd all your life-time in London; but I assure you, you are Cousin-Germans. Let me introduce you to each other.

BLISTER: Dear cousin Coupee.

COUPEE: Dear cousin Blister.

GOODWILL *(aside)*: It's but a blow and a kiss with these sparks, I find.

COUPEE: I thought there was something about him that would not let me hurt him. Dear cousin, I hope you will excuse my ignorance.

BLISTER: Yes, cousin, with all my heart, since there is no harm come on't; but if you will take my advice, you shall immediately lose some blood, and I will order you a gentle purge.

(*To them*, WORMWOOD.)

WORMWOOD: Your servant, cousin Goodwill. How do you do, Master Blister. The roads are very dirty; but I obey your summons, you see.

GOODWILL: Master Coupee, this is your cousin Wormwood, the attorney.

WORMWOOD: I'm glad to see you, Sir. I suppose by so many of our relations being assembled, this is a family law-suit I am come upon.

GOODWILL: I sent for you on the account of no law-suit this time. In short, I have resolv'd to dispose of my daughter to one of my relations: if you like her, cousin Wormwood, with 10,000 pounds, and you should happen to be her choice—

BLISTER: That's impossible; for she has promis'd me already.

COUPEE: And me.

WORMWOOD: How! Has she promised two of you? Why then the two that miss her will have very good actions against him that has her.

GOODWILL: Her own choice must determine; and if that fall on you, Mr. Blister, I must insist on your leaving off your trade, and living here with me.

BLISTER: No, Sir, I cannot consent to leave off my trade.

GOODWILL: Pray, Gentlemen, is not the request reasonable?

OMNES: Oh, certainly, certainly.

GOODWILL: Then let Robin, my butler, bring us the bottle. I shall show you, coz, the physic of a better apothecary.

WORMWOOD: Well, it is surprising that men should be such fools, that they should hesitate at leaving off their professions for ten thousand pounds.

GOODWILL: Ay, and the bottle is the best attorney, for it teaches men to speak glib. Cousin Wormwood, you will leave off your practise, I'm sure.

WORMWOOD: Indeed, Sir, but I will not. I hope you don't put me upon a footing with bleeders and dancing-masters.

GOODWILL: What is a lawyer but a bleeder? And what does he do in court but step nimbly? Nay, you are all alike.

Air VIII: *Mother, quoth Hodge &c.*

The doctor is fee'd for a dangerous draught,
  Which cures half a dozen, and kills half a score;
Of all the best drugs the dispensaries taught,
  'Twere well could each cure one disease, and no more.
    But here's the juice
    Of sovereign use,
  'Twill cure your distempers, whatever they be;
    In body or spirit,
    Wherever you bear it;
  Take of this a large dose, and it soon sets you free.

By cunning directors, if trick'd of your pelf,
  Your losses a dose of good claret can heal;
Or if you have been a director yourself,
  'Twill teach you no loss of your honour to feel:
    Stocks fall or rise,
    Tell truth or lies,
  Your fame or fortune here remedy find;
    If Silvia be cruel,
    Take this water-gruel,
  'Twill soon cure the fever that burns up your mind.

Recitativo:

  Rogues there are of each nation,
    Except among the divines;
  And vinegar, since the creation,
    Hath still been made of all wines.
  Against one lawyer Lurch
    A country scarce can guard;
  One parson does for a church,
    One doctor for a church-yard.

WORMWOOD: No man need be ashamed of marrying his daughter to a practitioner of the law. What would you do without lawyers? Who would know his own property?

BLISTER: Or without physicians? Who'd know when he was well?

COUPEE: If it was not for dancing-masters, men might as well walk upon their heads as their heels.

(*To them,* LUCY *and* MR. THOMAS.)

GOODWILL: Ha! confusion! what do I see! my daughter in the hands of that fellow!

LUCY: Pray, Papa, give me your blessing; I hope you won't be angry with me, but I am married to Mr. Thomas.

GOODWILL: Oh, Lucy! Lucy! is this the return you make to my fatherly fondness?

LUCY: Dear Papa, forgive me, I won't do so any more. But he met me when I was frightened, and did not know what I did.

GOODWILL: To marry a footman!

THOMAS (*helps himself to claret*): Why, look ye, Sir! I am a footman, 'tis true, but I have a good acquaintance in life. I have kept very good company at the hazard-table; and when I have other clothes on, and money in my pocket, they will be very glad to see me again.

GOODWILL (*aside*): This fellow drinks with ease, at least. Not like these other fellows. Ay, he has the makings of a gentleman.

WORMWOOD: Harkye, Mr. Goodwill, your daughter is an heiress. I'll put you in a way to prosecute this fellow.

BLISTER: Did you not promise me, Madam?

COUPEE: Ay, did you not promise me, Madam?

LUCY: You have none of you any reason to complain; if I did promise you all, I promis'd him first.

WORMWOOD: Lookye, Gentlemen, if any of you employ me, I'll undertake we shall recover part of her fortune.

COUPEE: If you had given your daughter a good education, and let her learn to dance, it would have put softer things in her head.

BLISTER: This comes of your contempt of physic. If she had been kept on a diet, with a little gentle bleeding, and purging, and vomiting, and blistering, this had never happened.

WORMWOOD: You should have sent her to town a term or two, and taken lodgings for her near the Temple, that she might have conversed with the young gentlemen of the law, and seen the world.

[173]

LUCY (*sings*):

Air: IX: *Bush of Boon*

Oh, dear papa! don't look so grum;
　　Forgive me, and be good:
For though he's not so great as some,
　　He still is flesh and blood.

What though he's not so fine as beaus,
　　In gold and silver gay:
Yet he, perhaps, without their clothes,
　　May have more charms than they.

THOMAS: Your daughter has marry'd a man of some learning, and one who has seen a little of the world, and who by his love to her, and obedience to you, will try to deserve your favors. As for my having worn livery let not that grieve you; as I have liv'd in a great family, I have seen that no one is respected for what he is, but for what he has; the world pays no regard at present to anything but money; and if my own industry should add to your fortune, so as to entitle any of my posterity to grandeur, it will be no reason against making my son, or grandson, a lord, that his father, or grandfather, was a footman.

Air X: *Lillibolera*

Let the foolish philosopher strive in his cell,
　　By wisdom, or virtue, to merit true praise;
The soldier in hardship and danger still dwell,
　　That glory and honour may crown his last days:
　　　　The patriot sweat,
　　　　To be thought great;
Or beauty all day at the looking-glass toil;
　　　　That popular voices
　　　　May ring their applauses,
While a breath is their only reward and their spoil.

But would you a wise man to action incite,
   Be riches propos'd the reward of his pain:
In riches is center'd all human delight;
   No joy is on earth but what gold can obtain.
      If women, wine,
      Or grandeur fine,
Be most your delight, all these riches can;
      Would you have men to flatter?
      To be rich is the matter;
When you cry he is rich, you cry a great man.

GOODWILL: Ha! thou talk'st like a pretty sensible fellow, and I don't know whether my daughter has not made a better choice than she could have done among her booby relations. I shall suspend my judgment at present, and pass it hereafter, according to your behaviour.

THOMAS: I will try to deserve it should be in my favour.

WORMWOOD: I hope, cousin, you don't expect I should lose my time. I expect six and eight-pence for my journey.

GOODWILL: Thy profession, I see, has made a knave of whom nature meant a fool. Well, I am not convinc'd 'tis less difficult to raise a fortune than to find one worthy to inherit it. Let us call in my other fellows, to hear the news. And the maids. Robin, William, Sweetissa, Margery!

(*To them:* ALL.)

Your mistress is marry'd, have you heard? And Mr. Thomas, the footman, is now my new son. And you shall all go to London on the wedding-trip.

WILLIAM: Do you mean, Sir, we shall delay the hunting for today?

GOODWILL: Well, it has been Lucy who went hunting today. And snar'd herself a husband.

LUCY: And shall you come to London with us too, Papa? La, I'm to see the world at last!

GOODWILL: I shall stay home at first. And come later. I must get used to this unexpected event.

[175]

Air XI: *The Yorkshire Ballad*

BLISTER: Had your daughter been physic'd well, Sir, as she ought,
With bleeding and blist'ring, and vomit and draught,
This footman had never been once in her thought,
    With his Down, down, &c.

COUPEE: Had pretty Miss been at a dancing-school bred,
Had her feet but been taught the right manner to tread,
Gad's curse! 'twould have put better things in her head,
    Than his Down, down, &c.

THOMAS: Had she learnt, like fine ladies, instead of her prayers,
To languish and die at Italian soft airs,
A footman had never thus tickled her ears,
    With his Down, down, &c.

LUCY: You may physic, and music, and dancing enhance,
In one I have got them all three by good chance,
My doctor he'll be, and he'll teach me to dance,
    With his Down, down, &c.

(*Dance here:* LUCY *and* COUPEE, *then* LUCY *and* THOMAS.)

CURTAIN

(*During the change of scene:* SQUIRE GOODWILL *may appear before the curtains as follows:*)

GOODWILL (*solus*): Well, my hunting is off, my only daughter marry'd and soon gone to London. All this is sudden and requires some thinking. But at least I can smoke. What a glorious creature was he who first discovered the use of tobacco!—the industrious retires from business—the voluptuous from pleasure—the lover from a cruel mistress—the husband from a curs'd wife—and I from all the world to my pipe.

Air XVIII: *Freemason's tune*

Let the learn'd talk of books,
    The glutton of cooks,
The lover of Celia's soft smack-o;
    No mortal can boast
    So noble a toast,
As a pipe of accepted tobacco.

[176]

Let the soldier for fame,
And a general's name,
In battle get many a thwack-o;
Let who will have most,
Who will rule the roast,
Give me but a pipe of tobacco.

The man whose chief glory
Is telling a story,
Had never arrived at the knack-o,
Between ev'ry heying,
And as I was saying,
Did he not take a whiff of tobacco.

The doctor who places
Much skill in grimaces,
And feels your pulse running tick-tack-o;
Would you know his chief skill?
It is only to fill,
And smoke a good pipe of tobacco.

The courtiers alone
To this weed are not prone;
Would you know what 'tis makes them so slack-o!
'Twas because it inclin'd
To be honest the mind,
And therefore they banish'd tobacco.

SCENE TWO: *In London. At Mrs. Midnight's.* TAWDRY *and* MRS.
MIDNIGHT.

MRS. MIDNIGHT: And he did not give you a single shilling?

TAWDRY: No, upon my honour.

MRS. MIDNIGHT: Very well. They spend so much money in show
and equipage, that they can no more pay their ladies than their
tradesmen.

TAWDRY: Virtuous women and gentlemen's wives come so cheap, that no man will go to the price of a lady of the town. Have you put a bill on your door, Ma'am, as you said you would?

MRS. MIDNIGHT: It is up, it is up. O Tawdry! that a woman who hath been bred, and always lived like a gentlewoman, and followed a polite way of business, should be reduced to let lodgings.

TAWDRY: It is a melancholy consideration, truly. (*Knocking.*) But hark! I hear a coach stop.

MRS. MIDNIGHT: Some rake or other, who is too poor to have any reputation. This is not a time of day for good customers to be abroad. (*To them,* SERVANT.)

SERVANT: Madam, a gentleman and lady to enquire for lodgings; they seem to be just come of the country, for the coach and horses are in a terrible dirty pickle.

MRS. MIDNIGHT: Why don't you shew them in? Tawdry, who knows what fortune has sent us?

TAWDRY: If she had meant me any good, she'd have sent a gentleman without a lady. (*Servant returns with* WILLIAM.)

SERVANT: This is my mistress, friend.

WILLIAM: Do you take folks in to live here? Because if you do, Madam and the Squire will come and live with you.

MRS. MIDNIGHT: Then your master is a squire, friend, is he?

WILLIAM: Ay, he is as good a squire as any within five miles o'en: tho'f he was but a footman before, what is that to the purpose? Madam has enough for both o'em.

MRS. MIDNIGHT: Well, you may desire your master and his lady to walk in. I believe I can furnish them with what they want. What think you, Tawdry, of the Squire and his lady, by this specimen of them?

TAWDRY: Why, I think if I can turn the Squire to as good account as you will his lady, (*I mean if she be handsome*) we shall have no reason to repent our acquaintance. You will soon teach her more politeness, than to be pleased with a footman, especially as he is her husband. (*To them:* MR. THOMAS, LUCY, *and* SERVANTS.)

THOMAS: Madam, your humble servant. My fellow here tells me you have lodgings to let, pray what are they, Madam?

MRS. MIDNIGHT: What conveniences, Madam, would your lady-ship want?

LUCY: Why, Good-woman, I shall want everything which other fine Ladyships want. Indeed, I don't know what I shall want yet: for I never was in town before: but I shall want everything I see.

THOMAS: I hope your apartments here are handsome, and that people of fashion used to lodge with you.

MRS. MIDNIGHT: If you please, Sir, I'll wait upon your honour, and shew you the rooms.

THOMAS: Ay, do, do so; do wait on me. Will, do you hear, do you take care of all our things.

LUCY: Ay, pray, Robin take care of the great cake and the cold turkey, and the ham and the chickens, and the bottle of sack, and the two bottles of strong beer, and the bottle of cyder.

WILL: I'll take the best care I can: but a man would think he was got into a fair. The folks stare at one as if they had never seen a man before.

(*Remain* TAWDRY *and* LUCY.)

TAWDRY: Pray, Madam, is not your ladyship infinitely tired of your journey?

LUCY: I tired! not I, I an't tired at all; I could walk twenty miles farther.

TAWDRY: O, I am surprised at that! most fine ladies are horribly fatigued after a journey.

LUCY: Are they?—Hum, I don't know whether I an't so too! yes, I am, I am horribly fatigued. (*aside*) Well, I shall never find out all that a fine lady ought to know.

TAWDRY: Was your ladyship never in town before, Madam?

LUCY: No, Madam, never before that I know of.

TAWDRY: I shall be glad to wait on you, Madam, and shew you the town.

LUCY: I am very much oblig'd to you, Madam: and I am resolved to see everything that is to be seen: the Tower, and the crowns, and the lions, and Bedlam, and the parliament-house, and the Abbey—

TAWDRY: O fie, Madam! these are only sights for the vulgar; no fine ladies go to these.

LUCY: No! why then I won't neither. Oh odious Tower and filthy lions. But pray, Madam, are there no sights for a fine lady to see?

TAWDRY: O yes, Madam; there are ridottos, masquerades, courts, plays, and a thousand others, so many, that a fine lady has never time to be at home but when she is asleep.

LUCY: I am glad to hear that; for I hate to be at home: but, dear Madam, do tell me—for I suppose you are a fine lady.

TAWDRY: At your service, Madam.

LUCY: What do you fine ladies do at these places? What do they at masquerades now? for I have heard of them in the country.

TAWDRY: Why they dress themselves in a strange dress, and they walk up and down the room, and they cry, *Do you know me?* and then they burst out laughing, and they sit down, and then they get up, and then they walk about again, and then they go home.

LUCY: Oh this is charming, and easy too; I shall be able to do a masquerade in a minute: well, do tell me a little of the rest. What do they do at your what d'ye call 'ems, your plays?

TAWDRY: Why, if they can, they take a stage box, where they let the footman sit the first two acts, to shew his livery; then they come in to shew themselves, spread their fans upon the spikes, make curtsies to their acquaintance, and then talk and laugh as loud as they are able.

LUCY: O delightful! by gole, I find there is nothing in a fine lady; anybody may be a fine lady if this be all.

(*To them*, THOMAS *and* MRS. MIDNIGHT.)

THOMAS: My dear, I have seen the rooms, and they are very handsome, and fit for us people of fashion.

LUCY: O, my dear, I am extremely glad on't. Do you know me? Ha, ha, ha, ha, my dear. (*stretching out her fan before her*) ha, ha, ha!

THOMAS: Heyday! What's the matter now?

LUCY: I am only doing over a fine lady at a masquerade or play, that's all.

(*She coquets apart with her husband.*)

TAWDRY (*to Midnight*): She's simplicity itself. A card fortune has dealt you. You may bring her to any purpose.

MRS. MIDNIGHT: I am glad to hear it: for she's really pretty, and I shall scarce want a customer for a tit-bit.

THOMAS *and* LUCY (*Duet*):

Air XVI: *Young Damon once the happiest swaim*

When mutual passion hath possess'd,
With equal flame, each amorous breast,
How sweet's the rapt'rous kiss!
While each with soft contention strive,
Which highest ecstasies shall give,
Or be more mad with bliss!

LUCY: Well, my dear, you won't stay long, for you know I can hardly bear you out of my sight; I shall be quite miserable till you come back, my dear, dear, Tommy.

THOMAS: Who else could speak those words so sweetly?

THOMAS *and* LUCY (*Duet*):

Air XVII: *All in the Downs*

Would you my love in words display'd,
    A language must be coin'd to tell;
No word for such a passion's made,
    For no one ever lov'd so well.
Nothing, Oh! nothing's like my love for you,
And so my dearest, and so my dearest, and my dear, adieu.

THOMAS: My dear Lucy, I will but go find out a tailor, and be back with you in an instant.

LUCY: Pray do, my dear.—Nay, t'other kiss; one more—O! thou art the sweetest creature. (*Exit* THOMAS.) Well, Miss, fine lady, how do you like my husband? Is he not a charming man?

TAWDRY: Your husband! Dear Madam, and was it your husband that you kiss'd so?

LUCY: Why, don't fine ladies ever kiss their husbands?

TAWDRY: No, never.

LUCY (*aside*): That's what my cousin Blister said, but my cousin Coupee said t'opposite.—O la! but I don't like that, though. By gole, I believe I shall never be a fine lady, if I must not be kiss'd.

ACT ONE

Air XXI (*see* Appendix)

How happy are the nymphs and swains,
Who skip it and trip it all over the plains:
  How sweet are the kisses,
  How soft are the blisses,
Transporting the lads, and all melting their misses!
If ladies here so nice are grown,
Who jaunt it and flaunt it all over the town,
  To fly as from ruin,
  From billing and cooing,
A fig for their airs, give me plain country wooing.

TAWDRY: O, you mistake me, Madam; a fine lady may kiss any man but her husband.—You will have all the beaus in town at your service.

LUCY: Beaus! O gemini, those are the things Miss Jenny used to talk of.—And pray, Madam, do beaus kiss so much sweeter and better than other folks?

TAWDRY: Hum! I can't say much of that.

LUCY: And pray, then, why must I like them better than my own husband?

MRS. MIDNIGHT: Because it's the fashion, Madam. Fine ladies do everything because it's the fashion. They spoil their shapes, to appear big with child, because it is the fashion. They lose their money at whist, without understanding the game; they go to auctions, without intending to buy; they go to operas, without any ear; and slight their husbands without disliking them; and all—because it is the fashion.

LUCY: Well, I'll try to be as much in fashion as I can: but pray when must I go to these beaus; for I really long to see them. For Miss Jenny says, she's sure I shall like them; and if I do, i'facks! I believe I shall tell them so, not withstanding what our parson says.

MRS. MIDNIGHT: Bravely said; I will shew you some fine gentlemen which I warrant you will like.

LUCY: And will they like me?

TAWDRY: Like you! they'll adore you, they'll worship you.

[182]

Madam, says my Lord, you are the most charming, beautiful, fine creature that ever my eyes beheld!

LUCY: What's that? Do say that over again. And will they think all this of me?

TAWDRY: No doubt of it. They'll swear it.

LUCY: Then to be sure they will think it. Yes, yes, to be sure they will think so. I wish I could see these charming men.

MRS. MIDNIGHT: O, you will see them everywhere. Here in the house I have had several to visit me, who have said the same thing to me and this young lady.

LUCY (aside): Did they call you charming and beautiful? By gole, I think they may very well say so to me.—But when will these charming men come?

MRS. MIDNIGHT: They'll be here immediately: but your ladyship will dress yourself? I see your maids have brought your things. I suppose your ladyship has your clothes with you.

LUCY: O yes, I have clothes enough; I have a fine thread satin suit of clothes of all the colours in the rainbow; then I have a fine red gown, flower'd with yellow, all my own work; and a fine lac'd suit of pinners, that was my greatgrandmother's! that has been worn but twice these forty years, and my mother told me, cost almost four pounds when it was new, and reaches down hither. And then I have a great gold watch that has continu'd in our family, I can't tell how long, and is almost as broad as a moderate punchbowl; and then I have two great gold earrings, and six or seven rings for my finger, worth about twenty pounds all together; and a thousand fine things that you shall see.

MRS. MIDNIGHT: Ay, Madam, but these things would have drest your ladyship very well an hundred years ago: but the fashions are alter'd. Lac'd pinners, indeed! You must cut off your hair, and get a little perriwig and a French cap; and instead of a great watch, you must have one so small, that it is impossible it should go; and—but come, this young lady will instruct you. Pray, Miss, wait on the lady to her apartment, and send for proper tradesmen to dress her; such as the fine ladies use. Madam, you shall be drest as you ought to be.

LUCY: Thank you, Madam; and then I shall be as fine a lady as the best of them. By gole, this London is a charming place. If ever my husband gets me out of it again, I am mistaken.

Air XXII (*see* Appendix)

Farewell, ye hills and valleys;
Farewell, ye verdant shades;
I'll make more pleasant sallies
To plays and masquerades.
With joy, for town I barter
Those banks where flowers grow;
What are roses to a garter?
What lilies to a beau?

Come, dear Miss, I am impatient. *Do you know me?* ha, ha, ha!
(*Exeunt* LUCY *and* TAWDRY.)
(ZOROBABLE *brought in: in a chair: with the curtains drawn.*)
MRS. MIDNIGHT: O here's my best customer—Mr. Zorobable, is it you? I am your worship's most obedient servant.
ZOROBABLE: How do you do, Mrs. Midnight? I hope nobody sees or overhears. This is an early hour for me to visit at. I have but just been at home to dress me, since I came from the alley.
MRS. MIDNIGHT: But you have dressed yourself in new style! Now that is a handsome silk coat!
ZOROBABLE: You've an eye for whatever shews money. Ay, a nice coat. And why?

Air XXIII (*see* Appendix)

ZOROBABLE: A man if he would dignify
                     His person, should first signify
              His station with a coat as fine as mine;
                     To find himself a mistress fair
                     With patch, and powder in her hair,
              He really needs a tailor to accomplish his design!

MRS. MIDNIGHT: He really needs a tailor . . .

ZOROBABLE: If he only be a male, or . . .

MRS. MIDNIGHT: A tenor *sans* regalia . . .

ZOROBABLE: Or a bombardier or sailor, who has come from
               off the line:

BOTH: He really needs a tailor to accomplish his design!

Recitativo:

ZOROBABLE: A starling loves her darling for the dark sheen of his throat . . .

MRS. MIDNIGHT (*sings*): And a lady loves a tenor for the beauty of his note . . .

ZOROBABLE: And the lady robin-redbreasts on the robin's redbreast dote—

(*sings*):   Thus nature gives instruction
In the old art of seduction,
That a man is loved quite largely for the splendour of his coat.

A man, if he would catch the eye
Of ladies, when they're passing by,
Should garb himself with caution in a coat well-lac'd as mine:

The tailor's very special art
Will reach the oft well-guarded heart
Of virgins and rich widows, and accomplish his design!

ZOROBABLE: He really needs a tailor . . .

MRS. MIDNIGHT: If he only be a male, or . . .

ZOROBABLE: A tenor *sans* regalia . . .

MRS. MIDNIGHT: Or a bombardier or sailor, who has come from the line:

BOTH: He really needs a tailor to accomplish his design!

(*Dance here.*)

MRS. MIDNIGHT: I suppose your worship's hands are pretty full there now with your lottery-tickers?

ZOROBABLE: Fuller than I desire, Mrs. Midnight, I assure you. We hoped to have brought them to seven pounds before this; that would have been a pretty comfortable interest for our money.

MRS. MIDNIGHT: But your loans—?

ZOROBABLE: Ah, they are better.

Air XXIV: (*see* Appendix)

ZOROBABLE:
When lending money, I have found
There's many a shilling to the pound
That was not there, somehow, before I lent it.
And when it comes their turn to pay
My debtors find, in the same way,
A pound is somehow less when they have spent it.

MRS. MIDNIGHT: And they repent it. . . !

ZOROBABLE:
Though they repent, I'll not relent;
They pay for pleasures and their rent
With guineas from my pocket—
With quite an air, but not a groat
My Lord displays his bright lac'd coat,
But he'll soon face the docket.

MRS. MIDNIGHT: A coat? He should go hock it!
And ev'ry ring and locket!

ZOROBABLE:
By lending money, I have grown
To wealth, and fame, and am well-known
For my non-Euclidean, legal usury:
For two and two, when lent, is five;
And every borrower alive
Knows two and two, when spent, is only three.

MRS. MIDNIGHT: And three's a crowd,
But one and one, if you ask me,
Is company—

ZOROBABLE: And that's no lie—

MRS. MIDNIGHT: For you can add—
And I can multiply
My ev'ry gainful opportunity!

[186]

(*Dance here.*)

ZOROBABLE: But have you anything worth seeing in your house?

MRS. MIDNIGHT: O, Mr. Zorobable! such a piece! such an angel!

ZOROBABLE: Ay, ay, where? where?

MRS. MIDNIGHT: Here in the house.

ZOROBABLE: Let me see her this instant.

MRS. MIDNIGHT: Sure nothing was ever so unfortunate.

ZOROBABLE: What now?

MRS. MIDNIGHT: O Sir! not thinking to see your worship at this busy time, I have already promised her a lord.

ZOROBABLE: How, Mrs. Midnight, promised her a lord without offering her to me first?

MRS. MIDNIGHT: Marry forbid! Don't utter curses against me.

ZOROBABLE: You are a very ungrateful woman. I know a woman of fashion at St. James's end of the town, where I might deal cheaper than with yourself.

MRS. MIDNIGHT: But the girl hath never seen a lord as yet.

ZOROBABLE: Hath she not? Why then she never shall, till I have done with her: she'll be good enough for a lord half a year hence. Come, fetch her down. How long hath she been in town?

MRS. MIDNIGHT: Not two hours. Pure country innocent flesh and blood—But what shall I say to her?

ZOROBABLE: Say anything: does she want only a lord? Then tell her I am one.

MRS. MIDNIGHT: I will.—What name shall it be?

ZOROBABLE: Why, Lord Bawble.

MRS. MIDNIGHT: Well, I'll do the best I can; though, upon my honour, I could easily have had two hundred guineas from Lord Formal, if he should ever see her.

ZOROBABLE: Two hundred promises you mean; but had it been in ready cash, I'll make you ready amends if I like her; we'll never differ about the price; so fetch her, fetch her.

MRS. MIDNIGHT: I will, an't please your worship. (*A noise without.*) O Sir, here is some noisy person coming this way; slip into the next room: I am as tender of your reputation as of my own.

ZOROBABLE: You are a sensible woman, and I commend your care; for reputation is the very soul of a money-lender.

G   [187]

MRS. MIDNIGHT: Go in here, I will quickly clear the coast for you again. (*Exit* ZOROBABLE.)

(*Enter* LORD FORMAL.)

LORD FORMAL: So, Old Midnight, what schemes art thou plotting on?

MRS. MIDNIGHT: O fie! my Lord; I protest if Sir Robert and you don't leave off your riots, you will ruin the reputation of the house forever. I wonder, too, if you have no more regard for your own characters.

LORD FORMAL: Why, thou canting offspring of hypocrisy.

MRS. MIDNIGHT: We ought all to be ashamed of our sins. O my Lord, my Lord, had you heard the excellent sermon on Kensington Common, it would have made you ashamed: I am sure it had so good an effect upon me, that I shall be ashamed of my sins as long as I live.

LORD FORMAL: Why don't you leave them off then, and lay down your house?

MRS. MIDNIGHT: Alas, I can't, I can't, I was bred up in the way: but I repent heartily; I repent every hour of my life; and that I hope will make amends.

LORD FORMAL: Well, where is my Susie Ranter?

MRS. MIDNIGHT: Ah, poor Susie! Poor Susie is gone. I shall never see her more; she was the best of girls: it almost breaks my tender heart to think on't. (*crying*) My Lord, Sir Robert and you forgot to pay for that bowl of punch last night.

LORD FORMAL: Damn your punch, is my dear Susie dead?

MRS. MIDNIGHT: Nay, not dead . . . She is turn'd methodist, and married to one of the brethren.

LORD FORMAL: O, if that be all, we shall have her again!

MRS. MIDNIGHT: Alas! I fear not.

(*To them:* LUCY. *She hesitates.*)

LORD FORMAL: Heyday! I see a girl—

MRS. MIDNIGHT (*waves* LUCY *back*): Nay, my Lord, nay . . . Do not go near her! You'll frighten her. She's just arrived out of the country!

LORD FORMAL: I know how to deal with country ladies. I learnt the art of making love to them at my election.

MRS. MIDNIGHT: This one is as pure a virgin—upon my soul!

LORD FORMAL: Then I shall not miss Susie!

MRS. MIDNIGHT: Nay, my Lord, nay. . . . Do not speak to her. You'll scare the dear thing. For I have known her whole bringing up: she's a relation of mine; her father left me her guardian. I have just brought her from a boarding-school to have her under my eye, and complete her education.

LUCY (*aside*): Why is that old man staring at me? And what does the Madam mean with all this waving her arms?

LORD FORMAL: Her education? There are some things, Old Midnight, you cannot teach her, but I shall be glad to help you in that.

MRS. MIDNIGHT: Not a step without the R*eady*. I told you I was her guardian and I shall not betray my trust. Though I am grateful for your Lordship's offer—

LORD FORMAL: If I like her—upon my honour—

MRS. MIDNIGHT: I have too much value for your Lordship's honour, to have it left in pawn. Besides, I have more right honourable honour in my hand unredeemed already, than I know what to do with. However, I think you may depend upon my honour; deposit a cool hundred and you shall talk to her; and then take either the lady or the money. But the lady is three hundred, if she goes.

LUCY (*aside*): I wonder, what do they whisper so long?

LORD FORMAL: I know thee to be inexorable. First let me converse, and then I'll step home and fetch the money. I gave that sum to my wife this morning to buy her clothes. I'll take it back from her again and let her tic, with the tradesmen. Lookye, if this be stale goods, I'll break every window in the house.

MRS. MIDNIGHT: I'll give you leave. (*to* LUCY) Come here, my dear. I am going to introduce your ladyship to one of our fine gentlemen whom I told you of.

LUCY (*surveying him awkwardly*); Is this a beau, and a fine gentleman? —By goles, Mr. Thomas is a finer gentleman, in my opinion, a thousand times.

MRS. MIDNIGHT (*aside*): What am I to do? But Mr. Zorobable will be tired of her in a week, and then I may dispose of her again. I did wrong, I'm afraid, in putting her off for a virgin, for Lord Formal will certainly discover she is married. However, I can forswear the knowing of it.

LORD FORMAL: Madam, your humble servant; I shall always think myself obliged to Mrs. Midnight for introducing me to a young lady of your perfect beauty. Pray, Madam, how long have you been in town?

LUCY: Why, I have been in town about three hours: I am but a stranger here, Sir; but I was very lucky to meet with this civil gentlewoman and this fine lady, to teach me how to dress and behave myself. Sir, I would but be a fine lady for all the world.

LORD FORMAL: Madam, you are in the right on't: and this soft hand, this white neck, and these sweet lips were formed for no other purpose.

LUCY: Let me alone, Mun, will you; I won't be pull'd and haul'd about by you, I won't.—For I am very sure you don't kiss half so sweet as Mr. Thomas.

LORD FORMAL: Nay, be not coy, my dear; if you will suffer me to kiss you, I will make you the finest of ladies; you shall have jewels equal to a woman of quality:—nay, I will furnish a house for you in any part of town, and you shall ride in a fine gilt chair, carried by two stout fellows, that I will keep for no other purpose.

(*Sings: aside.*)

Air LV: *Giminianis' minuet*

Sweet's the little maid
That has not learnt her trade,
Fears, yet languishes to be taught;
Though she's shy and coy.
Still she'll give you joy,
When she's once to compliance brought.
Women full of skill
Sooner grant your will;
But often purchas'd are good for nought.
Sweet's the little maid, &c.

MRS. MIDNIGHT: Madam, if you will but like this gentleman, he'll make you a fine lady; he is Lord Formal. 'Tis he, and some more of his acquaintance, that make half the fine ladies in the town.

LUCY: Ay! Why, then I will like him. (*aside*)—I will say I do, which I suppose is the same thing.—But when shall I have all these fine things? For I long to begin.

LORD FORMAL (*offering to kiss her*): And so do I, my angel.

LUCY:—Nay, I won't kiss any more till I have something in hand, that I am resolved of.

MRS. MIDNIGHT (*to Lord Formal*): Fetch her some baubles; any toys will do. And don't forget to bring me the *Ready*.

LUCY: But if you will fetch me all the things you promised me, you shall kiss me as long as you please.

LORD FORMAL: But when I have done all these things, you must never see any other man but me.

LUCY: Must not I?—But I don't like that.—And will you stay with me always then?

LORD FORMAL: No, I shall only come to see you in the evening.

LUCY (*aside*): O then it will be well enough, for I will see whom I please all the day, and you shall know nothing of the matter.—Indeed I won't see anybody else but you; indeed I won't. But do go and fetch me these fine things.

MRS. MIDNIGHT (*aside*):

Air XXV: *Soldier Laddy*

When a virgin in love with a brisk jolly lad
You match to a spark more fit for her dad,
'Tis as pure, and as sure, and secure as a gun,
The young lover's business is happily done:
Though it seems to her arms he takes the wrong rout,
    Yet my life for a farthing,
       Pursuing
       His wooing,
The young fellow finds, though he go round about,
    It's only to come
    The nearest way home.

LORD FORMAL: I go, my dear. Mrs. Midnight, pray take care of her. I never saw anyone so pretty nor so silly. (*Exit.*)

LUCY: Well, Miss Jenny may stay in the country if she will; and see nothing but the great jolly parson, who never gives anything but a nosegay, or a handful of nuts for a kiss. But where's the young lady that was here just now? for to my mind I am in a new world, and my head is quite turn'd giddy.

MRS. MIDNIGHT: It is a common effect, Madam, which the town air hath on young ladies, when they first come into it. (*Sounds without.*) And here come some more gentlemen; and I mistake not their voices, one is an opera-singer, and the other a singer in one of our playhouses. You had better step out a moment; look, go into the closet. (*Shows her into room where Zorobable waits.*)

(*Enter* SIGNOR CANTILENO *and* MR. BALLAD.)

What is the matter, gentlemen? What is the matter?

CANTILENO: *Per dio:* I will have the woman. I will have her.

BALLAD: You must win her first, Signor; and if you can gain her affections, I am too much an Englishman to think of restraining her from pursuing her own will.

CANTILENO: Never fear, I shall win her. No Englishwoman can withstand the charms of my voice.

MRS. MIDNIGHT: If he begins to sing, there will be no end on't. I must go look after my young lady. (*Exits.*)

BALLAD: Ha, ha, ha! What the devil should an Italian singer do with a mistress?

CANTILENO: Ask your women, who are in love with the Italian singer.

(*To them: a* PORTER.)

PORTER (*to Cantileno*): Sir, the lady's in the next room.

CANTILENO: Very well. *Per dio*, I will have her.

BALLAD: I'll follow you, and see how far the charms of your voice will prevail. (*Exeunt.*)

(*Enter* ZOROBABLE, MRS. MIDNIGHT, *and* LUCY, *from closet.*)

ZOROBABLE (*to* MRS. MIDNIGHT): Upon my soul, a fine girl! I suppose this is she you told me of?

MRS. MIDNIGHT (*aside*): This is difficult.—Yes, yes, your worship, this is the same: But pray come away; for I can't bring her to anything yet: she is so young, if you speak to her, you will frighten her out of her wits; have but a little patience, and I shall bring her to my mind.

ZOROBABLE: Don't tell me of patience; I'll speak to her now; and I warrant I shall bring her to my mind. She wants a lord, does she? Then, remember that I am Lord Bawble.

LUCY (*aside*): O. la! this is a fine gentleman, indeed;—I wonder if he'll speak to me again, before the old fellow will be back. O, it had better be quick.

ZOROBABLE: I like her the better. It is in vain to contend; for by Jupiter, I'll at her.

MRS. MIDNIGHT: What will become of me? I'll get out of the way, and swear to Lord Formal, I know nothing of Mr. Zorobable's seeing her. (*Exits.*)

ZOROBABLE: It is generous in you, Madam, to leave the country, to make us happy here with the sunshine of your beauty.

LUCY: Sir, I am sure I shall be very happy if anything in my power can make the beaus and fine gentlemen of this fine town happy.— (*aside*) He talks just like Mr. Thomas, before I was married to him, when he first come out of his town-service.

ZOROBABLE (*aside*): She seems delightfully ignorant.—O, Madam, can you doubt of your power, which is as extensive as your beauty; which lights such a fire in the heart of every beholder, as nothing but your frowns can put out.

LUCY: I'll never frown again; for if all the fine gentlemen in town were in love with me, icod,—with all my heart, the more the merrier.

ZOROBABLE: When they know you have my admiration, you will soon have a thousand other adorers. If a lady hath a mind to bring custom to her house, she hath nothing more to do but hang one of us lords out for a sign.

LUCY: A lord?—Gemini, and are you a lord too? (*aside*) This one is younger and handsomer.

ZOROBABLE: My Lord Bawble, Madam, at your service.

LUCY: Well, my Lord Bawble is the prettiest name I ever heard: the very name is enough to charm one.—My Lord Bawble!

ZOROBABLE: Why, truly, I think it has something of a quality-sound in it.

LUCY: Heigh-ho!

ZOROBABLE: Why do you sigh, my charmer?

LUCY: At what, perhaps, will make you sigh too, when you know it. (*aside*)—No, I will not tell him I am married to an odious footman, and can never be my Lady Bawble. I'm afraid he won't like me, should I inform him o' that.

ZOROBABLE: What are you considering, my dear?

LUCY: I must not stay with you any longer, for I expect an old gentleman every minute, who promised me a thousand fine things, if I would not speak to anybody but him: he promised me two tall lusty fellows, for no other business but to carry me up and down in a chair.

ZOROBABLE: I will not only do that but I will keep you two other tall fellows for no other use but to walk before your chair.

LUCY: Will you? Nay, I assure you, I like you better than him, if I shall not lose any fine thing by the bargain.—But hold, now I think on't: suppose I stay here till he come back again with his present, I can take the things, promise him, and go with you afterwards, you know, my Lord. O, how pretty Lord sounds!

ZOROBABLE: No, you will have no need on't! I will give you variety of fine things. (Till I am tired of you: and then I'll take them away again.) But, my dear, these lodgings are not fine enough: I will take some finer with you.

LUCY: O la! what are there finer houses than this in town? Why, my father hath five hundred a year in the country, and his house is not half so fine.

ZOROBABLE: O, my dear, gentlemen of no hundred pound a year scorn such a house as this: nobody lives now in anything but a palace.

LUCY: Nay, the finer the better, by goles, if you will pay for it.

ZOROBABLE: Pugh, pshaw, pay! never mind that: (*that word put many a real lord in the vapors.*)—Come, my dear girl—(*Kisses her.*)

LUCY: O fie, my Lord, you make me blush. He kisses sweeter than my husband, a thousand times; I did not think there had been such a man as my husband in the world, but I find I was mistaken.

ZOROBABLE: Consider, my dear, what a pride you will have in hearing the man you love call'd lordship.

LUCY: Lordship! it is pretty. Lordship! But then you won't see me above once in a twelvemonth.

ZOROBABLE: I will see you every day, every minute: I like you so well, that nothing but being married to me could make me hate you.

LUCY: O Gemini! I forgot it was the fashion.

ZOROBABLE: Let us lose no time, but hasten to find some place where I may equip you like a woman of quality. And I shall show you the town.

LUCY: The ridottos?

ZOROBABLE: Ay!

LUCY: The play-houses?

ZOROBABLE: I'faith, I shall take you to a rehearsal of Mr. Fielding's new play this very afternoon.

LUCY: I am out of my wits. My Lord, I am ready to wait upon your lordship whenever your lordship pleases—Lordship! Quality! I shall be a fine lady immediately now.

ZOROBABLE: Then I shall call my chair. And come you after me in a moment, my dear. (*Exits.*)

(*Enter* CANTILENO.)

CANTILENO: *Hèlas,* that damn English ballad-singing dog has got away my woman—*ah, pardie—voila un autre—*(*going toward her*).

LUCY: This is certainly one of those operish singers Miss Jenny used to talk of.

(*To them:* MRS. MIDNIGHT.)

MRS. MIDNIGHT: Hold, hold, Signor; this lady is not for you— She is a woman of quality, and her price is a little beyond your pocket.

(*She takes* LUCY *by the hand and draws her from the room: just as* BALLAD *enters.*)

BALLAD: There goes a pretty piece! Ay—! But how quickly Midnight makes off with her—

CANTILENO: Your luck was no better than mine? This is a poor day for us, my friend.

BALLAD: Maybe a good day. (*Sings.*)

Air XXIX (*see* Appendix)

BALLAD: A man, if he is truly wise,
     Will stay away from women;
     But damn my eyes, if I am wise,
     I fear I'm merely human.

CANTILENO: You never spoke more true, man!

BALLAD: Oh Venus without arms for me
            Is Venus without charms for me,
              A goddess cold in stone;
            My goddess must be kind to me
            To warrant her divinity—

CANTILENO: I'll say that for my own!

BALLAD: Oh woman is meant for love,
              And love is meant for woman,
            And though, in fine, she be divine,
              She must then prove she's human.

CANTILENO: I'll say that for me too, man!

(*To them:* MRS. MIDNIGHT.)

MRS. MIDNIGHT: Gentlemen, I must beg you would go into another room; for my Lord Formal is just coming.

CANTILENO: The devil! one of our directors! I would not have him see me here for the world.

(*Exeunt* CANTILENO *and* BALLAD. *Enter* LUCY.)

LUCY: Is my Lord come? How eagerly I long to see him. But not my Lord Formal. No, my Lord Bawble. And now I remember! he told me he waited below.

MRS. MIDNIGHT: You go to Lord Bawble?

LUCY: To his pretty lordship! Immediately. (*She runs off.*)

MRS. MIDNIGHT: What shall I say? I am ruin'd forever. Mr. Zorobable hath carried away the girl. Lord Formal will never forgive me: I shall lose him, and after the money-lender, he is the best support of my house. I should have kept the girl against her will. Alas! women never know how to make their market till they are so old no one will give anything for them.

(*To her:* LORD FORMAL.)

LORD FORMAL: Well, I have kept my word; I have brought the *Ready.*

MRS. MIDNIGHT (*aside*): And I must lose that too?—My dear, gentle, noble Lord Formal, how shall I tell you?

LORD FORMAL: What is this?

MRS. MIDNIGHT: That ungrateful girl has run off. But never worry, I shall soon have her back. I think she was frightened by your grand manners.

LORD FORMAL: Run off! With another man?

MRS. MIDNIGHT: I fear so, my Lord.

LORD FORMAL: Who would take advantage of a country miss so pure, so innocent? 'Sdeath, I'll thrash the rascal! What man?

MRS. MIDNIGHT: Why, I am not sure, but I think it was Mr. Zorobable, the money-lender, though he called himself my Lord Bawble.

LORD FORMAL (*aside*): Zorobable? 'Ifaith, I owe the fellow so much money, I'll do no thrashing there.—Then mark ye. If they are in London, I shall find them. And I shall persuade the girl to change her mind.

MRS. MIDNIGHT: No violence, I pray you. She is delicately bred.

LORD FORMAL: Nay. I shall use soft words. My heart may still be young and impetuous, but my head is old and has been taught a thing or two. And I have seen the world.

Air XXX (*see* Appendix)

LORD FORMAL: When first from off these shores I went
In search of pleasures continent—

MRS. MIDNIGHT: Continent—?

LORD FORMAL: I mean in search of pleasures continental:
My manly strength I straightway prov'd
In many an amorous interlude—

MRS. MIDNIGHT: Lewd—?

LORD FORMAL (with *cosi-cosa* gesture):
Inter-lewd—
And passage sentimental;
And learned,
Though he be spurned,
The bravest soldier wins if he is gentle.

MRS. MIDNIGHT: Ah, gentle . . .

LORD FORMAL: When maids resist, you should withdraw,
The mildest summer sun will thaw
In time the frosty heart of any virgin:
With flattery and soulful sighs
You shall at length obtain your prize:
She only needs a little skilful urgin'.

MRS. MIDNIGHT: And learned,
Though he be spurned,
The bravest soldier wins if he is gentle.

LORD FORMAL: The lass is stern? you should retrench;
And be she Spanish, Dutch, or French,
The tactic is the same in every land:
Outwait the modest, early blush,
Your eye on two birds in the bush
Than one not quite in hand!

MRS. MIDNIGHT: And learned,
Though he be spurned,
The bravest soldier wins if he is gentle,
And continent—

LORD FORMAL: —'Tal

LORD FORMAL: Old Midnight, I take my leave. I shall recover your niece for you. (*Exits.*)
MRS. MIDNIGHT: But I shall never recover the *Ready.*

ACT TWO

SCENE ONE: The Playhouse. Enter several players.

FIRST PLAYER: Mr. Emphasis, good day; you are early at the rehearsal.

SECOND PLAYER: Why, faith, Jack, our beer and beef sat but ill on my stomach, so I started out to try if I could not walk it off.

FIRST PLAYER: I wish I had any thing in my stomach to walk off; if matters do not get better with us shortly, my teeth will forget their office.

SECOND PLAYER: Who knows what our author Fielding may produce that's new? Faith, I like my part very well.

FIRST PLAYER: Nay, if variety will please the town, I am sure there is enough of it; but I could wish, methinks, the satire had been a little stronger, a little plainer.

(*Enter* MARPLAY *and* MARPLAY JR. *Then* MR. ZOROBABLE *and* LUCY.)

MARPLAY: My Lord, your most obedient servant; this is a very great and unexpected favour indeed, my Lord. (*aside*) So our money-lender now calls himself Lord Bawble, does he? Many a bauble of mine he's had! But he is a man to humour. Zounds, if he can play a lord's part, perhaps I can use him for an actor. Madam, I kiss your hand; I am very glad to see you here. This is my son, Marplay Junior.

MARPLAY JR.: Madam, I kiss your hand.

LUCY: Is this gentleman too an actor? You promised to shew me some actors.

ZOROBABLE: We are come to attend your rehearsal, Sir; pray, when will it begin?

MARPLAY: That is hard to say, for the author Mr. Fielding was arrested as he was going home from King's coffee-house; and as I heard it was for upward of four pound, I suppose he will hardly get bail.

[199]

SECOND PLAYER: Is there anything to be done?

MARPLAY (*to First Player*): Jack, you are the prompter. What else have you besides this farce?

FIRST PLAYER: There is Mr. Marplay Jr's new tragedy. And this third play to be cast.

MARPLAY: Give it to my son. I'll see what can be done about my missing author. (*Exits.*)

MARPLAY JR.: It's another tragedy. *The Life and Death of King John*, written by Shakespear. Here are a parcel of English lords.

FIRST PLAYER: Their parts are but of little consequence; I will take care to cast them.

MARPLAY JR.: Do; but be sure you give them to actors who will mind their cues:—Faulconbridge—what sort of character is he?

FIRST PLAYER: Sir, he is a warrior, my cousin here will do him very well.

LUCY (*aside*): That man—he does not look like a warrior to me.

MARPLAY JR.: Can you look fierce, and speak well?

FIRST PLAYER (*with great effort*): Bah!

LUCY (*aside*): O la, the man is mad!

(*Enter* MARPLAY SR.)

MARPLAY: What are you doing here?

MARPLAY JR.: I am casting the parts in the tragedy of *King John*.

MARPLAY: Then you are casting the parts in a tragedy that won't do.

ZOROBABLE: How, Sir! Was it not written by Shakespear, and was not Shakespear one of the greatest geniuses that ever liv'd?

MARPLAY: No, Sir, Shakespear was a pretty fellow, and said some things which only want a little of my licking to do well enough; *King John*, as now writ, will not do—But a word, I will make him do.

LUCY: How shall you do that?

MARPLAY: By alteration, Madam: it is a maxim of mine, since I am at the head of theatrical affairs, that no play, however good, will do without alteration.

ZOROBABLE: I should only be afraid as Shakespear is so popular an author—

MARPLAY: Ay, Sir, but as Shakespear is already good enough for people of taste, he must be alter'd to the palates of those who have none.

ZOROBABLE: Ay, you are the man for that.

MARPLAY: That I am. Let any play be brought to me, and if I can make any alterations in it that will be for its advantage, I will stage it freely. Was you to see the plays when they are brought to us—a parcel of crude undigested stuff. We are the persons, Sir, who lick them into shape. The poet make a play, indeed! the colour-man might be as well said to make the picture, or the weaver the coat. My son and I, Sir, are a couple of poetical tailors. When a play is brought to us we consider it as a tailor does his coat: we cut it, Sir— we cut it; and let me tell you we have the exact measure of the town; we know how to fit their taste. The poets, between you and me, are a pack of ignorant—

MARPLAY, JR.: Hold, hold, Sir. Am I not a tragedy poet?

ZOROBABLE (to Marplay): And yet, as I take it, you have done the town the honour of writing yourself?

MARPLAY: I did, as you say, once make a small sally into Parnassus— took a sort of flying leap over Helicon; but if ever they catch me there again—Sir, the town have a prejudice to my family; for, if any play could have made them ashamed to damn it, mine must. It was all over plot. It would have made half a dozen novels: nor was it crammed with a pack of wit-traps, like Congreve and Wycherly, where every-one knows when the joke was coming. I defy the sharpest critick of them all to have known when any jokes of mine was coming. The dialogue was plain, easy, and natural, and not one single joke in it from beginning to the end; besides, Sir, there was one scene of tender melancholy conversation—enough to have melted a heart of stone; and yet they damned it—and they damned themselves; for they shall have no more of mine.

LUCY: O, you must take pity on the town, Sir.

MARPLAY: I! No, Madam, no. I'll write no more. No more: unless I am forced to it.

MARPLAY JR.: I have been chid for putting off my tragedy so long. I hope you are all quite perfect, for the town will positively stay for it no longer. I have been obliged, at their own requests, to wait upon some half-dozen persons of the first quality with tickets. I think I may very well put upon the bills, At the particular desire of several ladies of quality, the first night.

(*The Players consult together.*)

LUCY: This tragedy-writer is not so melancholy looking.

ZOROBABLE: You have only to sell tickets for him, and the author's tragedy is straightway over.

FIRST PLAYER: Mr. Marplay Jr., Sir, we must defer the rehearsal of your tragedy, for the gentleman who plays the first ghost is not here yet; and when he will come, he has got such a churchyard cough he will not be heard to the middle of the pit. We hope you will give us leave to rehearse the comedy first.

MARPLAY JR.: Ay, ay, you may rehearse it first, if you please, and act it first too. If it keeps back mine above three nights, I am mistaken. I don't know what friends the author may have; but if ever such stuff, such damned, incoherent, senseless stuff was ever brought on any stage—if the audience suffer it to go through three acts—Oh, he's here. (*to them:* MR. FIELDING) Dear Mr. Fielding! your most humble servant, Sir; I read your comedy over last night, and a most excellent one it is; if it runs as long as it deserves you will engross the whole season to yourself.

FIELDING: Sir, I am glad it met with your approbation, as there is no man whose taste and judgment I have a better opinion of. (*To* MARPLAY SR.) I assure you, Sir, I had much difficulty to get hither so early.

SECOND PLAYER (*aside*): Yes, faith, I believe you had.

FIELDING: The truth is, I was in gaol for a little bill at the tavern—and had to send my hat to the pawnbroker's.

LUCY: Your hat?

FIELDING: One way or other, I find my head must always provide for my belly.

LUCY (*aside*): This one is better looking, but though he does comedy, he seems sadder than the tragedy-writer. What a strange place London is!

MARPLAY: Well, thou are not cured of scribbling yet?

FIELDING: No, scribbling's as impossible to cure as the gout. Yea, and as sure a sign of poverty as the gout of riches. 'Sdeath, in an age of learning and true politeness, where a man might succeed by his merit, there be some encouragement. But now, when party and prejudice carry all before them; when learning's decried, wit not understood; when the theatres are puppet-shows, and the comedians ballad-singers; when fools lead the town, would a man think to thrive by his wit? If you must write, write operas, put on pantomimes, set up an oratory and preach nonsense, and you may meet with encouragement enough. Be profane, be scurrilous, be immodest: if you'd receive applause, deserve to receive sentence at the Old Bailey; and if you'd ride in a coach, deserve to ride in a cart.

MR. ZORABLE: You're warm, my friend.

FIELDING: It comes from hearing true men ridiculed by fools—by idiots. To hear a fellow who, had he been born a Chinese, had starved for sufficient genius to've been even the lowest mechanick, toss up his empty noodle with an affected disdain of what he hasn't understood; and women abusing what they've neither seen nor heard, from an unreasonable prejudice to an honest fellow whom they have not known. If thou wilt write against all these reasons, get a patron, be pimp to some worthless man of quality, write panegyricks on him, flatter him with as many virutes as he has vices. Then, perhaps, you'll engage his lordship, his lordship engages the town on your side, and then write till your arms ake, sense or nonsense, it'll all go down.

LUCY: O la, this man talks with passion.

MARPLAY JR.: Thou art too satirical on mankind. It is possible to thrive in the world by justifiable means.

FIELDING: Ay, justifiable by custom. What does the soldier or physician thrive by but slaughter?—the lawyer by quarrels?—the courtier by taxes?—the poet by flattery? I know of none that thrive by profiting mankind, but the husbandman and merchant; and yet these are represented as mean and mechanical, and the others as honourable and glorious.

FIRST PLAYER (aside): I've heard some of this before.

MARPLAY JR.: Sir, your comedy's to be rehearsed first.

FIELDING: Excuse me, Sir, I know the deference due to tragedy.

MARPLAY JR.: Sir, I'd not have you think I give up the cause of tragedy; but my ghost, being ill, cannot get up without danger, and I would not risque the life of my ghost on any account.

MARPLAY: As we are for this once to give the precedence to comedy, let us begin. And since both the Prompter and I are to have parts, Sir, perhaps you'll hold the script?

FIELDING: This very instant; gentlemen, I beg you'll be ready, and let the Prompter bring me some copies for this gentleman and this lady.

LUCY: O, I am very oblig'd to you, I'm sure.

MARPLAY JR.: Mr. Fielding, you know I'm a plain speaker, so you will excuse any liberties I take.

FIELDING: You can't oblige me more.

MARPLAY JR.: Then I must tell you, Sir, I am a little stagger'd at the name of your piece: *The Historical Register of* 1736; doubtless you know the rules of writing, and I can't guess how you can bring the actions of a whole year into the circumference of four and twenty hours.

FIELDING: Sir, if I comprise the whole actions of the year in half an hour, will you blame me, or those who had done so little in that time? My register's not to be fill'd like those of vulgar news-writers, with trash for want of news.

ZOROBABLE: Well, Sir, and pray what is your design, your plot?

FIELDING: Why, I have several plots, some pretty deep, and some shallow.

ZOROBABLE: I hope they all conduce to the main design.

FIELDING: Yes, Sir, they do.

MARPLAY JR.: Pray, what's that?

FIELDING: To divert the town and bring full houses.

MARPLAY JR.: Pshaw! you misunderstand me, I meant what's your moral, your, your, your—

FIELDING: Oh, I comprehend you—Why, my design's to ridicule the vicious and foolish customs of the age, and that in a fair manner, without fear, favour, or ill-nature, and without scurrility, ill-manners, or common-place; I hope to expose the reigning follies in such a manner, that men shall laugh themselves out of them before they feel that they're touched.

ZOROBABLE: But what thread or connection can you have in this history? For instance, how is your political connected with your theatrical?

FIELDING: O very easily—When my politics come to a farce, they very naturally lead me to the play-house, where, let me tell you, there're some politicians, too, where there's lying, flattering, dissembling, promising, deceiving, and undermining, as well as in any court in Christendom.

LUCY (*aside*): O la, I do love to hear this man talk. A rehearsal's a fine thing.—But Mr. Playwright, who's to be married?

FIELDING: Why, Madam, I have a marriage; I hope you think I understand the laws of comedy better than to write without marrying somebody.

FIRST PLAYER: Sir, the prologue's ready.

(*Enter* PLAYER *for the Prologue*.)

FIELDING: Come, Sir, make a very low bow to the audience; and shew as much concern as possible in your looks.

PLAYER (*speaks Prologue*):

> Bold is th'attempt in this nice-judging age
> To try at fame, by pleasing on the stage.
> So eager to condemn as you are grown,
> Writing seems war declar'd against the town.
> Which ever way the Poet seeks applause,
> The Critic's ready still to damn his cause.

FIELDING: Oh! dear sir, seem a little more affected, I beseech you; advance to the front of the stage, make a low bow, lay your hand upon your heart—for you're speaking to the Critics!—, fetch a deep sigh, and pull out your handkerchief. "If for new characters he hunts abroad. . ."

PLAYER:

> If for new characters he hunts abroad
> And boldy deviates from the beaten road,
> In monsters then unnatural he deals;
> If they are known and common, then he steals.
> If wit he aims at, you the traps can shew;
> If serious, he is dull, if humorous, low.
> Some would maintain one laugh throughout a play,
> Some would be grave, and bear fine things away.
> How is it possible at once to please
> Tastes so directly opposite as these?
> Nor be offended with us if we fear,
> From us—some seek not entertainment here.
> 'Tis not the Poet's wit affords the jest,
> But who can catcall, hiss, or whistle best!

MARPLAY JR.: That's a rare prophecy.

FIELDING: Pray go on.

ZOROBABLE: Is there more?

FIELDING: A few lines, in which I define the essence of farce.

PLAYER:

> As Tragedy prescribes to passion rules,
> So Comedy delights to punish fools;
> And while at nobler games she boldly flies,
> Farce challenges the vulgar as her prize.
> Some follies scarce perceptible appear
> In that just glass, which shews you as you are.
> But farce still claims a magnifying right
> To raise the object larger to the sight
> And shew her insect fools in stronger light.

ZOROBABLE: Methinks your man should breathe a bit stronger on the insect. That's a good word.

MARPLAY JR.: And you don't intend to flatter the audience?

FIELDING: No, Sir, for I flatter myself they shall like my play without it.

MARPLAY JR. (*aside*): And I flatter myself they won't. —

FIELDING: But, besides the prologue, I've a song to start my play; and as mine's the history of the year, what can be properer than an ode?

THE PLAYERS:

Air XXXIX (*see* Appendix)

> This is a day, in days of yore
>   Our fathers never saw before:
> This is a day, 'tis one to ten,
>   Our sons will never see again.
>   Then sing the day,
>   And sing the song,
>   And thus be merry
>   All day long.

> This is the day,
> And that's the night,
> When the moon shall be gay,
> And the sun shall be bright.

The sun shall rise,
All in the skies;
The moon shall go,
All down below.
Then sing the day,
And sing the song,
And thus be merry
All day long
Ay, ay, come on, and sing it away.

LUCY : Icod, that doesn't make much sense to me, Mr. Playwright.

FIELDING: Madam, there is very little sense in it. But I do like a good lively tune, and so, I think, does the audience. So our songs do not always have to make sense. Besides, you'll notice, by my saying this play is about a day such as was never seen, and'll never be seen again, I'm implying that everything in it is but fictitious.

ZOROBABLE: Is that necessary?

FIELDING: It is, Sir, under our present ministry. I should not want anyone in the ministry to think I meant him.

ZOROBABLE: Then it's all fictitious? Every part of it?

FIELDING: Ay, Sir, but it is drawn close to nature.

ZOROBABLE: I hope there's no harm in it, for I am a commercial man and prefer to be discreet. (*Sings.*)

LXXII

A man on business bound
Must be politically sound,
On the outs with the outs,
On the in with the ins;
Jump quick to the side
Of whoever wins,
It's the business man's tradition.
If you'd be rich,
Take heed to switch
At once from the opposition!

LUCY (*sings aside*):
A girl who's pleasure bound,
Must be politically sound,

For shows and beaux
And silken clothes
Are soon to be had
By the miss who knows
To say yes to a lord's petition;
If you'd advance
You should entrance
A man of high position!

ZOROBABLE (*sings aside*):
A man of many a pound,
When he is mistress-bound,
Though she be neat
On twinkling feet,
Should tell himself
To be discreet
In the business man's tradition.
When you're not rich,
She'll promply switch
From you to the opposition!

LUCY (*sings aside*):
In love, like politics,
A mistress never sticks
To the losing side;
She can't abide
A keeper poor
Who'll not provide
For her in the best tradition.
When in is out,
It's turnabout
For him and the opposition!

DUET (*but sung aside*):
Together, we are clever,
And never, never, never
Choose wrong, who might
Be choosing right. . .

LUCY: He likes his due-bills
         Paid on sight...
BOTH: That's quite the best provision.
LUCY: For he loves trade ...
ZOROBABLE: And she trades love ...
BOTH: In the business man's tradition!

MARPLAY JR.: And how do you begin, Mr. Fielding?

FIELDING: Mr. Marplay Jr., you'll observe that I don't begin this play, like most of our modern comedies, with three or four gentlemen who're brought on to talk wit; for, to tell you the truth, ladies and gentlemen, I've very little, if any, wit in this play. No, Sir, this's a play consisting of humor, nature, and simplicity. It's written, I believe, in the exact and true spirit of Molière: and this I'll say for it, that, except for about a dozen, or a score or so, there's not one impure joke in it. But come, clear the stage, and draw the back scene! Mr. Marplay Jr., if you please to sit down by me.

(MAYOR *and* ALDERMEN *discovered.*)

LUCY: Who're these characters?

FIELDING: Madam, they're Mr. Mayor of the town and his brethren, consulting about the election. Mr. Mayor, you begin.

MAYOR: Gentlemen, I have summoned you together to consider the proper representatives for this borough: you know the candidates on the court side are my Lord Place and Colonel Promise; the country candidates are Sir Henry Fox-chace and Squire Tankard; all worthy gentlemen, and I wish with all my heart we could choose all four.

FIRST ALDERMAN: But since we cannot, Mr. Mayor, I think we should stand by our neighbors; gentlemen whose honesty we are witnesses of, and whose estates in our own neighborhood render 'em not liable to be bribed.

MAYOR: Mr. Alderman, you've a narrow way of thinking; honesty's not confined to a country; a man that lives a hundred miles off may be as honest as him who lives but three.

ALDERMEN (*shaking their heads*): Ay, ay, ay, ay.

MAYOR: Besides, gentlemen, are we not more obliged to a foreigner for the favours he does us than to one of our own neighbors? For my part, I never saw or heard of either my lord or the colonel till within this fortnight; and yet they're as civil and familiar as if we had been born and bred together.

FIRST ALDERMAN: Nay, they are very civil, well-bred men, that's the truth on't.

MAYOR: But, mum! here are my lord and the colonel.

(*Enter* LORD PLACE *and* COLONEL PROMISE.)

LORD PLACE: Gentlemen, your most humble servant; I have brought the colonel to take a morning's whet with you.

MAYOR: Your lordship and the colonel do us great honour; pray, my lord, be pleased to sit down; pray, colonel, be pleased to sit. More wine here.

MARPLAY JR.: I wish, Mr. Fielding, your actors don't get drunk in the first act.

FIELDING: Dear sir, don't interrupt the rehearsal.

LORD PLACE: Gentlemen, prosperity to the borough!

MAYOR: My lord, we're sensible of your great power to serve this borough.

LORD PLACE: Gentlemen, you may depend on me; I shall do all in my power. I shall do you some services which are not proper at present to mention to you; in the meantime, Mr. Mayor, give me leave to squeeze you by the hand, in assurance of my sincerity.

FIELDING: You, Mr., that act my lord, bribe a little more openly, if you please, or the audience will lose that joke, and it's one of the strongest in my whole play.

LORD PLACE: Sir, I cannot possibly do it better at the table.

FIELDING: Then all get up, and come forward to the front of the stage. Now, you gentlemen that act the mayor and aldermen, range yourselves in a line; and you, my lord and the colonel, come to one end and bribe away with right and left.

LUCY: Is this wit, Mr. Fielding?

FIELDING: Yes, it is wit; and such wit as will run all over the kingdom. Gentlemen, are you all bribed?

OMNES: Yes, Sir.

FIELDING: Then, my lord and the colonel, you must go off and make room for the other candidates to come on and bribe too.

(*Exeunt* PLACE *and* PROMISE.)

[210]

ZOROBABLE: Is there nothing but bribery in this play of yours, Mr. Fielding?

FIELDING: Sir, this play's an exact representation of nature; I hope the audience will date the time of action before the bill of bribery and corruption took place; but now, Mr. Marplay Jr., I shall shew you the art of a writer, which is, to diversify his matter, and do the same thing several ways. You must know, Sir, I distinguish bribery into two kinds, the direct and the indirect: the first you've seen already; and now, Sir, I shall give you a small specimen of the other. Prompter, call Sir Harry and the Squire. But, gentlemen, what're you doing? How often shall I tell you that the moment the candidates are gone out you are to retire to the table, and drink and look wise; you, Mr. Mayor, ought to look very wise.

LUCY: And he does, truly.

MAYOR (to her): Thank'ee, ma'am. (to the others) Come, here's a round to my lord and the colonel's health; a Place and a Promise, I say!

FIELDING: Come, enter Sir Harry and the Squire. Where are they?

(Enter SIR HARRY and SQUIRE.)

SIR HARRY: Halloo, hark forwards; hark, honest Ned, good-morrow to you; how dost, Master Mayor? What, are you driving it about merrily this morning? Come, come, sit down; the squire and I will take a pot with you. Come, Mr. Mayor, here's—liberty, and property, and no taxes.

MAYOR: Sir Harry, your health.

SIR HARRY: What, won't you pledge me? Won't you drink no taxes?

MAYOR: I don't love party healths, Sir Harry.

ALL ALDERMEN: No, no; no party healths, no party healths.

SIR HARRY: Say ye so, gentlemen? I begin to smoke you; your pulses have been felt, I perceive: and will you be bribed to sell your country? Where do you think these courtiers get the money they bribe you with, but from yourselves? Do you think a man who will give a bribe won't take one? If you would be served faithfully, you must choose faithfully, and give your vote on no consideration but merit.

MAYOR: I do believe you, Sir Harry.

SIR HARRY: Mr. Mayor, I hope you received those three gifts of venison I sent you, and that they were good.

MAYOR: Sir Harry, I thank you for them; but 'tis so long since I ate them that I have forgot the taste.

SIR HARRY: We'll try to revive it—I'll order you three more to-morrow morning.

MAYOR: You'll surfeit us with venison: you will indeed; for it's a dry meat, Sir Harry, a very dry meat.

SIR HARRY: We'll find a way to moisten it, I'll warrant you, if there be any wine in town. Mr. Alderman Stitch, your bill is too reasonable; you certainly must lose by it: send me in a half-dozen more greatcoats, pray. Mr. Timber, I shall get into your books too.

FIELDING: Go on, go on, Sir.

SIR HARRY: For you must know, gentlemen, that I intend to pull down my old house, and build a new one.

FIELDING: Pray, gentlemen, observe all to start at the word *house*.

MAYOR: Gentlemen, methinks Sir Harry's toast still stands; will nobody drink liberty, property, and no taxes?

(*They all drink and huzza.*)

SIR HARRY: Give me thy hand, mayor; I hate bribery and corruption: if this borough will not suffer itself to be bribed, there shall not be a poorman in it.

FIRST ALDERMAN: Come, gentlemen, here's a Fox-chace and a Tankard!

OMNES: A Fox-chace and a Tankard! huzza!

FIELDING: This is the end of the first scene, Sir.

LUCY: Is this all a play is? Why it's just the same as when Squire Jones and Squire Western were our candidates last year.

FIELDING: My next scene, Sirs, lies in the island of Corsica, being at present the chief scene of politics of all Europe. I call it "The Coffee-house Politicians".

(*Scene draws and discovers* MR. POLITIC *at a table reading the news-papers. To him:* MR. DABBLE.)

MR. POLITIC: Mr. Dabble, good morrow.

DABBLE: Are the mails come in?

MR. POLITIC: Just arrived.

DABBLE: I've not slept one wink for reflecting on what you told me last night about the Continental situation; perhaps this Dutch mail may give some insight into those affairs. But what says the Lying Post?

MR. POLITIC: I've had no time to read it yet, I wish you would. I have only read the London Journal, the Country Journal, the Weekly Journal, Applebee's Journal, the British Journal, the British Gazetteer, the Morning Post, the Coffee-House Morning Post, the Daily Post-boy, the Daily Journal, the Daily Courant, the Evening Post, and the St. James's Evening Post. So, if you please, begin the Lying Post.

MARPLAY JR.: Am I to believe all these papers are received in Corsica?

FIELDING: Why not, Sir? Why not?

DABBLE (reads): "Moscow, January the 5th. We learn from Constantinople that affairs continue still in the same doubtful way: it's not yet known what course our court will take. The Empress having been slightly indisposed, the other day, took the air in her own coach, and returned so well recovered, that she eat a very hearty supper."—

MR. POLITIC: Hum!—There's no mention of the supper in any other papers.

DABBLE:—"Berlin, January the 20th. We hear daily murmurs here concerning certain measures taken by a certain northern potentate; but cannot certainly learn either who that potentate is, or what are the measures which he hath taken—meantime we are well assured that time will bring them all to light."

MR. POLITIC: Pray read that last over again.

DABBLE: "Meantime, we are assured that time, &c."

MR. POLITIC: Hum! hum!

DABBLE: "Marseilles, January the 18th. The affairs in regard to Italy continue in the same uncertain condition."

MR. POLITIC: Hum!

DABBLE: "The talk of a large embarkation still runs high."

MR. POLICIC: Hum!

DABBLE: "The Spaniards continue still encamped near Barcelona."

MR. POLITIC: Hum! (Shakes his head.)

DABBLE: "And everything seems tending to a rupture—meantime

we expect the return of a courier from Vienna, who, 'tis generally expected, will bring the news of a general pacification."

MR. POLITIC: All's well again!

DABBLE: I like this, and some other papers, who disappoint you with good news. Where the beginning of a paragraph threatens you with war, and the latter part of it ensures you peace.

MR. POLITIC: Please to read on—

DABBLE: "However, notwithstanding these assurances, 'tis doubted by most people, whether the said courier will not rather bring a confirmation of war; but this's all guess work, and, until such time as we see an actual hostility committed, we must leave our readers in the same uncertain state we found them."

ZOROBABLE: Methinks this can go on forever.

FIELDING: So it can, Sir; so let's call a halt. Read no farther, gentlemen, if you please. I have observ'd, in the past ten years, the dawnings of this political humour among some of our people. They spend all their time reading the papers. Why, were their wives to leave them, or their daughters be seduced and ruin'd, I do not believe they themselves would credit it, unless they read that too in the papers. The greatest part of mankind labour under one delirium or other: and Don Quixotte differed from the rest, not in madness, but the species of it. The covetous, the prodigal, the superstitious, and the coffee-house politican, are all Quixottes in their several ways.

FIELDING, LUCY, OMNES:

Air XL: *Country Bumpkin*

FIELDING: All mankind are mad, 'tis plain;

> Some for places,
> Some embraces;
> Some are mad to keep up gain,
> And others made to spend it.
> Courtiers we may madmen rate,
> Poor believers
> In deceivers;
> Some are mad to hurt the state,
> And others mad to mend it.

> Lawyers are for bedlam fit,
>   Or they never
>   Could endeavour
> Half the rogueries to commit.
> Which we're so mad to let 'em.
> Poets madmen are no doubt,
>   With projectors,
>   And directors;

LUCY: Women are all mad throughout—

OMNES: And we more mad to get 'em?

(*Dance here.*)

LUCY: Mr. Playwright, you promis'd us a marriage.

FIELDING: I did, Madam, I did.

LUCY: But so far, we've seen no ladies at all.

FIELDING: True, Madam, true. Do you think I'm like your shallow writers of comedy, who publish the bans of marriage between all the couples in their play in the first act? No, Madam, I defy you to guess my couple till the thing's done, slap all at once; and that too by an incident arising from the main business of the play, and to which everything conduces.

ZOROBABLE: That will, indeed, surprise me.

FIELDING: Sir, you're not the first man my writings have surprised. But since you asked for ladies, Madam, we shall have a council of them now.

LUCY: Does this scene lie in Corsica too?

FIELDING: No, no, this lies in London—(*to Zorobable*) You know, Sir, it would not have been quite so proper to have brought English politicians (of the male kind, I mean) on the stage, because our politics are not quite so famous: but in female politicians, to the honour of my countrywomen I say it, I believe no country can excel us; come, draw the scene and discover the ladies.

(*The scene draws and discovers four ladies.*)

ZOROBABLE: What're these ladies assembled about?

FIELDING: Affairs of great importance, as you'll see—Please to begin all of you.

(*The ladies all speak together.*)

ALL LADIES: Was you at the opera, Madam, last night?

[215]

SECOND LADY: Who can miss an opera while Farinello stays?

THIRD LADY: Sure he's the charmingest creature.

FOURTH LADY: He's everything in the world one could wish.

FIRST LADY: Almost everything one could wish.

SECOND LADY: They say there's a lady in the city has a child by him.

ALL LADIES: Ha, ha, ha!

LUCY (aside): That's just how Miss Tawdry told me to do it.

FIRST LADY: Well, it must be charming to have a child by him.

MARPLAY JR.: Mr. Fielding, Sir, is this history?

FIELDING: Upon my word, Sir, it's fact. I take it to be ominous, for if we go on to improve in luxury, effeminacy and debauchery, as we've done lately, the next age, aught I know, may be more like the children of squeaking Italians than hardy Britons.

ALL LADIES: Don't interrupt us, dear Sir.

LUCY (aside): I must meet one of these Italians. There was one at Mrs. Midnight's, but all he did was sing.

FIELDING: Come, enter Beau Dangle.

(Enter DANGLE.)

DANGLE: Fie upon it, Ladies, what're you doing here? Why are you not at the auction? Mr. Hen will be in his pulpit a half hour by the time you get there.

FIRST LADY: O, dear Mr. Hen, I never miss him.

SECOND LADY: What's to be sold today?

FIRST LADY: Oh, I never mind that; there'll be all the world there.

DANGLE: You'll find it almost impossible to get in.

ALL LADIES: Oh, I shall be quite miserable if I don't get in.

FIELDING: There, they're gone to the auction.

MARPLAY JR.: I am glad on't with all my heart.

ZOROBABLE: Upon my word, Mr. Fielding, that last's an exceeding good scene, and full of a great deal of politeness, good sense, and philosophy.

LUCY (aside): Were these fine ladies?

FIELDING: It's nature; it's nature.

ZOROBABLE: Faith, Sir, the ladies are much obliged to you.

FIELDING: That's more than I desire such ladies, as I represent here, should be; as for the nobler part of the sex, for whom I have the greatest honour, their characters can be no better set off, than by ridiculing that light, trifling, giddy-headed crew, who're a scandal to their own sex, and a curse on ours.

ZOROBABLE: I should like to ask you, Mr. Fielding, the same question which one of your ladies did just now; what do you intend to sell at this auction, the whole stock in trade of some milliner or mercer who's left off business?

FIELDING: I intend to sell such things as were never sold in any auction before, nor ever will again: I can assure you, this scene, which I look upon as the best in the whole performance, will require a very deep attention, Sir; if you should take one pinch of snuff during the whole scene, you'll lose a joke by it; and yet they lie pretty deep too, and may escape observation from a moderate understanding, unless very closely attended to.

ZOROBABLE: I hope, however, they don't lie as deep as the dumb gentleman's politics did in the second act; if so, nothing but an inspir'd understanding can come at 'em.

PROMPTER: Sir, everything's ready.

FIELDING: Then draw up the curtain—Come, enter the ladies.

(*Scene: an Auction room: a pulpit and Forms placed: and several People walking about: some seated near the Pulpit. Enter* DANGLE *and the Ladies.*)

FIRST LADY: Dear Mrs. Barter.

SECOND LADY: Dear Madam, you're early today!

FIRST LADY: Oh, if one doesn't get near the pulpit, one does nothing, and I intend to buy a great deal today. You won't bid against me?

SECOND LADY: You know I never bid for anything.

(*Enter* MR. HEN, *Auctioneer. Bowing.*)

THIRD LADY: Oh! dear Mr. Hen, I'm glad you're come, you're horrible late today.

HEN: I'm just mounting the pulpit; I hope you like the catalogue, Ladies?

DANGLE: Boy, give me a catalogue.

HEN (*in the pulpit*): I dare swear, Gentlemen and Ladies, this auction'll give general satisfaction; it's the first of its kind which I ever had the honour to exhibit, and I believe I may challenge the world to produce some of the curiosities which this choice cabinet contains. A catalogue of curiosities, collected by that celebrated virtuoso, Peter Humdrum, Esq., which'll be sold by auction, by Christopher Hen, on Monday, the twenty-first day of March, beginning at lot 1. Gentlemen and Ladies, this's lot 1. A most curious remnant of Political Honesty. Who puts it up, Gentlemen? It'll make you a very good cloak, you see it's both sides alike, so you may turn it as often as you will—Come, five pounds for this curious remnant: I assure you several great men have made their birth-day suits out of the same piece— It'll wear forever, and never be the worse for wearing—Five pounds's bid—nobody more than five pounds for this curious piece of Political Honesty, five pounds, no more—? (*Knocks*) Lord Both-sides. Lot 2. A most delicate piece of Patriotism. Gentlemen, who bids? ten pounds for this piece of Patriotism?

FIRST COURTIER: I wouldn't wear it for a thousand pounds.

HEN: Sir, I assure you, several gentlemen at court have worn the same; it's quite a different thing within to what it is without.

FIRST COURTIER: Sir, it's prohibited goods, I shan't run the risk of wearing it.

HEN: You take it for the Old Patriotism, whereas it's indeed like that in nothing but the cut; but alas, Sir, there's a great difference in the stuff—But, Sir, I don't propose this for a town-suit, this is only proper for the country; consider, Gentlemen, what a figure this'll make at an election—Come, five pounds—one guinea—put Patriotism by.

FIELDING: Ay, put it by, one day or other it may be in fashion.

HEN: Lot 3. Three grains of Modesty: Come, Ladies, consider how scarce this valuable commodity is!

FIRST LADY: Yes, Mr. Hen, and out of fashion too.

HEN: I ask your pardon, Madam, it's true French, I assure you, and never changes colour on any account—Half a crown for all this Modesty—Is there not one lady in the room who wants any Modesty?

SECOND LADY: Pray, Sir, what is it? for I can't see it at this distance.

HEN: It cannot be seen at any distance, Madam, but it's a beautiful powder which makes a fine wash for the complexion.

FIRST LADY: I thought you said it was true French, and wouldn't change the colour of the skin?

HEN: No, it will not, Madam; but it serves mighty well to blush

behind a fan with, or to wear under a lady's mask at a masquerade—
What, nobody bid—Well, lay Modesty aside—Lot 4. One bottle
of Courage, formerly in the possession of Lieutenant-colonel Ezekiel
Pipkin, citizen, alderman and tallow-chandler—

FIRST OFFICER: Is the bottle whole? is there no crack in it?

HEN: None, Sir, I assure you—it'll never waste while you stay at
home, but it evaporates immediately if carried abroad.

FIRST OFFICER: Three shillings for it.

HEN: Three shillings are bid for this bottle of Courage.

DANGLE: Four.

FIRST COURTIER: What do you bid for Courage for?

DANGLE: Not for myself, but I've a commission to buy it for a
lady.

FIRST OFFICER: Five.

HEN: Five shillings, five shillings for all this Courage; nobody
more than five shillings? (*knocks*) Your name, Sir?

FIRST OFFICER: Mackdonald O'Thunder.

HEN : Lot 5, and Lot 6. All the Wit lately belonging to Mr. Hugh
Pantomime, composer of entertainments for the play-houses, and
Mr. William Goosequill, composer of political papers in defence
of a ministry; shall I put these up together?

FIRST COURTIER: Ay, it's a pity to part them, where are they?

HEN: Sir, in the next room, where any gentleman may see them,
but they're too heavy to bring in; they are near three hundred volumes
in folio.

FIRST COURTIER: Put them by, who the devil would bid for them,
unless he was the manager of some theatre or other? The town has
paid enough for their works already.

HEN: Lot 7. A very clear Conscience, which has been worn by a
judge and a bishop.

FIRST LADY: Is it as clean as if it was new?

HEN: Yes, no dirt'll stick to it, and pray observe how capacious it is;
it has one particular quality, put as much as you will into it, it's never
full; come, Gentlemen, don't be afraid to bid for this, for whoever
has it will never be poor.

DANGLE: One shilling for it.

HEN: O fie, Sir, I'm sure you need it, for if you'd any Conscience,

H　　　　　　　　　[219]

you'd put it up at more than that: come, fifty pound for this Conscience.

DANGLE: I'll give fifty pound to get rid of my Conscience, with all my heart.

HEN: Well, Gentlemen, I see you're resolv'd not to bid for it, so I'll lay it by: come, lot 8, a very considerable quantity of Interest at Court; come, a hundred pounds for this Interest at Court.

OMNES: For me, Mr. Hen.

HEN: A hundred pound's bid in a hundred places, Gentlemen.

DANGLE: Two hundred pound.

HEN: Two hundred pound, two hundred and fifty, three hundred pound, three hundred and fifty, four hundred, five hundred, six hundred, a thousand; a thousand pound's bid, Gentlemen; nobody more than a thousand pounds for this Interest at Court; nobody more than one thousand? (*knocks*) Mr. Littlewit.

DANGLE: Damn me, I know a shop where I can buy it for less.

ZOROBABLE: Egad, you took me in, Mr. Fielding, I couldn't help bidding for it.

FIELDING: It's a sure sign it's nature, Sir, and I shouldn't be surpris'd to see the whole audience stand up and bid for it too.

HEN: All the Cardinal Virtues, lot 9. Come, Gentlemen, put in these Cardinal Virtues.

DANGLE: Eighteen pence.

HEN: Eighteen pence's bid for these Cardinal Virtues; nobody more than eighteen pence? Eighteen pence for all these Cardinal Virtues, nobody more? All these Virtues, Gentlemen, are going for eighteen pence; perhaps there's not so much more Virtue in the world, as here is, and all going for eighteen pence. (*knocks*) Beau Dangle.

DANGLE: Sir, here's a mistake; I thought you had said a Cardinal's virtues; 'sblood, Sir, I thought to've bought a pennyworth; here Temperance and Chastity, and a pack of stuff that I wouldn't give three farthings for.

(*The curtains draw.*)

ZOROBABLE: Yours is certainly a modern comedy, Mr. Fielding.

MARPLAY JR.: Modern, why modern? Your common-place satirists are always endeavouring to persuade us that the age we live in is worse than any other has been, whereas mankind have differ'd very little since the world began; for one age has been as bad as another.

FIELDING: Sir, I don't deny that men've always been bad enough; vice and folly are not the invention of our age.

ZOROBABLE (*aside*): This play is damn'd stuff surely.

(*Enter* CANTILENO.)

CANTILENO: Mr. Fielding, your servant. And a thousand apologies I'm very late.

FIELDING: Fie upon't, fie upon't, make no excuses.

CANTILENO: Consider, Sir, I'm my own enemy.

LUCY (*aside*): Gemini cancer, it's the Italian singer.

CANTILENO: Lord Bawble, your servant. And Lady Bawble, I presume.

ZOROBABLE (*aside*): How does this happen? Mr. Marplay must've been at him.—If I'm Lord Bawble, you may expect this to be my lady.

FIELDING (*aside*): I don't know what's his game, but surely imposture is no new phenomenon in the town. He has picked a strange part. I've known lords to borrow money, but I've never known them to lend any.

LUCY (*aside*): Lady Bawble. By goles! How gentle that sounds!

CANTILENO: Really this's a very bad house.

FIELDING: It's indeed not so large as the others, but I think one hears better in it.

CANTILENO: Pox of hearing, as you English say; one can't see— one's self, I mean; here're no looking-glasses; I love Lincoln's Inn Fields for that reason better than any house in town.

ZOROBABLE: Ay, ay, I could say that too. A man's coat is wasted on him here.

LUCY (*aside*): Such a pretty coat! I should like to see my Thomas in a coat like that.

FIELDING: Very truly, my Lord; but I wish your lordship would think our project worthy your consideration; as the morals of a people depend, as has been so often said and well prov'd, entirely on the public diversions, it'd be of the greatest consequence that those of the sublimest kind should meet with your lordship's and the rest of the nobility's countenance.

ZOROBABLE (*aside*): Why I can, if the occasion calls, speak as well as any lord!—Sir, I'm always ready to give my countenance to anything of that kind.

FIELDING (*aside*): What airs this moneylender puts on!—No one's a better judge of what's a good play than your lordship.

LUCY (*aside*): La, what polite conversation!

ZOROBABLE: Not I, indeed, Mr. Fielding—but as I'm one half of the play in the Green-room talking to the actresses, and the other half in the boxes talking to the women of quality, I have an opportunity of seeing something of the play, and perhaps may be as good a judge as another.

FIELDING (*aside*): There's lordly wisdom in that answer.

CANTILENO: I hope I've not miss'd much—

FIELDING: The play's partly over, but the plot's just beginning to open.

MARPLAY JR.: Isn't the fifth scene a little late to open the plot, Mr Fielding?

FIELDING: Perhaps, but 'tis an error on the right side: I've known a plot to open in the first act, and the audience, and the poet too, to forget it before the third was over: now, Sir, I'm not willing to burden either the audience's memory or my own. Madam, thank you for your applause of my last scene. I have promis'd you a marriage, and now you shall have it. The romance, which has hitherto been only carried on by hints, and opened itself like the infant spring by small and imperceptible degrees to the audience, will display itself like a ripe matron, in its full summer's bloom; and cannot, I think, fail with its attractive charms, like a lodestone, to catch the admiration of everyone like a trap, and raise an applause like thunder, till it makes the whole house like a hurricane. I must desire a strict silence through this whole scene. (*The curtains withdraw and discover* COLONEL PROMISE *and a young lady*.) Sir, stand you still on this side of the stage; and, miss, do you stand on the opposite.—There, now look at each other. (*A long silence here*.)

LUCY: Pray, Mr. Fielding, is nobody ever to speak again?

FIELDING: Oh! the devil! You've interrupted the scene; after all my precautions the scene's destroyed; the best scene of silence that was ever penned by man.

ZOROBABLE: Would it be too much to ask, Mr. Fielding, who these lovers are supposed to be?

FIELDING: Why, Sir, this's Colonel Promise, who appear'd in my first scene—

ZOROBABLE: Ay, but you've had the same actors appear in so many parts, how's a man supposed to know anything of that?

FIELDING: It shall all be revealed again.

CANTILENO: And the young Lady? Who's she?

FIELDING: Why, the mayor's daughter. (*to the players*) Come, come, you may speak now; you may speak as fast as you please.

COLONEL PROMISE: Madam, the army's very much obliged to you for the zeal you shew for it; me, it has made your slave forever; nor can I ever think of being happy unless you consent to marry me.

LUCY: Oh! It is pretty, Mr. Fielding.

MISS MAYOR: Ha! and can you be so generous to forgive all my ill usage of you?

ZOROBABLE: What ill usage, Mr. Fielding! For, if I mistake not, this's the first time these two lovers spoke to one another.

FIELDING: What ill usage, Sir? a great deal, Sir.

LUCY: When? where?

FIELDING: Why, behind the scenes. What, would you have everything brought upon the stage? I intend to bring ours to the dignity of the French stage; and I have Horace's advice on my side. We've many things both said and done in our comedies which might be better performed behind the scenes: the French, you know, banish all cruelty from their stage; and I don't see why we should bring on a lady in ours practising all manner of cruelty upon her lover: besides, Sir, we don't only produce it, but encourage it; for I could name you some comedies, if I would, where a woman's brought in for four acts together, behaving to a worthy man in a manner for which she almost deserves to be hanged; and in the fifth, forsooth, she's rewarded with him for a husband: now, as I know this hits some tastes, and am willing to oblige all, I've given every lady the latitude of thinking mine has behaved in whatever manner she would have her.

CANTILENO: Pray let's have the scene.

FIELDING: Go on, miss, if you please.

MISS MAYOR: I've struggled with myself to put you to so many trials of your constancy: nay, perhaps have indulged myself a little too far in the innocent liberties of abusing you, tormenting you, coquetting, lying, and jilting; which as you are so good to forgive, I do faithfully promise to make you all the amends in my power, by making you a good wife.

FIELDING: That single promise, gentlemen, is more than any of my brother authors had ever the grace to put into the mouth of any of their fine ladies yet.

CANTILENO: Faith, Signor Fielding, you're right.

COLONEL PROMISE: And can you be so generous, so great, so good? Oh! could I live a hundred thousand years, I never could repay the bounty of that last speech! Oh! my paradise!

FIELDING: Open your arms, miss, if you please; remember you're no coquette now: how pretty this looks! Let me have one of your best embraces, I desire: do it once more, pray—There, there, that's pretty well; you must practise this behind the scenes.

(*Enter* MAYOR *and* MRS. MAYORESS.)

COLONEL PROMISE *and* MISS MAYORESS (*kneeling*): Sir, and Madam, your blessing.

MAYOR and MRS MAYOR: Ha!

LUCY: What, are they married already?

FIELDING: Ay, they are, if you please.

ZOROBABLE: Upon my word, they've been very expeditious.

FIELDING: Yes, Sir; the parson understands his business; he has plyed several years at the Fleet.

COLONEL PROMISE: Your daughter, Sir and Madam, has made me the happiest of mankind.

MAYOR: Colonel, you know you might have had my consent; why did you choose to marry without it? However, I give you both my blessing.

(*Enter* LORD PLACE.)

LORD PLACE: Then call my brother candidates; we'll spend this night in feast and merriment.

MARPLAY JR.: What has made these two parties so suddenly friends?

FIELDING: What? why the marriage; the usual reconciler at the end of a comedy. This, Sir, has been, I think, a very pretty pantomime trick. But, then, the public want pantomime tricks and nothing else, it seems.

(*The curtains draw apart. The company appears.*)

CHORUS:

Air XLVIII: *Abbot of Canterbury*

You wonder, perhaps, at the tricks of the stage,
Or that pantomime miracles take with the age;
But if you examine court, country, and town,
There's nothing but harlequin feats will go down.
Derry down, &c.

From Fleet-street to Limehouse the city's his range,
He's a saint in his shop, and a knave on the Change;
At an oath, or a jest, like a censor he'll frown,
But a lie or a cheat slip currently down,
Derry down, &c.

In the country he burns with a politic zeal,
And boasts, like knight-errant, to serve commonweal;
But once return'd member, he alters his tone,
For, as long as he rises, no matter who's down,
Derry down, &c.

At court, 'tis as hard to confine him as air,
Like a troublesome spirit he's here and he's there;
All shapes and disguises at pleasure puts on,
And defies all the nation to conjure him down,
Derry down, &c.

FIELDING: And so ends my play, my farce, or what you please to call it; may I hope it has your approbation?

ZOROBABLE: A bit on the quiet side, methinks, but pretty, indeed, very pretty.

FIELDING: And that Madam hasn't found the rehearsal too dull?

LUCY: Nay, I lik'd best the marriage, and the kissing and hugging.

CANTILENO: It'll be the vogue, I'faith. It'll be the vogue.

FIELDING: I pray so. And now I must go to the publisher, to see about having my play printed, and perhaps your lordship and my lady would care to accompany me, if they've never yet been to see a publisher?

LUCY: O la! Shall I see a book printed?

FIELDING: No, but you may see one written.

(*Enter* MR. BOOKWEIGHT.)

BOOKWEIGHT: Madam, and gentlemen, your servant. This's Mr. Fielding?

FIELDING (to Lucy): This's my publisher now. He waits upon me.

BOOKWEIGHT: I was told, Sir, that you had particular business with me.

FIELDING: Yes, Mr. Bookweight; I've something to put into your hands. A play.

BOOKWEIGHT: Is it accepted, Sir?

FIELDING: Ay, Sir.

BOOKWEIGHT: That's all right, then. A play, like a bill, is of no value until it is accepted; nor indeed when it is, very often. Besides, Sir, our playhouses are grown so plenty, and our actors so scarce, that really plays are become very bad commodities.

FIELDING: That's because all our players have become pantomime actors.

BOOKWEIGHT: You're in the right of that. But a play which'll do on the stage will not always do for us; there're your acting plays and your reading plays.

FIELDING: I do not understand that distinction.

BOOKWEIGHT: Why, Sir, your acting play is entirely supported by the merit of the actor; in which case, it signifies very little whether there be any sense in it or not. Now, your reading play's of a different stamp, and must have wit and meaning in it. These latter I call your substantive, as being able to support themselves. The former are your adjective, as what require the buffoonery and gestures of an actor to be joined with them to shew their signification.

ZOROBABLE: Very learnedly defined, truly.

FIELDING: Well, but, Mr. Bookweight, will you advance fifty guineas on my play?

BOOKWEIGHT: Fifty guineas! Yes, sir. You shall have them with all my heart, if you'll give me security for them. Fifty guineas for a play! Sir, I wouldn't give fifty shillings.

FIELDING: 'Sdeath, Sir! do you beat me down at this rate?

BOOKWEIGHT: No, nor fifty farthings. Fifty guineas! Indeed your name is well worth that.

FIELDING: You see, Madam, what're the rewards of authorship in our age.

[226]

LUCY: Well, you may have this, if it is worth anything to you. (*She kisses him.*)

CURTAIN

(During the change of scene, FIELDING, MARPLAY, MARPLAY JUNIOR, and MR. BOOKWEIGHT may appear before the curtains, and—with Mr. Bookweight maintaining in silence an appearance of obstinacy—the others may sing Air XLIX, to the tune of *Ye Commons and Peers:*)

FIELDING: How unhappy's the fate
     To live by one's pate,
     And be force to write hackney for bread!

MARPLAY JR.: An author's a joke
     To all manner of folk,

TRIO: Wherever he pops up his head, his head,
     Wherever he pops up his head.

MARPLAY SR.: Tho' he mount on that hack,
     Old Pegasus' back,
     And of Helicon drink till he burst,

FIELDING: Yet a curse of those streams,
     Poetical dreams,

TRIO: They never can quench one's thirst, &c.

FIELDING: Ah! how should he fly
     On fancy so high,
     When his limbs are in durance and hold?

MARPLAY JR.: Or how should he charm,
     With genius so warm,

TRIO: When his poor naked body's a cold, &c.
(MR. BOOKWEIGHT, *still adamant: leads them off.*)

SCENE TWO: *At the couturière's.* THE COUTURIÈRE, MR. ZOROBABLE, LUCY, MASTER COUPEE, SIGNOR CANTILENO, *the* LOTTERY SELLER, JEWELLER, *the* MASK-MAKER, *and* MANEQUINS.

THE COUTURIÈRE: I shall do as your worship requires and see that my lady's equipped as a woman of quality.

(MR. ZOROBABLE *waves a handful of bank-notes. The music begins softly. The manequins and tradesmen bring forward their offerings.*)

THE COMPANY:

Air LVI (*see* Appendix)

THE MASK-MAKER:

Does my lady wish a mask? I've a very pretty
mask, for my lady.

THE COUTURIÈRE:

Does my lady wish a gown? I've a very pretty
gown, for my lady.

OMNES:

Does my lady wish the town? We've a very pretty
town, for my lady.

LUCY:

I think this town is very fair,
And better far than country air!

OMNES:

Oh, my lady!

THE JEWELLER:

Does my lady wish a ring? I've a very pretty
ring, for my lady.

CANTILENO:

Does my lady wish to sing? I've a pretty song
to sing, to my lady.

LUCY:

If I had my choice,
I'd take your voice,
It's the very sweetest thing!

[228]

OMNES:

    Oh, my lady!

LUCY:

    I think this town is very fair,
    And better far than country air!

OMNES:

    Oh, my lady!

LOTTERY SELLER:

    Does my lady wish a chance? I've a very lucky
        chance, for my lady.

MASTER COUPEE:

    Does my lady wish to dance? I've a very pretty
        dance, for my lady.

LUCY:

    If I had my way,
    I'd dance all day,
      The country is dull, but the town is gay!

OMNES:

    Oh, my lady!
    My pretty lady!

(BALLET, *with solo dances by* LUCY *and* MASTER COUPEE. LUCY, *helped by the manequins: makes her pantomimic selections. Reprise of air by* CANTILENO. *The* COUTURIÈRE *adds up Lucy's purchases: gestures to* MR. ZOROBABLE, *and they exit. Enter* LORD FORMAL.)

LORD FORMAL: Ah, my dear! I knew where to find you. Have you purchas'd all these things? But I can take you to another place, twice as fine, and buy you gowns that cost twice as much.

LUCY (*aside*): O la! What shall I do?

LORD FORMAL: Just say you're going down to your chair, my dear. But, quite by chance, step into my chair, which's the next to it. I shall follow you. Then I shall bring you back here in an hour.

LUCY: This's the purest sport. I think I shall do it!

(*She runs off.* LORD FORMAL *is surrounded by the manequins: each competing for his attention.*)

[229]

LORD FORMAL: Zounds! My wife should see me! Nay, I cannot help myself!

Reprise

LORD FORMAL: A man, if he is truly wise,
   Will stay away from women;
  But damn my eyes, if I am wise,
   I fear I'm merely human.

OMNES: You never spoke more true, man!

LORD FORMAL: Oh Venus without arms for me
  Is Venus without charms for me,
   A goddess cold in stone;
  My goddess must be kind to me
  To warrant her divinity—

CANTILENO: I'll say that for my own!

LORD FORMAL: Oh woman is meant for love,
   And love is meant for woman,
  And though, in fine, she be divine,
   She must then prove she's human.

OMNES: Oh woman is meant for love,
   And love is meant for woman,
  And though, in fine, she be divine,
   She must then prove she's human!

CANTILENO: I'll say that for me too, man!

CURTAIN

(*During the change of scenes: three manequins may appear before the curtains and sing:*)

Air XIII: *Bessy Bell and Mary Gray*

In long pig-tails and shining lace,
  Our beaus set out a-wooing,
Ye maidens, never shew them grace,
  But laugh at their pursuing.
But let the daw, that shines so bright,
  Of borrow'd plumes bereft be,
Alas! poor beaus, how bare the sight!
  You'll find there's nothing left ye.

[230]

(*Enter* LORD FORMAL *with* CANTILENO. *The manequins see them and run off laughing.*)

LORD FORMAL: Where's the minx that was to be in my chair! She's got away from me.

CANTILENO: Again?

LORD FORMAL: That's no country girl. Old Midnight did not tell me truly. (*Sings.*)

Air XXXI: *Black Joke*

The more we see of human kind,
The more deceits and tricks we find,
   In every land, as well as Wales:
For would he ever hope to thrive,
Upon the mountains he would live,
   For rogues abound in all the vales.
The miser and the man will trick,
The mistress and the maid will nick.
    For rich and poor
    Are rogue and whore;
There's not one honest man in a score,
Nor woman true in twenty-four.

Nay, my Italian friend, to be disappointed twice in one day is enough. I'll have no more! (*Exits.*)

CANTILENO (*solus*): He's grown used to disappointment, I'll warrant. It's easy to be a cynic about women, when you've had as many of them as he's had. A plague on his cynicism, then!

Air XXXIV: *Sir Thomas: I cannot*

The worn-out rake at pleasure rails,
   And cries, 'Tis all idle and fleeting;
At court, the man whose int'rest fails,
   Cries, All is corruption and cheating.
    But would you know
    Whence both these flow?
Tho' so much they pretend to abhor 'em,
    That rails at court,
    This at love's sport,

Because they are neither fit for 'em,
fit for 'em,
Because they are neither fit for 'em.

(*Exits.*)

SCENE THREE: *The street.* MR. BALLAD *and* MR. SOTMORE.

BALLAD:

Air XXVIII (*see* Appendix)

I must be sad tonight, I think,
My lips would taste of more than drink.
Ah, gentlemen, a sorry toast,
A bed to friends, a health to kings!
Sack will not red a tavern boast
With blushes and with murmurings!
No more! Kick back the bench!
The glass may frowse until the air
Has pricked and blown the yellow bubbles—
Canary cannot cure despair,
Wine will not wink heart's sober troubles—
And I am following after
The whiter skin, a melting wench
Who'll cozen me with laughter!

SOTMORE: Why, thou wilt not leave us yet, and sneak away again to some nasty little whore?

BALLAD: The dear charming creatures! Woman! It is the best word that ever was invented. There's music, there's magic in it. Mark Antony knew well to lay out his money, and when he gave the world for a woman—he bought a lumping pennyworth.

SOTMORE: If he'd given it for a hogshead of good claret, I would have commended the purchase more.

BALLAD: Wine's only the prologue to love: it only serves to raise our expectations. The bottle is but a passport to the bed of pleasure. Brutes drink to quench their appetites—but lovers to enflame them.

SOTMORE: 'Tis pity the generous liquor should be used to no better purpose.

BALLAD: It's the noblest use of the grape, and the greatest glory of Bacchus is to be page to Venus.

SOTMORE: Before I go into a tavern again with a man who'll sneak away after the first bottle, may I be cursed with the odious sight of a pint as long as I live: or become a member of a city club, where men drink out of thimbles, that the fancy may be heightened by the wine, about the same time the understanding's improved by the conversation: I'll sooner drink coffee with a politician, tea with a fine lady, or 'rack punch with a fine gentleman, than thus be made a whetstone of, to sharpen my friends' inclinations, that some little strumpet may enjoy the benefit of that good humor which I have raised.

BALLAD: Why, thou art as ill-natur'd and as angry as a woman would be, who was disappointed in the last moment, when her expectations were at the highest.

SOTMORE: And haven't I the same cause?

BALLAD: Truly, honest Nol, when a man's reason begins to stagger, I think him the properest company for women: one bottle more, and I'd been fit for no company at all.

SOTMORE: Then thou had'st been carried off with glory—An honest fellow should no more quit the tavern while he can stand than a soldier should the field; but you fine gentlemen are for preserving yourselves safe from both for the benefit of the ladies.—'Sdeath! I'll use you with the same scorn a soldier would a coward: so, Sir, when I meet you next, be not surprised if I walk on the other side the way.

BALLAD: Nay, prythee, dear Silenus, be not so enraged: I'll but take one refreshing turn, and come back to the tavern to thee. Burgundy shall be the word, and I will fight under thy command till I drop.

SOTMORE: Now thou art an honest fellow—and thou shalt toast whomsoever thou pleasest—We'll bumper up her health, till thou dost enjoy her in imagination. To a warm imagination, there's no bawd like a bottle. It shall throw into your arms the soberest prude or wildest coquette in town; thou shalt rifle her charms in spite of her art. Nay, thou shalt increase her charms more than her art: and, when thou art surfeited with the delicious pleasure, wake coolly the next morning without any wife by your side, or any fear of children.

BALLAD: What a luscious picture thou hast drawn!

SOTMORE: And thou shalt have it, boy! Thou shalt triumph over her virtue, if she be a woman of quality—or raise her blushes, if she be a common strumpet. I'll go order a new recruit upon the table, and expect you with impatience.—'Fill every glass.'

Air LIX (*see* Appendix)
(*Duet*)
Let a set of sober asses
Rail against the joys of drinking,
While water, tea
And milk agree,
To set cold brains a thinking.
Power and wealth,
Beauty, health,
Wit and mirth in wine are crown'd;
Joys abound,
Pleasure's found,
Only where the glass goes round.
The ancient sects on happiness
All differ'd in opinion.
But wiser rules
Of modern schools,
In wine fix her dominion.
Power and wealth, &c.
All virtues wine is nurse to,
Of ev'ry vice destroyer;
Makes bright the wit
By doubling it,
Truth forces from the lawyer.
Wine sets our joys a flowing,
Our care and sorrow drowning,
Who rails at the bowl,
Is a Turk in his soul,
And a Christian ne'er should own him.
Power and wealth, &c.

(*Exit* SOTMORE.)

BALLAD: Sure this fellow's whole sensation lies in his throat: for he's never pleased but when he is swallowing: and yet the hogshead will be as soon drunk with the liquor it contains as he. I wish it had no other effect on me. Pox of my paper scull! I've no sooner buried the wine in my belly than its spirit rises in my head.—I am in a very proper humor for another frolic; if my good genius, and her evil one, would but send some lovely female my way—ha, the devil hath heard my prayers.

(*Enter* LUCY.)

LUCY: Was ever anything so unfortunate! I meant to step into Lord Formal's chair, but chose a strange chair entirely, that belonged to a horrible old woman. And now I'm lost and know not a step of the way—What shall I do?

BALLAD: By all my love of glory, an adventure.

LUCY: Ha! who's that? who are you, Sir? (*aside*) I've seen this gentleman some place today, but O la, I've seen so many gentlemen, I cannot be sure.

BALLAD: A cavalier, Madam, a knight-errant rambling about the world in quest of adventures. To plunder widows and ravish virgins; to lessen the number of bullies, and increase that of cuckolds, are the obligations of my profession.

LUCY: I wish you all the success so worthy an adventurer deserves.

BALLAD: But hold, Madam, I'm but just sallied, and you're the first adventure I have met with. (*Takes hold of her.*)

LUCY: Let me go, I beseech you, Sir, I'll have nothing to say to any of your profession.

BALLAD: That's unkind, Madam: for, as I take it, our professions are pretty near allied, and we're proper company for one another. (*aside*) I recollect this one now. She was only this afternoon at Old Midnight's and look what an air of country innocence she puts on.

LUCY: My profession, Sir!

BALLAD: Yes, Madam, I believe I'm no stranger to the honourable rules of your order. Nay, 'tis probable I may know your abbess too. (How Old Midnight would like to be called an abbess!)

LUCY: Nothing but your drink, Sir, and ignorance of my quality, could excuse this rudeness.

BALLAD: Whu— (*whistles*) Ignorance of your quality!

[235]

LUCY: You look, Sir, so much like a gentleman, that I'm persuaded this usage proceeds only from your mistaking me. I own it looks a little odd for a woman of virtue to be found alone in the street, at this hour—

BALLAD: Yes, it does look a little odd indeed.

LUCY: But when you know my story, I'm confident you will assist me, rather than otherwise. I've this very moment escap'd from Lord Bawble, and am going to see Lord Formal—

BALLAD: I'm Lord Formal's very humble servant, I've no doubt he pays you better than can I. But I find I'm too much in love with you, to let you go. Had you proved what I first took you for, I should've parted with you easily; but I read a coronet in your eyes. (She shall have her grace if she pleases, I'd rather give her a title than money.)

LUCY: Nay, now you mistake me as widely as you did at first.

BALLAD: Nay, by this frolic, Madam Duchess, your grace, you must be either a woman of quality, or a woman of the town—Your low, mean people, who govern themselves by rules, dare not attempt these noble flights of pleasure. Flights only to be reached by those who boldly soar above reputation.

LUCY (*aside*): This's the maddest fellow.

BALLAD: So, my dear, whether you be of quality or no quality, you and I'll go drink one bottle together at the next tavern.

LUCY (*aside*): I've but one way to get rid of him.

BALLAD: Come, my dear angel. Oh! this dear soft hand.

LUCY: Could I be but assured my virtue'll be safe.

BALLAD: Nowhere safer. I'll give thee anything in pawn for it— (*aside*) But my watch.

LUCY: And then my reputation—

BALLAD: The night'll take care of that— (*aside*) Virtue and reputation. These whores have learnt a strange cant.

LUCY: But will you love me always?

BALLAD: Oh! for ever and ever, to be sure.

LUCY: But will you—too?

BALLAD: Yes, I will—too.

LUCY: Will you promise to be civil?

BALLAD: Oh! yes, yes! (I was afraid she'd have asked me for money.)

LUCY: Well, then I will venture.—Go you to that corner tavern, I'll follow you.

BALLAD: Excuse me, Madam, I know my duty better—so, if you please, I'll follow you.

LUCY: I insist on your going first.

BALLAD: And so you'll leave me in the lurch: I see you're frighted at the roughness of my speech, but fore gad, I'm an honest man, and the devil take me if I bilk you.

LUCY: I don't understand you.

BALLAD: Why, then, Madam, here's as yellow a sovereign as ever come out of the Indies; you understand that, I hope.

LUCY: I shall take no bribes, Sir.

BALLAD: Refuse a sovereign! I like you now indeed; for you can't have been long upon the town, I'm sure. But I grow weary of impatience. If you're a modest woman, and insist on the ceremony of being carried, with all my heart.

LUCY: Nay, Sir, do not proceed to rudeness.

BALLAD: In short, my passion will be dallied with no longer. A woman's as ravishing a sight to me as the returning sun to Greenland. I am none of your puisny beaus, that can look on a fine woman, like a surfeited man on an entertainment. My stomach's sharp, and you're a pretty bird; and, if I do not eat you up, may salt beef be my fare forever. (*Takes her in his arms.*)

LUCY: I'll alarm the watch.

BALLAD: You'll be better-natur'd than that. At least, to encounter danger's my profession; so have at you, my little Venus—if you don't consent, I'll ravish you.

LUCY: Help there! a rape, a rape!

BALLAD: Hush, hush, you call too loud, people'll think you are in earnest.

LUCY: Help, a rape!

(STAFF *and* WATCH *enter.*)

STAFF: That's he there, seize him.

BALLAD: Stand off, ye scoundrels!

STAFF: Ay, Sir, you shou'd have stood off—Do you charge this man with a rape, Madam?

LUCY: I am frighted out of my senses—

STAFF: A plain case!—The rape's sufficiently proved.—What, was the devil in you, to ravish a woman in the street?

LUCY: Oh! dear Mr. Constable, all I desire is you would see me safe to my lodgings.

STAFF (*aside to her*): Never fear, Madam, you shall not want evidence.

BALLAD: Nay, if I must lodge with these gentlemen, I'm resolved to have your company, Madam. Mr. Constable, I charge that lady with threatening to swear a rape against me, and laying violent hands upon my person, whilst I was inoffensively walking along the street.

LUCY: How! villain!

BALLAD: Ay, ay, Madam, you shall be made a severe example of. The laws are come to a fine pass truly, when a sober gentleman can't walk the streets for women.

LUCY: For Heaven's sake, don't believe him.

STAFF: Nay, Madam, as we've but your bare affirmation on both sides, we can't tell which way to incline our belief; that'll be determin'd in the morning by your characters— (*Aside to her*) I wouldn't have you dejected, you'll not want a character.

LUCY: This's the most unfortunate accident, sure, that ever befell a woman of virtue.

STAFF: If you're a woman of virtue, the gentleman'll be hanged for attempting to rob you of it. If you're not a woman of virtue, why you'll be whipped for accusing a gentleman of robbing you of what you hadn't to lose.

LUCY: Oh! this unfortunate fright—But, Mr. Constable, I'm very willing that the gentleman should have his liberty, give me but mine.

STAFF: That request, Madam, is a very corroborating evidence against you.

BALLAD: Guilt will ever discover itself.

STAFF: Bring them along.

FIRST WATCH: She looks like a modest woman, in my opinion.

BALLAD: Confound all your modest women, I say—a man can have nothing to do with a modest woman, but he must be married, or hang'd for't.

(*Exeunt.*)

ACT THREE

SCENE ONE: At Justice Squeezum's. JUSTICE SQUEEZUM *and*
MR. QUIVER.

SQUEEZUM: Did Mother Bilkum refuse to pay my demands, say
you?

QUIVER: Yes, Sir: she says she doesn't value your worship's protection of a farthing, for that she can bribe two juries a year to acquit
her in Hick's Hall for half the money.

SQUEEZUM: Very fine; I shall shew her that I understand something
of juries, as well as herself. Quiver, make a memorandum against
Mother Bilkum's trial, that we may remember to have the panel
No. 3; they're a set of good men and true, and hearken to no evidence
but mine.

QUIVER: Sir, here's Mr. Staff, the reforming constable.

STAFF: An't please your worship.—We went to the house where
your worship commanded us, and heard the dice in the street; but
there were two coaches with coronets on them at the door, so we
thought it proper not to go in.

SQUEEZUM: You did right. The laws're turnpikes, only made to
stop people who walk on foot, and not to interrupt those who drive
through them in their coaches.

STAFF: We've taken up a man for rape too.

SQUEEZUM: What's he?

STAFF: I fancy he's some great man; for he talks French, sings
Italian, and swears English.

SQUEEZUM: Is he rich?

STAFF: We can't get a farthing out of him.

SQUEEZUM: A certain sign that he is. Deep pockets are like deep
streams; and money, like water, never runs faster than in the
shallows.

STAFF: Then there's another misfortune too.

[239]

SQUEEZUM: What's that?

STAFF: The woman'll not swear to anything against him.

SQUEEZUM: Never fear that; I'll make her swear enough for my purpose. What sort of woman is she?

STAFF: A common whore, I believe.

SQUEEZUM: The properest woman in the world to swear a rape. A modest woman's as shy of swearing a rape, as a gentleman of swearing a battery.—We'll make her swear enough to frighten him into a settlement, a small part of which'll satisfy the woman. So go bring them before me.—The night's still young. This woman needs to be examin'd.

(STAFF *exits.*)

SQUEEZUM and QUIVER:

Air LX: *There was a jovial beggar*

The stone that all things turns at will
    To gold, the chemist craves;
But gold without the chemist's skill,
    Turns all men into knaves.
        For a cheating they will go, &c.

The merchant would the courtier cheat,
    When on his goods he lays
Too high a price—but faith he's bit,
    For a courtier never pays.
        For a cheating they will go, &c.

The lawyer, with a face demure,
    Hangs him who steals your pelf;
Because the good man can endure
    No robber but himself.
        For a cheating they will go, &c.

Between the quack and highwayman
    What difference can there be?
Though this with pistol, that with pen,
    Both kill you for a fee.
        For a cheating they will go, &c.

The tenant doth the steward nick
(So low this art we find),
The steward doth his lordship trick,
My lord tricks all mankind.
For a cheating they will go, &c.

(*Enter* STAFF, WATCH, MR. BALLAD, *and* LUCY.)

STAFF: An't please your worship, here's a gentleman hath committed a rape last night on this woman.

SQUEEZUM: How! a rape! Hath he committed a rape on you, Child?

LUCY: Sir, I've nothing to say against him. I desire you'd give us both our liberty. He was a little frolicsome tonight, which made me call for these peoples' help; and when once they'd taken hold of us, they'd not suffer us to go away.

SQUEEZUM: They did their duty.—The power of charging lieth in us, and not in them.

BALLAD: Sir.—

SQUEEZUM: Sir, I beg we mayn't be interrupted. Hark'ye, young woman, if this gentleman hath treated you ill, don't let your modesty prevent the execution of justice. Consider, you'll be guilty yourself of the next offence he commits; and upon my word, by his looks, it's probable he may commit a dozen rapes within this week.

LUCY: I assure you he's innocent.

SQUEEZUM: Mr. Staff, what say you to this affair?

STAFF: May it please your worship, I saw the prisoner behave in a very indecent manner, and heard the woman say he'd ravish'd away her senses.

SQUEEZUM: Fie upon you, Child, won't you swear this?

LUCY: No, Sir; but I'll swear something against you, unless you discharge us.

SQUEEZUM: That cannot be, Madam, the fact's too plain. If you won't swear now, the prisoner must be kept in custody till you will.

STAFF: If she'll not swear, we can swear enough to convict him.

BALLAD: Very fine, faith! This justice is worse than a grand inquisitor.

SQUEEZUM: Did you ever see such a ravishing look as this fellow hath? Sir, if I was a judge, I'd hang you without any evidence at all.

It's such fellows as these who sow dissension between man and wife, and keep up the names of cuckold and bastard in the kingdom.

BALLAD: Nay, if that be all you accuse me of, I'll confess it freely, I have employ'd my time pretty well. Though I don't remember ever to have done you the honour of dubbing.

SQUEEZUM: Well, Child, can you find anything to say against this gentleman?

LUCY: I've already answered that.

SQUEEZUM: The woman's difficult of confessing in public: but I fancy when I examine her in private, I may get it out of her.—So, Mr. Constable, withdraw your prisoner.

(*Exit all save* SQUEEZUM, LUCY.)

SQUEEZUM: Come, come, Child, you'd better take the oath, though you're not altogether so sure. Justice should be rigorous. It's better for the public that ten innocent people should suffer, than one guilty should escape.

LUCY: Would you persuade me to perjure myself?

SQUEEZUM: By no means. Not for the world. Perjury indeed! Do you think I don't know what perjury is better than you? He did attempt to ravish you, you own; very well. He that attempts to do you any injury, hath done it in his heart. Besides, many a woman hath been ravished, ay, and men've been hanged for it—when she hath not certainly known she hath been ravished.

LUCY: You may spare yourself any further trouble: for I assure you it'll be in vain.

SQUEEZUM: I see where your hesitation hangs; you're afraid of spoiling your trade.—You think severity to a customer may keep people from your house.—Pray, answer me one question—How long have you been upon the town?

LUCY: What do you mean?

SQUEEZUM: Come, come, I see you're but a novice, and I like you the better: for yours is the only business wherein people don't profit by experience.—You're very handsome.—It's a pity you should continue in this abandoned state.—Give me a kiss;—Nay, be not coy to me.—I protest, you're as full of beauty as the rose is of sweetness, and I of love as its stalk is full of briars—Oh! that we were as closely joined together too.

LUCY: O la, Mr. Justice.

SQUEEZUM: If I thought you'd prove constant, I'd take you into keeping: for I have not liked a woman so much these many years.

LUCY (*aside*): I'll humour this old villain, I'm resolved.

SQUEEZUM: What think you, could you be constant to a vigorous, healthy, middle-aged man, hey!—Let thy silence give consent: here, take this purse as an earnest of what I'll do for you.

LUCY: Well, and what shall I do for this?

SQUEEZUM: You shall do—You shall do nothing; I'll do. I'll be a verb active, and you shall be a verb passive.

LUCY: I wish you be not of the neuter gender.

SQUEEZUM: Why, you little arch rogue, do you understand Latin, hussy?

LUCY: A little, Sir! My father was a country parson, and gave all his children a good education. He taught his daughters to read and write himself.

SQUEEZUM: What, have you sisters, then?

LUCY: Alack-a-day, Sir! sixteen of us, and all in the same way of business.

SQUEEZUM: Ay, this it is to teach daughters to write. I would as soon put a sword into the hands of a madman, as a pen into those of a woman.—Sure, my dear, the spirit of love must run very strongly in the blood of your whole family.

LUCY: Oh, Sir, it was a villainous man of war that harboured near us.—My poor sisters were ruined by the officers, and I fell a martyr to the chaplain.

SQUEEZUM: Ay, ay, the sailors are as fatal to our women as the soldiers are. One Venus rose from the sea, and thousands have set in it—But not Venus herself could compare to thee, my little honeysuckle.

LUCY: Be not so hot, Sir.

SQUEEZUM: Bid the touchwood to be cold behind the burning glass. The touchwood's not more easily kindled by the sun, than I by your dear eyes.

LUCY: The touchwood's not drier, I dare swear.

SQUEEZUM: But hark, I hear my clerk returning.—Leave word with him where I shall come to you.—I'll be the kindest of keepers, very constant, very liberal.

LUCY: Two charming qualities in a lover!

SQUEEZUM: My pretty nosegay, you'll find me vastly preferable to idle young rakehells. Besides, you're safe with me.—I shall be faithful to the time we appoint.

LUCY: Be not afraid of me.

SQUEEZUM: Adieu, my pretty charmer. I shall burn with impatience. (*Exit* LUCY.) Go thy way for a charming girl.—Oh! here they come. I must deal with my gentleman now in a different style.

(*Enter* MR. BALLAD *and* QUIVER.)

BALLAD: Well, Sir, is the lady determined to swear stoutly?

SQUEEZUM: Truly, it's hard to say what she determines; she's gone to ask the advice of a divine and a lawyer.

BALLAD: Then the odds're against me: for the lawyer'll certainly advise her to swear; and it is possible the divine will not contradict her in it.

SQUEEZUM: It's indeed a ticklish point, and it were advisable to make it up as soon as possible. The first loss is always the least. It's better to wet your coat than your skin, and to run home when the clouds begin to drop, than in the middle of the storm. In short, it were better to give a brace of hundred pounds to make up the matter now than to venture the consequence. I'm heartily concerned to see gentlemen in such a misfortune. I'm sorry the age is so corrupt. Really I expect to see some grievous and heavy judgment fall on the nation. We're as bad as ever Sodom and Gomorrah; and I wish we may not be as miserable.

BALLAD: Heark'e, justice; I take a sermon to be the first punishment which a man undergoes after conviction. It's very hard I must be condemned to it beforehand.

SQUEEZUM: I speak for your good: my interest sways not one way or the other.—I would, were I in your circumstances, do what I advise you to do.

BALLAD: Faith, Sir, that I must doubt; for, were you in my circumstances, you wouldn't be worth the money.

SQUEEZUM: Nay, Sir, you jest with me; a gentleman can never be at a loss for such a trifle.

BALLAD: Faith, Sir, you mistake. I know a great many gentlemen not worth three farthings. He that resolves to be honest must resolve to be poor.

SQUEEZUM: A gentleman, and poor; Sir, they're contradictions. A man may as well be a scholar without learning, as a gentleman without riches. But I've no time to dally with you. If you do not understand good usage, while it's dealt you, you may, when you feel the reverse. The affair may now be made up for a trifle; the time may come when your whole fortune would be too little.—An hour's delay in the making up of an offence is as dangerous as in the sewing up of a wound.

BALLAD: Well, you've over-persuaded me; I'll take your advice.

SQUEEZUM: I'll engage you'll not repent it—I don't question but you'll regard me as your friend.

BALLAD: That I do, indeed. And to give you the most substantial instance of it I'll ask a favor, which is expected only from the most intimate friendship—that you'll be so kind to lend me the money.

SQUEEZUM: Alack-a-day, Sir, I've no such sum in my command. Besides, how must it look in me, who am an officer of justice, to lend a culprit money wherewith to evade justice!

QUIVER: I wonder how you could ask it.

BALLAD: Necessity obliges to anything, my friend. Mr. Squeezum was so kind to shew me the necessity of giving money, and my pockets were so cruel to shew me the impossibility of it.

SQUEEZUM: Well, Sir, if you can't pay for your transgressions like the rich, you must suffer for them like the poor.—Here, Constable.

(*Enter* STAFF, THE WATCH.) Take away your prisoner; keep him in safe custody till further orders. If you come to a wiser resolution within these two hours, send me word: after that, it'll be too late.

BALLAD: Heark'e Mr. Justice, you'd better use me as you ought, and acquit me: for, if you do anything which you cannot defend, hang me, if I'm not revenged on you.

SQUEEZUM: Hang you!—I wish there may not be more meaning in those words than you imagine.

BALLAD: 'Sdeath! you old rascal, I can scarce forbear rattling those old dry bones of thine till they crack thy wither'd skin.

SQUEEZUM: Bear evidence of this; I'm threatened in the execution of my office.

BALLAD: Come, honest Mr. Constable, let me go anywhere from this fellow—

(*Exits with* STAFF *and* WATCH.)

SQUEEZUM: I'm afraid I shall make nothing of this fellow at last. I've a mind to discharge him.

QUIVER: Try him a little longer, however.

(*Re-enter* STAFF.)

Your worship, the prisoner has changed his tune and begs that he be allowed to see his friend, Mr. Zorobable, the moneylender. This very night.

SQUEEZUM: That's good news. Let some one send for friend Zorobable at once. Meanwhile, I've another appointment.

(*During the change of scene,* SQUIRE GOODWILL *may appear before the curtains and encounter* WILLIAM.)

WILLIAM: Why, it's Squire Goodwill! Good evening to you, Sir!

GOODWILL: William, my man! I'm come to town. You'll direct me to the lodgings where I may find my daughter and my new son Thomas!

WILLIAM: That I will, Sir. At once. Though I was now on an errand that promis'd me some pleasure.

GOODWILL: The town's pleasure. Do you not miss, William, the country? The hunting?

WILLIAM: Ay, a country wench makes better hunting.

GOODWILL: The fox and hare, William! Who can love the city when dawn comes? In the country, you rise early.

Air XII: *Dutch skipper*

GOODWILL: The gaudy sun adorning
   With brightest rays the morning,
      the morning,
   Shines o'er the eastern hill;
   And I will go asporting,

WILLIAM: And I will go a courting,
      a courting,
   There lies my pleasure still.

GOODWILL: In gaffer Woodford's ground
                A brushing hare is found,
                A course which even kings themselves might see;

WILLIAM: And in another place
                There lies a blushing lass,
                Which will give one ten times more sport than she.

WILLIAM: This way, Sir. I will lead you.
(*Exeunt.*)

SCENE TWO: In gaol. MR. ZOROBABLE, MR. SOTMORE, and LUCY.

ZOROBABLE: Believe me, my dear, I'm distrest suddenly to come upon my country lady in a London gaol.

LUCY: If you'll but follow up the plan I suggest—(*aside*) Gemini cancer, am I glad to see my lord again, or not, in this place? What a town this London is, where there's something happening every moment! Nothing so dull as the country.

ZOROBABLE: It's a miraculous chance that this gentleman's friend, having known me in former years, sent for me straightaway.

SOTMORE: He comes!

LUCY: Sirs, be within call.

ZOROBABLE: I hope you're sober enough, Mr. Sotmore, to play your part.

SOTMORE: Ay, ay. This little mistress of yours is the most dextrous politician, if that scoundrel poppy doth not disappoint us.

(*Exeunt.*)

(*Enter* SQUEEZUM.)

Oh! you are here—you little, pretty, dear, sweet rogue!—I've been waiting for this these—these two hours at least.

LUCY: Young lovers are commonly earlier than their appointment.

SQUEEZUM: Give me a kiss.—Thou shalt find me a young lover, a vigorous young lover too.—Hit me a slap in the face, do—Bow-wow! Bow-wow! I'll eat up your clothes.—Come, what'll you drink?

White or red?—Women love white best.—Come, sit down; do, sit
down.—Come, now let's hear the story how you were first debauched.
—Come—that I may put it down in my history at home. I've the
history of all the women's ruin that ever I lay with, and I call it, The
History of My OWN Times.

LUCY: I'll warrant it's big.

SQUEEZUM: It's really a good reputable size. I've done execution
in my time!

LUCY: And may do execution still.

SQUEEZUM: Well—But now let me have the history—Where did
your amour begin?—at church, I warrant you. More amours begin
at church than end there.—Or, perhaps, you went to see the man of
war—? Going to see sights hath ruined many a woman.

LUCY: Ay, Sir, it was there indeed I saw him first; that was the
fatal scene of our interview.

SQUEEZUM: Well, and was the amour managed by letter, or by
word of mouth?

LUCY: By letter, Sir. I believe he writ two quires of paper to me
before I'd send him an answer: I returned him several unopened, and
then several others opened—But at last he obtained an answer.

SQUEEZUM: Well, and after your answer, what followed then?

LUCY: Oh! he thought himself sure of me as soon as I'd answered
his letter.

SQUEEZUM: Ah, I've always observed in my amours that when I
received an answer I never failed of the woman; a woman follows
her letter infallibly. Well, and what'd he say in the second letter?

LUCY: Oh! he swore a thousand fond things: his love'd last as long
as his life: his whole happiness depended on me—and a vast deal of
that nature.

SQUEEZUM: Ay, ay, just as I've done myself. I find whoring's
as methodical as the law.

LUCY (aside): And I fancy as tedious with you, old gentleman.

SQUEEZUM: Well, and how many letters did you write to him,
eh!—before—

LUCY: Not many. He didn't want much encouragement.

SQUEEZUM: Then, passing over the rest of the suit, let's come to
the last fatal meeting.

LUCY: It was of a Sunday morning—

SQUEEZUM: Right. My old method: when other people're gone to church.

LUCY: In an exceedingly hot day.—

SQUEEZUM: May or June?—Women and cherries are commonly gathered in the same month.

LUCY: I was fatigued with walking in the garden, and retired to an arbour to repose myself: guess what was my surprise when I found the dear perfidious had conveyed himself hither before me.

SQUEEZUM: A sly dog! My old way again. An ambush is as useful in love as war.

LUCY: At my first entrance he pretended a surprise at seeing me unexpectedly; but on my questioning him how and with what design he'd conveyed himself there, he immediately threw off the cloak and confessed all: he flew to me, caught me in his arms with the most eager raptures, and swore the most violent love and eternal constancy. I in the greatest agony of rage repelled him with my utmost force; he redoubled his attacks, I slackened my resistance; he intreated, I raved; he sighed, I cry'd; he press'd, I swooned; he—

SQUEEZUM: Oh!—I can bear no longer, my angel! my paradise! my honeysuckle! my dove! my darling!

LUCY: What do you mean, Sir?

SQUEEZUM: I mean to eat you up, to swallow you down, to squeeze you to pieces.

LUCY: Help there! a rape, a rape!

(*To them:* SOTMORE, ZOROBABLE.)

SOTMORE: Hey-day! what in the devil's name is here?—Justice Squeezum ravishing a woman in his own gaol!

LUCY: Oh! for Heaven's sake, Sir, assist a poor forlorn, hapless maid, whom this wicked man hath treacherously seduced.

SQUEEZUM: Oh, lud!—Oh, lud!

ZOROBABLE: Fie upon you, Mr. Squeezum; you who're a magistrate, you who're the preserver and executor of our laws, thus to be the breaker of them.

SQUEEZUM: Can'st thou accuse me?

LUCY: You know too well how barbarously you've used me. For pity's sake, Sirs, secure him; don't let him escape, till we send for a constable. If there be any law for a justice, I'm resolved to hang him.

SQUEEZUM: Oh, lud; what shame have I brought myself to! that ever I should've lived to see this day.

SOTMORE: If thou hadst stood to thy bottle like an honest fellow this had never happened; but you must go a whoring with a pox to you, at your years too; with these spindle shanks, that weezle face, that crane's neck of a body. Who would've imagined that such an old withered maypole as thou art should attempt to fall on a woman? Why thou wilt be the diversion of the whole town.—Grub-street will dine a month on your account. Thou wilt be ushered to Tyburn with more pomp than Alexander was ushered into Babylon. Justice never triumphs so universally as at the execution of one of her own officers.

SQUEEZUM: Sir, if there be truth on earth, I'm as innocent.

ZOROBABLE: All the innocence on earth won't save you.—A man doth not always draw the rope by the weight of his sins. Your innocence will not acquit you in a court of Justice against her oath; and, when you come to the gallows, it'll be vain to plead your innocence. All's fish that comes to the net there. The gallows so seldom gets its due, that it never parts with what it gets.

LUCY: Can you pretend to innocence? Were not these gentlemen eye-witnesses to your rudeness, to the injury you offered me?

SQUEEZUM: I see, Madam, your design's to extort money from me. I'm too well acquainted with the laws to contend; I hope you'll be reasonable, for I'm poor, very poor, I assure you; it's not for men of my honesty to be rich.

LUCY: Sir, if you'd give me millions, it should not satisfy my revenge! you should be hanged for an example to others.

SOTMORE: Hey-day! what vehicle is this? a vinegar bottle?—Half a pint, by Jupiter! Why, thou sneaking rascal, canst thou pretend to honesty, when this dram glass hath been found upon thee? Were I thy judge, or thy jury, this very sneaking vehicle should hang thee, without any other evidence. But come, since you're to be hang'd, I'll drink one bumper to your good journey to the other world.— You'll find an abundance of your acquaintance, whom you've sent before you.—And now, I'll go call a constable.

SQUEEZUM: Hold, hold, Sir; for mercy sake don't expose me so.—Will nothing content you, Madam?

LUCY: Nothing but the rigour of the law. Sir, I beseech you lose no time, but send for the constable immediately.

SQUEEZUM: I'll do anything; I'll consent to any terms.

LUCY: The constable! the constable!

SQUEEZUM: Stay, dear Sir; I'll give you a hundred guineas; I'll do anything.

LUCY: Remember your vile commitment of that gentleman this evening.—But I will revenge the injury of my friend.—Sir, I beseech you send for the officers.

SQUEEZUM: He shall be dismissed immediately.

LUCY: It's too late.

SOTMORE: Harkye, Sir, will you leave off whoring, and take to drinking for the future?

SQUEEZUM: I'll leave them off both.

SOTMORE: Then you shall be hang'd: but if you'll commence honest fellow, and get drunk every day of your life, I'll intercede with this lady, that, on your acquitting the gentleman, you shall be acquitted yourself.

SQUEEZUM: I'll do anything, I'll quit anything.

ZOROBABLE: Madam, let me persuade you to be merciful this time to this unfortunate and undutiful servant of justice.

LUCY: Sir, I can deny you nothing.

SQUEEZUM: Get me a pen and ink; I'll send an order to bring him hither, and discharge him instantly.

SOTMORE (calls): Bring pen, ink, and paper, and a bottle of old port.

SQUEEZUM (to Lucy): And could you have had the conscience to have sworn against a poor old man?

SOTMORE: Faith! 'twas a little cruel. Could you have had the heart to see him swinging like a gibbeted skeleton? Could you have served up such a dry dish to justice—The body of one of her own children too?—But there's the paper.—Come, Sir, write his discharge and your own.

(SQUEEZUM writes.)

You've managed this matter so well, that I shall have an opinion of your sex's understanding ever after.

ZOROBABLE: Leave a woman alone for a plot, Mr. Sotmore.

SOTMORE: Ay, Madam, a woman that'll drink a bumper. Wine is the fountain of thought: and

> The more we drink,
> The more we think.

It is a question with me, whether wine hath done more good, or physic harm in the world: I wou'd have every apothecary's shop in the town turn'd into a tavern.

LUCY: I am afraid, the more you have of the one, the more you will require of the other.

SOTMORE: Let me advise you, Madam, leave off your damn'd adulterated water, your tea, and take to wine. It'll paint your face better than vermillion, and put more honesty in your heart than all the sermons you can read.

SQUEEZUM: This letter, Sir, will produce the gentleman immediately.

(*Exit* MR. ZOROBABLE, *with letter.*)

SOTMORE: Come, honest justice, our acquaintance hath an odd beginning, but we may soon be very good companions. Let's sit down, and remember what you've bargained to do every day of your life. (*They sit.*) Here's a health to the propagation of trade, thy trade, I mean, to the increase of whores, and false dice.—Thou art a collector of the customs of sin, and he that would sin with impunity must have thy permit. Come, pledge me, old boy; if thou leavest one drop in the glass thou shall stay in gaol yet, by this bottle.

SQUEEZUM: I protest, Sir, your hand's too bountiful; you will overcome me with wine.

SOTMORE: Well, and I love to see a magistrate drunk; it's a comely sight. When justice is drunk, she can't take a bribe. Drink, like the game, was intended for gentlemen—and no one should get drunk who can't go home in a coach.—Come, Madam, it's your glass now.

LUCY: Dear Sir! I beg you'd not compel me to it.

SOTMORE: By this bottle I will; I'll ravish thee to it before the justice's face. Come, drink the justice's health, as a token of amity; the justice's a good honest fellow. (*to the Justice*) But let me give you some wholesome advice. Leave off fornicating; leave the girls to the boys, and stand to thy bottle; it's a virtue becoming your years; and don't be too hard on a wild honest young rake. Be as severe as you please to whores and gamesters, that offer to act without your license: but if ever you grant a warrant for a friend of mine again, you shall not only drink the wine, but eat the bottle too. Come, here's your health, in hopes of your amendment; thou shalt pledge thy own health, in a bumper.—Here, bring up a gallon of wine.

SQUEEZUM: Not a drop more.

SOTMORE: A drop! confound the name. Come, empty your glass; the lady is a-dry.

SQUEEZUM: This's worse than a prison!

SOTMORE: You'll get out of this with paying less fees. Drink, I say.

SQUEEZUM: Well—since I must.

(During the change of scene: LUCY *and* MR. BALLAD *may appear before the curtains to sing:)*

Air LIII: *Pierrot's tune*

BALLAD:	Great courtiers palaces contain,
LUCY:	While small ones fear the gaol;
BALLAD:	Great parsons riot in champagne,
LUCY:	Small parsons sot on ale;
BALLAD:	Great whores in coaches gang,
LUCY:	Smaller misses,
	For their kisses,
	Are in Bridewell bang'd;
BOTH:	While in vogue
	Lives the great rogue,
	Small rogues are by dozens hang'd.

(Exeunt.)

SCENE THREE: At Mrs. Midnight's. MRS. MIDNIGHT *solus.*

Air XXXIII, *Red House*

Ye virgins who would marry,
Ere you choose, be wary,
If you'd not miscarry,
Be inclin'd to doubting:

Examine well your lover,
His vices to discover,
With caution con him over,
And turn quite inside out him;
But wedding past,
The stocking cast,
The guests all gone,
The curtain drawn,
Be henceforth blind,
Be very kind,
And find no faults about him!

(*Enter* THOMAS.)

THOMAS: Your humble servant, Madam. Pray, Madam, how do you like my clothes?

MRS. MIDNIGHT: Your tailor hath been very expeditious, indeed, Sir.

THOMAS: Yes, Madam, I shouldn't have had them so soon, but that I met with an old acquaintance, Tom Shabby, the tailor in Monmouth Street, who fitted me with a suit—But where's my wife?

MRS. MIDNIGHT (*aside*): What shall I say to him?—I believe she's gone out to see the town.

THOMAS: Gone out! hey! what, without me! who's gone with her?

MRS. MIDNIGHT: Really, Sir, I can't tell. Here was a gentleman all over lace: I suppose some acquaintance of hers. I fancy she went with him.

THOMAS: A gentleman in lace! I'm undone, ruin'd, dishonored! Some rascal hath betray'd away my wife.—Zounds, why did you let her go out of the house till my return?

MRS. MIDNIGHT: The lady was only a lodger with me, I'd no power over her.

THOMAS: How, did any man come to see her? for I'm sure she did not know one man in town. It must be somebody that used to come here.

MRS. MIDNIGHT: May the devil fetch me, if ever I saw him before: nor do I know how he got in.—But there're birds of prey lurking in every corner of this wicked town: it makes me shed tears to think what villains there are in the world to betray poor innocent young ladies.

THOMAS: Oons and the devil; the first week of our marriage!

MRS. MIDNIGHT: That's a pity indeed—if you've been married no longer: had you been together half a year, it'd been some comfort. But be advised, have a little patience; in all probability, whoever the gentleman is, he'll return her soon again.

THOMAS: Return her! ha! stain'd, spotted, sullied! Who shall return me my honour?—'Sdeath! I'll search her through the town, the world—Ha! her father here!

(*Enter* MR. GOODWILL.)

GOODWILL: Son, I met your man William at the inn, and he shew'd me the way hither.—Where's my daughter, your wife?

THOMAS: Stolen! lost! everything's lost, and I'm undone.

GOODWILL: Hey-day! What's the matter?

THOMAS: The matter! O curse this vile town; I did but go to furnish myself with a suit of clothes, that I might appear like a gentleman, and in the meantime your daughter hath taken care that I'll appear like a gentleman all the days of my life; for I'm sure I shall be ashamed to shew my head among footmen.

GOODWILL: How! my daughter run away—

MRS. MIDNIGHT: I'm afraid it's too true.

GOODWILL: And do you stand meditating?

THOMAS: What shall I do?

GOODWILL: Go advertise her this minute in the newspapers—get my lord chief-justice's warrant.

MRS. MIDNIGHT: As for the latter, it may be advisable; but the former will be only throwing away your money; for the papers've been of late so crammed with advertisements of wives running away from their husbands, nobody now reads them.

THOMAS: That I should be such a blockhead to bring my wife to town!

MR. GOODWILL: That I should be such a sot as to suffer you!

THOMAS: If I was unmarried again, I'd not venture my honour in a woman's keeping, for all the fortune she could bring me.

MR. GOODWILL: And if I was a young fellow again, I'd not get a daughter, for all the pleasure any woman could give me.

(*Enter* LUCY *and* MR. BALLAD.)

LUCY: Such joy! such rapture! Well, I'll never go into the country again. Faugh! how I hate the name. Oh Father, I'm sure you don't know me; nor you, Mr. Thomas, neither;—nor I won't know you.—Ah, you old fusty fellow,—and I don't want anything that you can give; nor you shan't come near me,—so you shan't—Madam, I am very much oblig'd to you for letting me see the world. I hate to talk to anyone I can't call Lordship.

MRS. MIDNIGHT (*aside*): I'm an innocent woman, and shall fall a sacrifice to an unjust suspicion.

MR. GOODWILL: And is this be-powder'd, be-curl'd, be-hoop'd mad woman my daughter? (*She coquets affectedly.*) Why, hussy, don't you know your own father?

THOMAS: Nor your husband?

LUCY: No, I don't know you at all;—I never saw you before. I've got a lord, and I don't know anyone but my Lord.

THOMAS: And is this your Lord? I shall—

LUCY: No, he's not a lord. He is Mr. Ballad, a gentleman who was arrested for trying to rape me.

MRS. MIDNIGHT: Alack-a-day!

THOMAS and MR. GOODWILL: Rape! (*They start toward* MR. BALLAD, *who retreats.*)

LUCY: Pray do not touch him. It was all a mistake. I was not raped at all.

BALLAD: I assure you, gentlemen, there was a general error and, I'm here on behalf of my Lord Bawble, whom this lady has chosen as her keeper.

MR. GOODWILL: My daughter into keeping!

THOMAS: Lord Bawble? Who is he? And where does he keep himself? Pray what hath my Lord done to you, that hath put you in such raptures?

LUCY: Oh, by gole! who'd be the fool then? When I liv'd in the country, I used to tell you everything I did; but I'm grown wiser now, for I'm told, I must never let my husband know anything I do, for he'd be angry; though I don't much care for your anger, for I design always to live with my Lord now; and he's never to be angry, do what I will.—Why, prithee, fellow, do'st thou think I'm not fine lady enough to know the difference between a lord and a footman?

THOMAS: You call me footman! I own I was a footman; and had rather be a footman still, than a tame cuckold to a lord. I wish every man, who's not a footman, thought in the same manner.

GOODWILL: Thou art a pretty fellow, and worthy a better wife.

(*Enter* MR. ZOROBABLE.)

LUCY: O my dear Lord, are you come?

ZOROBABLE: Fie, my dear, you shouldn't have run away from me again, while I was in an inner room, promising the gaoler his reward, just as you did when I was paying for all those fine things I bought you.

LUCY: O my Lord, I only stept into a chair, as you call it, with Mr. Ballad, to make a visit to a fine lady here. It's pure sport to ride in a chair.

ZOROBABLE: Bless me! what's here! My old man Tom in masquerade?

THOMAS: Mr. Zorobable, Sir! And are you my Lord Bawble? (*To Lucy*) And is this your Lord? I give your lordship joy of this fine girl—

ZOROBABLE: Stay till I've had her, Tom. Egad she hath cost me a round sum, and I've had nothing but kisses for my money yet.

THOMAS: No, Mr. Zorobable! Then I'm afraid your lordship never will have anything more, for this lady's mine.

ZOROBABLE: How! what property have you in her?

THOMAS: The property of an English husband, Sir.

ZOROBABLE: How, Madam! are you married to this man?

LUCY: I married to him! I never saw the fellow before.

ZOROBABLE: Tom, thou art a very impudent fellow.

MR. GOODWILL: Mercy on me! what a sink of iniquity is this town! She hath been here but eight hours, and learn't assurance already to deny her husband.

ZOROBABLE: Come, Tom, resign the girl by fair means, or worse will follow.

THOMAS: How, Sir, resign my wife! Fortune, which made me poor made me a servant; but nature, which made me an Englishman, preserved me from being a slave. I've as good a right to the little I claim, as the proudest peer hath to his great possessions; and whilst I am able, I will defend it.

BALLAD: There speaks a man who has drunk English stout.

MR. GOODWILL: And eaten plain English fare. Ay! The roast beef of Old England!

GOODWILL, then OMNES:

Air LXVII: *The king's old courtier*

When mighty roast beef was the Englishman's food,
It ennobled our hearts, and enriched our blood;
Our soldiers were brave, and our courtiers were good:
    Oh the roast beef of old England,
    And old England's roast beef!

But since we have learnt from all-conquering France,
To eat their ragouts as well to dance,
Oh what a fine figure we make in romance!
    Oh the roast beef of England,
    And old England's roast beef!

Then, Britons, from all nice dainties refrain
Which effeminate Italy, France, and Spain;
And mighty roast beef shall command on the main.
    Oh the roast beef, &c.
    Oh the roast beef, &c.

MR. GOODWILL: Hold, Sir; this girl, ungracious as she is, is my daughter, and this honest man's wife.

ZOROBABLE (*to Mrs. Midnight*): The next time you ask me three hundred guineas for the sweetest kind of country innocence, pray see that her husband and father are not with her in the town.

THOMAS (*to Lucy*): And so you see, Madam, your Lord's no lord at all, but a stock-jobber and moneylender. And none knows it better than I, for I was three years in his service.

ZOROBABLE: All I ask is that your young mistress return my trinkets. I question not but these trinkets will purchase a finer lady.

Air LXVIII (*see* Appendix)
If men from experience a lesson could reap,
    To fly from the folly they'd seen,
What madman at forty a mistress would keep,
    What woman would love at eighteen!
    What woman, &c.

The levees of statesmen and courts of the law,
    Boys only would haunt very soon;
And all married brawls to conclusion would draw,
    At the end of the sweet honeymoon.
    At the end, &c.

Thomas, and Madam, your servant. (*Exits.*)

LUCY: What, was he no lord, and is he gone?

THOMAS: Yes, Madam, and you shall go, as soon as I can get horses put into a coach.

LUCY: Ay, but I won't go with you.

THOMAS: No, but you shall go without me: your good father here will take care of you into the country: where, if I hear of your amendment, perhaps, half a year hence I may visit you; for since my honour is not wrong'd, I can forgive your folly.

LUCY: I shall shew you, Sir, that I'm a woman of spirit, and not to be govern'd by my husband.—I shall have vapours and fits (these they say are infallible); and if these won't do, let me see who dares to carry me into the country against my will: I'll swear the peace against them.

MR. GOODWILL: Oh! oh! that ever I should beget a daughter!

THOMAS: Let all my things be pack'd up again in the coach they came in;—and you, bring here this instant your mistress's riding dress.—Come, Madam, you must strip yourself of your puppet-show dress, as I will of mine; they'll make you ridiculous in the country, where there's still something of Old England remaining. Come, no words, no delay! by Heaven! if you but affect to loiter, I'll send orders to lock you up, and allow you only the bare necessities of life. You shall know I'm your husband, and will be obey'd.

LUCY (*crying*): And must I go into the country by myself? Shall I not have a husband, or a lord, or anybody?—If I must go, won't you go with me?

THOMAS: Can you expect it? Can you ask me after what has happened?

LUCY: O, but nothing happened!

THOMAS: Hum!

LUCY: What I did, was only to be a fine lady, and what they tola

[259]

me other fine ladies do, and I should never've thought of in the country; but if you'll forgive me, I'll never attempt to be more than a plain gentlewoman again.

THOMAS: Well, and as a plain gentlewoman you shall have pleasures some fine ladies may envy. Come, dry your eyes; my own folly, not yours, is to blame; and that I'm only angry with.

LUCY: And will you go with me then, Tommy?

THOMAS: Ay, my dear, and stay with thee too; I desire no more to be in this town, than to have thee here.

MR. GOODWILL: Henceforth I'll know no degree, no difference between men, but what the standards of honour and virtue create: the noblest birth without these is but splendid infamy; and a footman with these qualities is a man of honour.

LUCY:

Air LXXI (*see* Appendix)
Welcome again, ye rural plains;
Innocent nymphs and virtuous swains:
Farewell town, and all its sights;
Beaus and lords, and gay delights:
　　All is idle pomp and noise;
　　Virtuous love gives greater joys.

Chorus

　　All is idle pomp and noise;
　　Virtuous love gives greater joys.

CURTAIN

APPENDIX

THE MUSIC

Airs XX, XXI, XXII, XXVI, XXVII, LXXI: Special music for these
songs was written for the original production of *Miss Lucy in
Town* and copies of the scores will be found in the first printed
version of the play, available in the Reference Room of the New
York Public Library.

Airs XLI, XLVII, LXVIII: Music for these songs, written by Seedo
for the original production of *The Lottery*, will be found in
early printed versions of this farce, also available in the Reference
Room of the New York Public Library.

Airs XXIII, XXIV, XXVIII, XXIX, XXX and LXII: These are
new songs, added by the collaborator. Music for them has not yet
been written. A melody for Air LVI has been suggested by the
collaborator and set down by Michele Wilt (see p. 156).

Air XXXIX is taken from the *Historical Register of 1736*; Air LIX
(presumably a well-known drinking song) is from *The Coffee-
house Politician*; Air LXI is from the *Grub-street Opera*. Later
versions of these plays do not mention the musical source of the
words; earlier versions, if available, may do so. A musical historian
could trace them, I believe, by their lilt.